DANGER

DANGER
MARKETING RESEARCHER AT WORK

Terry Haller

QUORUM BOOKS
Westport, Connecticut • London, England

Library of Congress Cataloging in Publication Data

Haller, Terry.
   Danger, marketing researcher at work.

   Bibliography: p.
   Includes index.
   1. Marketing research. I. Title.
HF5415.2.H27   1983   658.8'3   82-13261
ISBN 0-89930-026-X   (lib. bdg.)

Library of Congress Catalog Card Number: 82-13261
ISBN: 0-89930-026-X

First published in 1983 by Quorum Books

Greenwood Press
A division of Congressional Information Service, Inc.
88 Post Road West, Westport, Connecticut 06881

Printed in the United States of America

10 9 8 7 6 5 4 3 2 1

To my father, a chief operating officer
for longer than average, all without
benefit of marketing research.

Contents

Preface

In our approach to marketing research we resemble the lost space colony that has forgotten all its forebears once knew, and is now controlled by a mysterious computer. Hardly anyone today knows if his research is good or bad. Yet, like votaries, we do its bidding, whether sense or nonsense, because it has the cloak of probity and certitude.

But this is not so much a book about how to do marketing research (although there is much of that in it) as it is about the dangers, the many dangers, lurking beneath the surface (or between the pages, if you prefer cogent metaphors) every time you pick up a research report. And, of course, it has numerous pointers on how to avoid these dangers.

It's not a text book and it won't pretend to cover every marketing research field. Omitted are, principally, sales research, media research, and mathematical modes of analysis. The first is too tiring to think about, the second would be a book unto itself, and the third has been amply rendered by many others. So for those who cringe every time they see a mathematical formula, rest assured there will be none between these pages.

It is a book that examines aspects about the research business that the texts always omit. It's about the problems they never tell you about.

Mainly, it is about the dangers of assuming things work, when they usually don't.

Acknowledgment

I am indebted to everyone I ever worked for, to the many I have worked with, and to some who once worked for me. Mentioning their names would, I'm afraid, embarrass some and suggest ulterior motives to others. So we'll just leave it at that.

DANGER

1 • *Research in Decline*

That marketing research has not progressed toward its goal of becoming a true profession is evident to all who have observed its internal strife and self-doubts.

In this world, since prehistoric times, human activity either advances or disappears. Copper refining, established circa 3500 B.C., progressed to the manufacture of bronze alloy, then into iron and steel, and developments in this industry are still going on; more recently the electronics industry has branched off into refinements unimaginable even a decade ago. But marketing research has encountered a seemingly insurmountable hurdle.

It has surrendered its progress to other disciplines, especially recent intumescences in mathematics made inviting by more easily accessible computers, and has seen, therefore, its own inner progress halted and its full intellectual potential aborted.

As a consequence, the era of Promethean achievement it seemed on the verge of entering, the joy of discovery, the unquenchable yearning for cerebral refinement that once were its hallmarks have slipped away. Perhaps the remains of this are still found in a handful of companies, but it is not manifest in the research community at large. The product of all this is an engulfing stagnation and an alarming explosion of useless and probably dangerously misleading information.

CLASSIFICATION OF ERRORS

And so therefore, research, though superficially conducted with efficiency and certitude, lacks the underlying soundness that is truly necessary as a central basis for serious business decisions.

Our best estimate is that as much as 90 percent of all marketing research is so seriously flawed as to be of questionable value. (Of course it would be even worse in the less-developed nations.) These research inadequacies can be roughly classified as follows:

1. Logic error
2. Sequence error
3. Techniques proven unreliable
4. Use of wrong bases

These errors will be discussed in the context of specific applications in the ensuing chapters on the various research functions.

REAL-LIFE EXPERIENCES

As stated in the Preface, it is not the purpose of this book to review all known research techniques, or analytical approaches. Moreover, to avoid cascading along the paths of no return other writers invariably choose on this subject, I will strive to avoid dependency on academic works in this field. These do not contain the answers we are looking for. Instead, in order to be perfectly practical and aboveboard, all that I say will be derived from real-life experiences.

Through my own careful experiments and those of trusted and highly professional colleagues, certain insights have been gained that I feel the reader may enjoy sharing. As far as I know most of these have never before been the subject of any published document, and since all involve questions of proprietary interests, sources and identifying details cannot be divulged. Otherwise, publication would not be possible. However, all of these findings, once explained and thoroughly expounded, will have, I trust, a strong and readily perceptible intuitive appeal. All are logical; all will be communicated in plain language. As illustrative backup I will refer with sufficient detail to the environment that brought them to light. The only problem I can see emanating from this is that critics may deem it unscholarly; so be it. There is no alternative, other than remaining mute. Unfortunately, that is not an attractive or acceptable option: In a survey conducted by the American Marketing Association in 1981 among the top executives of fifty companies, marketing research fared the worst among all marketing activities, with only 8 percent of those surveyed giving it high ratings.[1] Until a better idea comes along, this book might make a tiny contribution to the advancement of the profession and, while it may not be scholarly, I prefer to press on with it because, if the ratings get any worse, the whole ball game could be over.

SOURCES OF THE TROUBLE

Perhaps no one knows where the trouble first started. The situation is complicated by the fact that there are many different sectors to the research business:

1. The dozen or so large consumer companies who care enough about their techniques to safeguard and develop them through careful experiments, which they refuse to talk about and keep very secret.

2. All the other manufacturers who tend to copy whatever they can pick up, mainly by hiring people trained in the above companies (who often later find they cannot transfer their sophistication to an alien shirt-sleeve environment). These

companies seldom originate or hold technique in high regard, being more concerned with just getting the job done.

3. The giant research firms whose experimental dollar goes mainly to improve production aspects of the business so as to make their costs lower and margins higher, or their service more competitive by lowering prices or decreasing turnaround times.

4. The thousands of smaller research firms who tend, by and large, to do the first thing that crosses their mind (or that they can sell to the client). They lack the resources to experiment.

5. Academia, which has little on-line experience and negligible budgets, so that whatever it can devise must come from untested intuition.

6. The service firms (field interviewing houses, data processing groups, etc.) that do just a small portion of the job and have virtually no understanding of the intellectual content of the craft.

Historians may speculate that the decline in the scientific integrity of marketing research was due to the spread of sophisticated marketing know-how to the newer and smaller company, which seldom was able to justify having a very ample research department of its own. Usually, they have none, or if they have any at all it's usually just one person with, as the want ads state, "at least two years' experience." The frequency with which they employ any given technique is so low they cannot generate any depth of experience or useful insights, and the harried environment and sudden changes in direction in a small firm make contemplation about the validity of results unlikely. Jobs are quickly conceived, commissioned, and executed, and everyone promptly goes on to the next project. Little reflection is allowed on technique.

When they turn to an outside research firm to have their research conducted, as they frequently must, they encounter people who have to make a profit from what they offer; people who have found that expertise (in things most clients would consider arcane) doesn't sell their services or help them acquire new clients. Their meagre budgets don't allow for any experimentation, which, if it were to be truly useful to all their clients, would have to be repeated across a number of different product categories.

The handful of companies that still conduct experiments in new techniques or in technique refinement never announce their results unless they are several years old, or if they feel they are about to leak out anyway (which can occur after being forced to reveal them in litigation or congressional hearings, or after presenting them to their agencies for internal purposes). By and large though, for competitive reasons, the best experiments are not divulged. Marketing research methodologies are not ascertainable from examining a company's products, nor can they be patented.

Secrecy, rather than serving as a stimulus for extra effort in technique development, has done the opposite: it results in an uncompetitive environment where only that which is visible (like computerization of analysis and cost-cutting tricks) enjoy the advantages of the free enterprise system. The system is not going to change, nor do I advocate any changes, but some of the items in the following chapters may provide some impetus for increased concern about the situation.

So, as a result, the environment for experimental research grows less and less favorable. The research firms seldom do it because there is no profit in it: the esoteric discoveries they might make are not sufficiently interesting to use in their sales programs. The companies don't do it because management is not interested in sponsoring what they judge to be navel-gazing by staff departments. The emphasis today is proletariat, which eliminates the opportunity to worry about whether a technique is any good or not.

The fact, though, is that many techniques—even those used every day—are *not* any good. Slight variations in design or question-wording or sequence can produce earth-shattering differences in results. Since this may vary dramatically by product category and as companies become more diversified, the need for experimentation is even greater now than in the past.

Everyone whose career is touched or affected by it should start thinking about research again—about what they may be doing wrong, about how it could be better, safer, and less riddled with scientific error.

MISPLACED EMPHASIS

Research is not a field in which science has had a very firm or established hold of late. Those whose bent is more mechanical or scientific, who prefer knowing the ultimate truths from precision and hard data, tend to be lured toward the mathematical aspects of the craft.

Now, I would be the first to confess that it is a lot more fun to see multicolored geographic-spatials pop up on your desk tube and to press a few keys and summon forth elaborate factorial matrices plus an army of coefficients that will astound any lay client, and that, with suitable manipulation, will answer any question. Clearly, this is more amusing than mulling over questionnaire design or writing letters to the group handling your interviewing. It's like superscience and it makes one feel a sense of sharing in some sci-fi scenario. But, alas, in the cold light of the dawning demise of marketing research, it is not enough; this is not all there is to research. Even Han Solo had to get out his monkey wrench and bang his photon engines now and then. Researchers cannot delegate all the work to the machinery; they must still use their brains, as arduous and mundane as that may seem in the last quintile of the twentieth century.

The Luddites (1811–16) were, of course, quite right: the increased use of machines displaces human labor, perhaps not in the aggregate, but certainly in given industries or localities. In research, part of the mind has been replaced by the computer. The Luddites, sensing danger, tried to destroy the machines. The researcher has chosen another track—he has married his machines.

Management thinks this is grand. "More sophistication can't hurt anyone," they thought. In theory, they are right. But subtle things occurred. The computer and its handmaidens at first started to influence the design of the questionnaires; and then, having won everyone's trust, they turned the research planners into pod people and went on to destroy the entire philosophical underpinnings on which the system had been built. "Surely," we thought at the time, "we could accommodate the computer and the programs and switch our questioning around slightly, especially if this means we intensify the power of our mathematical analysis and lets us get the same statistical reliance on smaller bases and give our users answers where heretofore none have been forthcoming?"[2] It sounded good, and it was infinitely better than the old way and its clumsy dependence on hand tabulation and card-sort equipment that just caused a lot of grief and too many errors to contemplate.

But once over the raptures of such promising beginnings things began to fall apart fast. After sacrificing a few paltry standards for the sake of expediency, and after growing increasingly addicted to elaborate multivariate analyses instead of simpler forms of assessments, it was only natural that a whole new emphasis would emerge.

The emphasis was now on the analysis itself. Technology made it attractive and easy. Moreover, it was the only thing new enough, or bright enough, to excite the researcher, who, it must be admitted, has a very boring job most of the time. Now that computers perch on everyone's desk (unlike the old days when researchers could only get on the computer weekends—providing payroll did not need it), every researcher has total freedom to invest his whole workday in analysis (or computer games; it's hard to tell what some people do in their offices all day without checking the log).

SCIENCE ABANDONED

Forgotten in this odyssey toward heightened technical proficiency were some of the things that really count: submission to a few principles spelled out hundreds of years ago on how to do a scientific experiment—proper controls, replicability, logic, and so on. Also dismissed from the lexicon was that healthy skepticism which all good scientific researchers must have, and which, sadly, only a handful have today. The analytic emphasis has replaced the design emphasis and, as a result, much of what passes for research today is hobbled by all kinds of questionable assumptions and lapses of logic that, in many cases, make it as dubious as pure guesswork. This is the root cause of the continued high failure rate in new products. It underlies the continued low success rate of marketing plans (one estimate says 80 percent of all marketing plans fail to achieve their key objectives) and the prevalence of fiscal failure at the profit-center level (two-thirds have negative cash flows).

The computer is one of the few joys left in research, but it unwittingly introduced a relaxed and unquestioning atmosphere that, if not eradicated, will cause further declines in esteem for the entire research community. There are dangers, clear and present dangers, threatening the very destiny of the marketing mission, which come from the way research is conducted today. As we explore them, some of these dangers may seem overly obvious to readers, others will seem surprising or unexpected, but nothing will be addressed that is merely a product of someone's imagination. None of it was invented just for the purpose of filling a book. All happened or were seriously feared for cause; most of them cropped up in several different companies, in many different countries, and were spotted by researchers with superior levels of intelligence or expertise. Some of them may sound like nit-picking and of more concern to a maiden aunt/celibate uncle than to fast-track executives. Unfortunately, that's the climate in most research organizations today. The researcher who is concerned about the foibles and fallacies of his methodologies is regarded a poor manager, a technocrat, or one who doesn't know how to get on with the job. His attempts to resolve technical disputes are characterized as "professional bickering." This is not only unfortunate for the researchers who take these matters seriously, but catastrophic for the users, who cannot possibly be expected to know about this and who are thus doomed to an unreliable—potentially poisonous—diet of information. To continue in this way is perilous . . . if marketing research is to play any major role in corporate decision-making.

NOTES

1. *Advertising Age*, September 21, 1981, p. 36.

2. In retrospect, I'm not even sure these momentous concessions were necessary. In those days you simply couldn't find any mathematicians who could speak English. C. P. Snow was probably right about the two separate cultures and the gulf between the sciences and the humanities. If a common language could have been found, both sides could have given a little. And if we could start all over again now that we can, more or less, speak the same language, it might be a lot better.

2 • *Logic, Empiricism, and Common Sense*

It is easy to lose one's sense of proportion. On the one hand, marketing research is a key purveyor of information central to crucial plans and milestone decisions. If it is not right, if it cannot be trusted, then the road ahead will be strewn with the rubble of marketing disasters. But, on the other hand, research cannot be made the sole culprit in the search for blame. Its admonitions are not always followed or understood. And it is not always requested at the right time, or for the right reasons.

And so, just in case some readers may suspect this to be the scribblings of a latter-day knight-errant whose self-designated mission to rescue research methods in distress comes armed only with a few sad tales and technical platitudes, which will mordantly succeed only in alerting industry to dangers too trivial to contemplate, let me begin with something more momentous than the small change of technological introspection.

At the root of the problem is the depressingly flimsy thought structure on which most marketing research is built. Though fancifully billing itself as a *science*, marketing research, in the main, much like some of its sister branches of the humanities, has developed into little more than a *system of beliefs*. At the basis of every misguided methodology examined in later chapters are a sinister absence of skepticism and a presence of excessive and unquestioning acceptance bordering on superstition. As with superstition, its paramount benefit is the provision of emotional comfort and the removal of the need for thought. Methods that were never strongly challenged when first devised have become craft orthodoxies.

With the need for thought eliminated, with dogmas defined and permanently in place as with an established religion, research has waxed intellectually flabby. The logic content of the average project would be an embarrassment to any college debating team. Logic, which must be openly manifest in the conduct of real scientific management, is no longer regarded a necessary constituent of good research design.

Even with just casual observation, most research projects can be challenged on purely intellectual grounds. Shockingly, most research studies—up to 90 percent of them—have conspicuous lapses in logic. Without impeccable logic any piece of research is suspect. And the analysis of such research is an opus in futility. Therefore, before I go on to dissect the myriad of individual research techniques that give rise to so many specific dangers within the marketing community, I will explore these underlying weaknesses in logic and indicate how they can be eradicated. Clearly, unless this can be accomplished, unless sound basic thinking can be introduced at the very core of the planning process, no amount of methodological face-lifting will save the day.

While I honestly doubt that this message, if given at a press conference, would have reporters bolting to the doors and phoning the wire services, I sincerely believe this whole mess is worthy of the most serious brow-scrunching. It may not make you suddenly shout "Eureka!" or stir you to embark on a crusade to revitalize your research program (and it may not even interest you very much) but it is exceedingly important. It cuts to the guts of research, and without it no research project is even worth doing.

MR. SPOCK

When you think of logic, you naturally think of Mr. Spock. Avid Trek-kies might speculate on the semi-Vulcan's impressions of marketing research on Planet Earth; and, true to his "Star Trek" persona, his com-ments would be something like: "It is most illogical . . . perhaps hopeless. Beam me up immediately!"

In all likelihood, Spock would find the foremost irritant to be that vast phylum of errors that logicians, as they wink imperiously at one another, call *post hoc, ergo propter hoc*, which means, literally, "after this, there-fore because of this." It is the cardinal sin of marketing research. Eliminate it, and you remove most of the poison infecting the craft.

Post hoc, for readers mercifully spared the agonies of college logic courses, is when you impute from mere correlations cause-and-effect con-clusions. As miserable earthlings, in our everyday nonchalance, we do it all the time. At the turn of the century, the medical profession claimed a corn diet would cause pellagra; later they learned that corn had little to do with it, that the disease was due to a deficiency of Vitamin B. Those who had this deficiency just happened frequently to eat a lot of corn. Corn did not cause pellagra. An example of *reversed post hoc* is the teenage girl who believes, as many of them do, that one can't get pregnant the first time "you do it." Spock could probably forgive our doctors circa 1900 and teenage girls (since prudence of intellect is not anticipated from such a source), but when the modern researcher poses as scientist, when he sets out to establish Truth where once only crude speculation existed, he presents a false facade and would receive Spock's disapproval.

In the perfect world of the Vulcan, the researcher would either come clean and confess he is no scientist or recognize that he owes his *clients* the assurance that he is adhering to commonly accepted standards of logical, scientific inquiry. On Earth, unfortunately, the laws of logic are honored only in the breech.

TEST MARKET SANS CONTROL .

The most costly renditions of *post hoc* syndromes are found in test markets. On any day of the week a test market is launched somewhere without due regard for the scientific method, and based on such faulty test markets companies subsequently *go national* with markedly changed formulas; with tremendous advertising *heavy-ups*.

The typically flawed test market design consists of a *test area* (for example, Grand Rapids, Michigan), sales audits, and some kind of usage-and-attitude study. The latter will be conducted several weeks or months after the marketing event was begun, where the research planner has a room-temperature IQ, and where his IQ is *dull-normal* it is preceded by a *prestudy* which allows him to compare *before-and-after* glimpses of attitudes and so on. The intellectual progression from the poststudy *only* to the pre-and-post-study format is, to some companies, so close in impact to the cartoon light bulb suddenly materializing over corporate headquarters that a researcher, upon introducing this, is fulsomely congratulated and referred to as "our research genius."

I suppose, superficially, this may seem okay to some; after all, in many less-enlightened companies no consumer research would be done at all. Others might skip the prestudy but compare the poststudy to some national tracking study and not look too audaciously for those pesky geographic differences that always seem to plague the rest of us.

What these test market designs leave out is the "control." To anyone familiar with laboratory or medical experiments (excepting those elaborately orchestrated by Bela Lugosi, et al. in the Gothic horrors from Universal), faithful devotion to the sanctity of the scientific method always mandates the use of a control. And so, Kalamazoo could be designated control to our Grand Rapids test (thus forming a classic city combination dating back to the dawn of marketing history), and the pre-and-post studies must be conducted in each.[1]

To those who scoff at such fastidiousness, let them talk with the legion of marketers who have had their promotional schemes emasculated by stray competitive events, and they will find that the pre-post/test-control format is the only one that instills them with much confidence. But even though these simple principles have been commonplace in scientific circles since before the days when Michael Faraday was hooking up electric wires to frogs' legs, they still have little currency with today's research community.

Now, I've intentionally chosen an easy and obvious illustration to introduce the subject of logic and consequently am in danger of arousing disbelief as to the gravity of the situation. In companies where researchers are pure of heart and sterling of character, readers with arched eyebrows are asking: "Does Haller really think people are that dense?"[2] Conversely, in even more companies (particularly those who barely make it to the Fortune 500) marketing directors are storming into their research departments, book in hand, and demanding: "Read this, turkey, and then tell me what you're going to do to salvage our Tulsa test?!" Believe me, the logic-starved test market is par for the course.

THE PERPETUAL RATIO

Manifestly, marketing can make no claim to being obsessed with logic, but when it comes to the analysis of marketing data, logic cannot safely be neglected. The strong researcher must not allow his instinct to avoid analytical sand traps to stop once his project has been reported. His vigilance must extend to those who use his report in order to ensure that they do not misconstrue his data because, if he relaxes his circumspection, his clients will, out of cleverness or ignorance, perform strange rites with his numbers. One common illicit numerical machination is when clients get the urge to work up their own ratios. They love indexing because it lets them get by with one number instead of several and they are not intimidated by the shaky nature of generating percentages on top of percentages. In the interest of promoting goodwill, this can usually be tolerated until they start ascribing an illogical permanency to some of these ratios.

The most common trap here is in the assumption of constancy between trial level and purchase level, which leads to a strong pitch for more promotional funding—with the argument that a major increase in trial (induced by couponing, etc.) would guarantee a commensurate increase in purchases, ergo the brand's market share would climb. For example, if a trial level of 55 percent produced a purchase level of 11 percent then a hyped trial of 80 percent would render a purchase level of 16 percent which would—they eloquently argue—more than pay for the extra promotional support required to generate it. Their proposals are usually made more subtly than this, but this is what it comes down to, and countless marketing plans have been framed on the basis of such erroneous conclusions and funding been allocated. A company doesn't have to be near the bottom of the Fortune 500 list to be cursed with this paucity of thinking; I've seen it in companies on the list's first page.

The flaw is immediately apparent to the armchair logician: you never have any guarantee that the relationships between two bits of independent data are linear and not exponential. The trial-purchase relationship is not a linear one. The consumers who were successfully propelled by your first wave of commercials and inducements to buy and then repurchase your product are probably *not* the same types of people as those who wouldn't get around to trying it until bombarded with further inducements. The first group could be composed of a lot of people who are vulnerable to anything new; the next group may be virtually immune to product innovations. Or, the first wave of triers could be a special minority group with a clear need for such a product—hence a disproportionate number of them who try it find it worthy of adoption for sustained usage. You may not be so lucky with the second wave, where you may pick up only triers motivated by curiosity and not by some profound need.

This is always an insidious kind of logic trap because when you read through a marketing plan—where such traps lurk—you usually do it in good faith, and presentations of this sort seem eminently reasonable: the numbers look sound and the thinking appears to be on an even higher plane than you usually encounter in most business documents. At first reading, it smacks of intelligence. So unless you assume the role of cynic and skeptic when you embark on a perusal of such documents, you could miss it.

ASSUMPTIONS OF CONSUMER'S LOGIC

A prevalent variation on the above is the superficially understandable presumption that a housewife's attitudes govern her behavior.[3] It sounds right, though; why else would a person do anything if there were not some kind of mental state that said it was desirable or permissible, etc. Awareness precedes attitudes, which precede trial, which precedes repeat purchasing. If you monitor any one of these and stimulate the consumers with marketing activities you should be able to assess the success of this effort, hence one of your management by objective (MBOs) becomes, for example, a significant improvement in brand awareness. The value of achieving this lies in its immanent impact on sales. At least that is the theory. Unfortunately, the consumer never made any commitment to logic, probably wouldn't recognize it as a component of her world, and would never tolerate it standing between herself and her shopper's entitlements.

It's still vital to try to improve attitudes toward your brand—if they're negative, you've got to do something; but they are not singular determinants of behavior. There are many other possibilities. Trial, in fact, can precede the formation of attitudes; consumers can be lured into trying a product purely out of curiosity. Or, more complexly, attitudes can remain flat and brand usage can still drop off if, for example, the entire product category begins to be replaced by another (e.g., a peanut-butter loving kid may still rave about Jif, though he has recently discovered tuna-salad sandwiches and no longer eats peanut butter). In the absence of other information—which, of course, the sophisticated and well-heeled marketer would have—you cannot always be sure what changes in consumer measurements mean. (See discussion on "DAGMAR," page 61.)

The foregoing introduction to research logic was general and not focused on particular methodological aspects. The following specific examples should be more vivid.

CLIENT RESEARCH REVIEW

A major U.S. company once had me review its entire marketing research program. Giving me a couple of file drawers full of reports, they instructed me to comment on the techniques they had used. Apart from serving as an intriguing respite from my workaday chores I felt a sense of mission in this assignment: they wanted to know why all the research made their products look so mediocre while, as a company, they were actually prospering. "How come," they asked, "the research fails to put a finger on why we are successful?"

In the files I found forty-five major studies with a total value of about $1 million. Among these, in all candor, I could only locate four studies with flawless logic.

At the risk of making it sound like a gossip column, I'd like to run through the kinds of logic errors I bumped into here. In prefacing this, I'd like the reader to know that most of these studies were performed by well-known, reputable research firms. They were conducted with seriousness and objectivity. While I hope (and trust) most readers will immediately see that the errors are obvious, I wish to make it clear—as obvious as they may be—they are not exceptional . . . they rather accurately reflect the kind of thinking that is ubiquitous. As pessimistic as it may seem, I maintain if you had a random sample of all the research conducted worldwide in the past twelve months you would find roughly the same incidence of blemished planning and analysis. Only a few examples are required to accurately reflect on the current state of the art.

1. The dialectic of the photographic memory

The first of my client's reports on my hit list is an attitude study whose sin against the norms of logic was in asking respondents where and how their attitudes about the product were formed. I could see what they were getting at, since this was planned as a prestudy for an advertising test (which apparently never was executed) and they had hoped to have people tell them on the poststudy that their attitudes were a result of the commendable and pervasive advertising efforts, etc. Some hope.[4] Few people can ever trace the origins of their thoughts, or the source of their brand awareness. There are far too many factors involved. Only rarely are attitudes formed by a conscious act of the will. Hence, it is illogical to assume that they can relate the process by which their attitudes were shaped. If asked, they will of course try to respond to such questions, but their responses will be utter nonsense.

2. The dialectic of permanently traceable causes

Next, I looked at a study that purported to measure "advertising effectiveness." I always groan when researchers state their intentions this way
and then laconically measure recall and attitudes (which was roughly all this
project amounted to). The thumping logic error, though, was asking where
the brand's advertising was seen and heard. Informed researchers, ever
since the famous Hershey case, have realized that most people will say they
saw it on television, whether or not there ever was any TV spending, and regardless of the weight you had in other media.[5] The point here, as in the
above example, is that people do not consciously categorize communications by the media that conveyed them. Moreover, since they spend so much
of their time watching TV, and given the intrusive power of the medium,
they will invariably credit it as the vehicle for any recall they can muster up.
Analytically, you will never be able to derive any serious nourishment from
this line of questioning. The responses it produces never line up with relative
media weights—even allowing for variances in effectiveness—and, as far as
I can determine, the top consumer goods companies stopped analyzing it
long ago. Still, I guarantee that if you look closely at any pedestrian questionnaire for a study on advertising you will find it included somewhere. It
is one of the more unremitting examples of unthinking research design and
the craft's most prevalent violation of the simplest rules of logic and good
sense.

3. The dialectic of balanced samples #1

This study was called a "customer satisfaction study." The research firm
asked how much consumers liked the client's brand, then compared these
responses to those from a similar group of competitive-brand consumers.
They made no allowance for recency of purchase, even though the most recent buyers, as a general rule, will have more favorable attitudes than less
recent buyers. By neglecting to check for that in your data processing you
can never be sure whether any detectable differences in attitudes are due to
the product or to recency of purchase. Normally, I would not get too upset
about this kind of oversight, but the report happened to indicate that my client's product was not as well liked as competition, and, recalling that I was
examining these studies to determine why their research always showed
gloom in the face of success, the results could have been pure illusion.

4. The dialectic of balanced samples #2

This was a study to determine how the client's dealers rated them compared to how the competition's dealers rated their suppliers. (In the product
category under study retailers carried only one brand.) My quibble with the
study's design logic centers around the likelihood of unequal samples. If my
client had garnered the best and the brightest of the retailers (as they proba-

bly had), then surely they would have been more demanding and more sharply critical than the competitor's less mentally agile group of retailers, who (not being on the same frequency) may have been too dull to come up with any penetrating or constructive criticism about their suppliers. Comparisons of attitudes between the two groups were not very flattering to my client, but, at the same time, not very actionable for engineering any improvements because of the built-in bias. I'm not saying the study was a total loss, but it would have been dangerous to take what it said at face value.

5. The dialectic of the objective respondent

This was an attitude study that began with a very lengthy (120) spate of agree-disagree questions covering just about everything you could possibly say about the product. Fatigue would be one evident problem, but the logic error was in their ending the interview with an open-ended attitudinal section. How they expected anyone to be able to answer this impartially after just being clued in by a 120-attribute preamble is beyond me. A self-respecting Vulcan would most certainly have reversed the order of these questions.

6. The dialectic of the creative consumer

Next was an image study in which, for some bizarre reason, respondents were enlisted to tell what would constitute the ideal advertising for this product. Common sense should dictate that since you have to sell your product to frequently indifferent or even hostile characters you would not be likely to benefit from their notions on how you should go about this. The suggestion that consumers would ever come up with useful ideas for ad copy, when most agencies go through purgatory just trying to do the same thing, is insupportable.

7. The dialectic of third-party informants

This purported to be an image study of the company but was stymied by a very confusing question. They asked, "What is the reputation of (company name)?" Now, normally when you want to find out what people think of your company, you can just go out and ask them. But when you ask what your *reputation* is, contextually, you cannot be sure whether people tell you what they think or what they imagine their friends think. (Of what value would the latter be?) I suspect this infringement of logical thought occurred at the study's very instigation, when its purpose was articulated. Thereafter, the job was probably delegated to a junior technician who innocently carried out what he thought to be a faithful execution of the proposal's wording. Never being asked or challenged by his superiors to state the logic in asking strangers to tell you what other strangers thought, when that could easily have been obviated by just asking the *strangers* himself, he went on to field, analyze, and report sheer absurdities.

8. The dialectic of extracting meaning from ambiguity

Then came a study evaluating a new ad campaign, with the main measurement being top-of-the-mind awareness plus this strangely worded question: "If you can recall any (brand name) advertising, what did you find *notable* about it?" Two logic problems here: One, top-of-the-mind awareness ("Name the brands of (product category) that come to mind") can signify such a diversity of things that, logically, you would never be able to interpret the results . . . at least not without grievous self-deception. High top-of-the-mind mentions, for example, accrue to brands with either highly offensive or very entertaining advertising, or to freshly introduced brands, or to the oldest brands on the market. Two, this study's worst inadequacy was in asking what was *notable* in the brand's advertising. A more ambiguous word could not be found; it has so many potential meanings (good, visible, useful, visually memorable, exceptional, very bad, tasteless, etc.) that nothing concrete can be ascertained from the responses, which in this study, by the way, happened to consist mainly of visual or situational elements.

9. The dialectic of pure exposure and instant motivation

I would skip this one, an advertising pretest, but for the fact that it was conducted by such a highly regarded research house, because its postulate is so ridiculous. Consider it comic relief if you will. After being shown some test ads consumers were asked which was *most persuasive . . .* and why. Ads deemed most persuasive were so judged because they "were eye-catching" and because they "showed a picture of the product." The logic error is embodied in the initial premise that such garbage would be even remotely helpful. After two minutes of contemplation anyone with an average intelligence level could see that such research serves as no guidance in marketing. No known system of logic could absorb data like that and continue on to a meaningful conclusion.

10. The dialectic of the impartial respondent (revisited) plus the dialectic of the value of useless knowledge

Here's another advertising *effectiveness study* in which viewers first were asked to name the sponsor of a given TV show (it was my client, naturally) and then were asked what brand they would buy. The first error is that, in an interview, whenever you appear to be searching for compliments, that's exactly what you'll get from a lot of folks. If they guess correctly on the sponsorship issue they'll feel you want them to also grant you a vote of thanks and endorse your brand. The truth, under the circumstances, might be pretty hard to proffer if your brand was not their real choice. The researchers could have reversed the question, but they really should have asked themselves if sponsorship knowledge was an actionable piece of information. Advertising has a more direct goal than that, and the study failed to address it.

11. The dialectic of the self-selected sample

Again, we had another advertising evaluation study wherein people were asked to volunteer what brands (in the appropriate category) they had recently seen advertised. Then they asked for detailed recall. This looked okay to me at first glance, but on reflecting for a minute I saw a glaring logic error: the sample is self-screened. If you want to know how well your advertising communicates a message you have to quiz a sample of the entire market, not just people who, for the vaguest of reasons, volunteer seeing your advertising right off the bat. They will give you distortingly high recall, while interviewing everyone would produce something much closer to the truth . . . as it affects marketing success.

12. The dialectic of the crystal ball through large samples

"Even if it's wrong if you do it enough it'll be okay." In this study over a thousand people were interviewed and asked to predict their future needs associated with a given product. It resulted in wild speculation involving robots and the total computerization of house and community. Logically, if teams of economists and sociologists can't get their forecasts right, it follows that the average housewife will fare no better. And it doesn't matter how many interviews you do, it still won't be reliable.

13. The dialectic of best meaning motivation

Here is a tricky one. This study attempted to learn why people bought certain brands, but the questionnaire went like this: Consumers were asked which brand they thought was best (*not* which they had bought) and why. Then, without grounds to substantiate any linkage, it was assumed this was the reason why the respondent would buy that brand. The important attributes thus obtained for one brand may be numerically superior to those of another, but the inference that this governs purchase decisions is dangerous. The data could be only an artifact of the questioning method. I might say that I thought a Mercedes the best automobile because of its craftsmanship and reliability, although I bought a Seville because it was cheaper and looked a lot better. My next-door neighbor also votes for the Mercedes, but he has a Saab because he thinks he is too young for the Benzie.

14. The universal dialectic of generic error

I saved this for the last because it is so universal and so serious that I wanted to make sure it received the best send-off. Throughout these studies I was asked to examine there was a pervasive tendency to ask closed-end questions about product attributes consisting of *generic* features. For example, in the shampoo category "cleans the hair" would be generic—it's an important feature but it's pretty common to all brands and thus not a serious basis for brand differentiation. There are better factors used in the shampoo business for this purpose: "stops dandruff," "does not leave hair greasy," "makes hair more manageable,"[6] "gives hair better texture/body," etc. The generic reason is usually why the product is bought but is seldom the basis for brand selections. Hence, these studies, by concentrating on mainly generic types of features, failed to reveal the true source of brand differentiation in this product category. (That may be the key reason why my client's research made them look so mediocre.)

They never gave the consumer a chance to tell what she really thought of their brand, which their sales volume indicated would have to be relatively favorable. Most of these studies put words in her mouth, instead of shutting up and letting her speak freely in response to open-end and nondirected types of questions. The logic in making a priori determinations about what the consumer seeks in the product was unjustified and flimsy. The generic approach fails to offer any useful guidance. (See section on open ends, Danger Number 59, pages 116–19.)

CONCLUSIONS

Logic, then, takes on many forms, ranging from formal structures of thought and Sherlockian deduction to an almost neurotic skepticism about how things really work vs. how they are often assumed to work.

Logic is really just common sense. Sometimes it helps if it is based on empirical evidence, but it is readily apparent to anyone who takes the time to apply a little mental effort.

If there is one single message or admonition in this book that should come through in the remaining chapters it is this: be skeptical of everything you first want to do. Examine every detail, in every step, in every project. Do not do anything just because it was done that way in the past, and neither should you do it because it *sounds* logical or correct. Every single project harbors some gaucherie, faux pas, or outrageous oversight. Most embody logic errors so momentous that, at first, you won't see them. Research isn't ever going to be perfect; new experiences will continually illuminate your procedures. But, by being skeptical and thorough in every matter, you will be able to improve your research quality immensely.

Still I fear that to most researchers this concern is rather arid. No one questions their logic, so there is no compulsion to do anything about it. But I say that logic—or its abuse—permeates every facet of the universe, and research cannot be excepted from its governance. It is a basic requirement, a *sine qua non*. It is at the very foundation of everything you must know in order to be a good judge of research. The basic principle of all scientific investigation and technical progress is, and always shall be, crystal clear thinking and an unfailing skepticism.

I will keep coming back to this as I pounce upon the specific dangers found in various marketing research practices and methodologies.

NOTES

1. The careful researcher would probably want more than one test area, and more than one control, as a contingency against the unforeseen local *disturbances*.

2. Not think . . . know from many sad experiences.

3. To preserve literary sanity, *housewife* is defined to mean anyone who is considered a consumer. The pronoun *she* and related variants are not indications of gender. While this is a book for global purposes, readers should be made aware that in the United States adult females have deserted the home front for positions in industry and government, and there are no traces of what was once termed a *housewife*. But the term sticks in the profession as a synonym for *consumer* in the United States, and in less-enlightened nations it remains in possession of its ancient meaning and connotations.

4. Advertising agencies like to work this line of questioning into their studies. If the poststudy has a lot of consumers crediting their campaign with motivational powers they will make a big to-do about it, take a few bows, and instinctively recommend increased media weight. If, on the other hand, as is more likely, nothing noteworthy emerges from this question, they simply ignore it.

5. The story goes that years ago, even though Hershey had no media advertising, consumers, when asked where they saw Hershey "advertising," invariably reported having seen it on television. This may, indeed, be an apocryphal story, but it is often told as gospel.

6. Procter & Gamble used to couple this with something called "more combable," which, on first exposure to it, few readers could pronounce correctly.

3 • *Product Research: The* Sine Qua Non

The product test is the most important thing the researcher does. We in marketing delude ourselves when we think our advertising, promotions, package graphics, shelf displays, and sales-force efforts match the product in importance. While our marketing skills get us our high trial levels, it is all—in the end analysis—merely recremental, for it is the product that largely generates its own repeat business and is the *sine qua non* of free enterprise.

And while our marketing skills certainly set in motion more favorable consumer perceptions, it is, ultimately, the quality of the product itself that propels our business and makes it abide and endure against competitive forces.

In the many factorial analyses of business success, the determinants of return on investment (ROI) have consistently highlighted the paramount nature of *product quality*, but none have ever given equal weight to advertising, promotional activity, or any of the other components of the marketing mix. They are the icing, the product is the cake.

It is, therefore, perplexing that product research is considered the domain of the drudge, while other research tributaries assume the fulgid glamor of a Vegas lounge act. The cold truth is that if the product research is not performed with surgical precision and unassailable thoroughness, the rest of the research package might as well be forgotten. In fact, nothing in the entire marketing pantheon equates with the business of testing the product.

Alarmingly, given its central significance, relatively little is known about the art and science of product testing. The analytical methods used in product tests have been thrashed around enough, but the task of planning the actual, detailed designs has been largely overlooked. There are many dangers and risks connected with product testing, many of which I will discuss. Many more have been left unexplored and must remain unanswered questions until someone comes forth with the funding for experimentation. Most companies assume a blasé posture about the methods applied in evaluating their products . . . and almost certainly are making far-reaching decisions with faulty information. It therefore seems exigent to explore this in considerable detail, and also to hope that in the future others will carry this task forward.

At the risk of breaking a promise made in the Preface and appearing that I am trying to transform this book into a text, I'd like to start with a structural overview of the subject. Veteran research professionals will be familiar with much of the content of the next few pages, but novices and lay persons may find something useful in it.

The usual product research project is none other than the blind test which, as everyone knows, is when you conceal the brand identity of a product and allow (and on this there is a need for faith and hope) the consumer to focus only on the *product* per se, or, in some rare cases, on the product *plus* the package. There are four major classifications of blind tests: evaluation, discrimination, association (*halo*), and market positioning. It helps to keep these straight in your mind because the purpose of the test dictates the method you will use.

MAJOR CLASSIFICATION OF BLIND TESTS

Evaluation tests

This is the most important piece of research you will ever do. Its purpose is simple and pure: to judge how well the consumer likes your product. Usually this is framed in terms of how it compares with its major competitor. Sometimes there is no competition (e.g., in the case of a totally new kind of product) and then the purpose more properly becomes one of determining how acceptable it is to the consumer. Since it is customary to invest a fair amount of money in such important tests (good random samples, in-home locales, etc.), you should be sure there are adequate grounds for such a test. In other words, make sure before you spend the money that the consumer can discriminate, which can be determined via a less expensive mode of testing (e.g., in a central location rather than in-home) in a *discrimination test*.

Discrimination tests

These usually involve formula changes you hope the consumer won't notice, such as a cheaper way of making the product which allegedly does not alter the way it performs. You have to be careful in defining the purpose of a discrimination test. Sometimes what you really want is a *cheap* evaluation test, but, bound by clumsy wording, you may end up with elaborate designs extending way beyond the level of sophistication your company may want. For example, some say it's perfectly adequate to use the simple paired comparison test design (new formula vs. old formula) even though, strictly speaking, this doesn't tell you if your consumers can *discriminate* between the two formulas. But if they break even in overall preference, does this say that most people could not see the difference, or just that they could and did not care, or that everyone could see a clear difference but split evenly on which they liked better . . . ? (More on this later.)

The design gymnastics that you get when you set out to do a *real* discrimination test (the double triangle, the pair-repeat, the reversed duo-trio, and so on) run into a pile of trouble in the field. Respondents can easily get confused about the real purpose of such tests and try to pick the *odd product*, rather than give honest indications of their preferences. Also, there is the problem of *inconsistency of preference*, which, as I will discuss later, accompanies virtually all product tests.

The sharpest, and probably safest, discrimination test could very well be the directed interest, which is also examined later in this chapter.

Association (halo) test

Although there are more precise ways of describing it, the term *halo effect*, though now sounding a little bit creaky in the postpsychoanalytical era, still has a slick pseudoscientific ring to it. Whenever you have an incidental, nonoperative element that imposes itself on the product's performance with such finesse that users perceive it to perform better than it really does (can you really tell one vodka brand from another?), you have grounds for conducting a halo effect test. It doesn't really look different than the evaluation test, but there are some special risks involved in it, which is why I list it separately.

It does differ from the discrimination test, however. The halo effect feature must be so unquestionably easy to discriminate that no preliminary discrimination test would be necessary. For example, if you want the cooling effect or *sting* in your after-shave lotion heightened by changing from yellow to blue, you don't have to test it to prove that men can perceive the color difference. You would go right into your association test.

Market positioning tests

These include tests to show that a given product change is directionally right for a brand—a question of product-strategy fit. Some researchers use these to detect market segments: this usually entails placing respondents with several different brands at the same time or sequentially. The technical problems and dangers connected with market positioning tests are not all that different from the other classifications mentioned above. The major departure is in the forms of analysis used, these being much more dependent on multivariate programs than the others . . . they are almost impossible to decipher without them. Not included in this classification would be the highly specialized in-home placements used to forecast market share; since these are traditionally accompanied by some form of advertising stimulus, they are not—strictly speaking—product tests.

OBVIOUS DANGERS

Product testing is beset with a number of concealed dangers and the last two-thirds of this chapter will be exclusively dedicated to their eradication.

For right now, just to alert the starry-eyed to the ominous presence of apprehension tormenting the more conscientious product-testing professionals, here are a couple of very general pitfalls needing no empirical effort to validate.

One is the failure to draft a precise enough definition of the problem to let you determine into which of the above classifications the test should fall. If only for budgetary purposes, this is an all-important first step, but one that many skip. Another is trying to get the respondent to use the product in some manner that is quite alien to her regular usage pattern. This may be acceptable if it is integral to the product formulation, but a lot of researchers inject it into test designs willy-nilly. One of the more common variations on this is asking her to keep notes while she does the test, so that she can have something to refer to on the call-back interview. These are all considerations that have commonsense appeal. . . . Most of those that I will cover later are not always so evident.

CHECKLIST

Before planning a blind test some of the following questions should be asked: Is there a sound argument for doing the test in the first place . . . i.e., is there a plausible chance that your consumers will be able to differentiate between the products; and what is the quality of evidence you have on this? Is the problem under study one of pure discrimination, which would not call for expensive full-scale fieldwork but could be done instead via a shopping mall intercept, etc.? Is this a one-shot test or is it a piece of a much broader program? If part of a larger undertaking, can we economize by possibly combining it with other tests . . . or can we wait until other tests are finished before seeing if we need to do this one? Have certain marketing circumstances been taken into account that would be necessary to exploit the product, and are these reflected in your usage instructions, etc.? Are you choosing the right sample of users? Can you keep the number of product comparisons down to a manageable level so that your management will be able to grasp the results of the test—given the very brief amount of time they will have to devote to reading your report or listening to your presentation . . . ? Can some formulas proposed for testing be discounted for purely marketing reasons without having to go through a blind test? Have you allowed for the inclusion of a competitive product somewhere in the test design? If all of these issues are considered at planning time money can often be saved, and, in some cases, entire tests can be eliminated altogether.

NO SUCH THING AS A SIMPLE TEST

The researcher is often thrown off his course by sudden shifts in the winds of testing rationales. The classic test of the marketing research textbook seldom graces his desk. Instead, he tends to get product tests couched in marketing terms, forcing him to turn his back on what he regards as his standard product testing techniques.

Consider the following exemplifications of the real world. (My versions of the answers are provided in the Notes.)

• The product manager on Mellow Instant Pudding wants to find out if his product is superior to his main competitor, Jello Instant Pudding. He cannot wait for you to field the test in your normal, snail-paced, in-home manner, he says, because that would take at least a week or two. Instead, he asks you to run it through a central location facility where he can arrange for a food technician to prepare the product and you can line up an interviewing service to haul in the housewives and get them to taste it. As a concession to your well-known desire for in-home conditions, he says, if you feel it is really necessary you can have the respondents actually prepare the pudding themselves in the test kitchen before they eat it. He has thus thrown you several curves. How do you handle it?[1]

• The latest Nielsens show that Prim Diet Cola is rapidly losing share. Tab is gaining. The product manager on Prim, in conspicuous panic, demands a quick test to see which flavor consumers prefer—Prim or Tab. He wants a paired comparison taste test, at a mall; and to speed the process along, he wants the questionnaire limited to one question: "Which flavor do you like better?" To make absolutely certain everyone gives you a valid, considered answer on the flavor issue, he wants you to tell each respondent, prior to tasting the products, to look only for flavor differences.[2]

• The grape crop was really awful, but R&D—like viticulturists of old—have played around with some *blending options* and have about a dozen or more variations they'd like you to test. But they want to use the company panel for security reasons. This panel is composed of employees trained in how to articulate product differences and to report on organoleptic sensations better than the average wine imbiber could (they romanticize the product too much). R&D promises to test the winning version in-home just like you always say they have to, but they do feel the company panel should be used for these variations, and they vow that the results will only be used for rough guidance and not to make important product decisions.[3]

• Product management is proposing to reduce the maple syrup level on Farm House Table Syrup to almost zero, but they hope neither the trade nor the consumer will notice this. Unfortunately, they will have to note the change on the label. Lately, they point out to you, the *Consumer Reports* people have been off on one of their crusades against the product category, deploring the wholesale disappearance of maple syrup from such products.[4]

• You are in a test market with Zing Beverage Mix and R&D comes along with a new formula that they feel will appeal to kids more than the current one. So far the test market has been disappointing, and marketing is very tempted to replace the current formula with the latest effort but are conservative enough to suggest doing some kind of product test first. So R&D drafts up a job request in which they ask for a paired comparison blind test of the current vs. the new, among children six to fourteen years of age.[5]

The stalwart researcher flushes out the extraneous hogwash and sets up only that product test design that fits perfectly with the given marketing situation. Most of this is not in the textbooks, because the marketing variations are too diverse or too *insider*. Marketing people cannot be expected to have the same frames of reference as the researcher. They will often introduce elements that are not relevant, or that simply cannot be accommodated within the framework of a product test. At the same time, the wise researcher will be quick to appreciate that a product test serves no one if carried out within a technician's vacuum. It must fit into the real world somehow. This augurs in favor of a flexible approach, balanced with the longer view that realizes the importance of having normative data.

For our present purposes it is enough to establish that there seems little opportunity—or need—to set one's product-testing methodologies in concrete, but the urge to veer away from standardization entirely increases the likelihood of embarking on a course fraught with immense and unforetold dangers. The slipperier curves that are tossed at the product researcher will be explored later in this chapter as we examine these dangers.

CRITICAL COMPONENTS OF THE PRODUCT TEST QUESTIONNAIRE

Perhaps I am merely a prisoner of my own experience, but if a paired comparison blind test contains, first of all, a question on *overall preference* ("Considering everything about them, which of the two products did you like better?") and, secondly, voluntary *reasons for preference* ("What is there about the [preferred product] that you liked better than the [nonpreferred product]?"), then I seldom care what comes next . . . as long as the damn interview doesn't get too long. I don't feel a lot of *direct questions* ("Which flavor did you like better?") are essential, and I would resist all attempts to do away with reasons for preference by substituting a list of direct questions.[6]

Reasons for preference are a key part of any product test and in some cases the most important part. Direct questions are a squalid substitute for them since (1) they force everyone to answer where, in actual fact, many respondents might consider some—or all—of the particular factors in question totally irrelevant, and (2) they only tell why a product was preferred if you were smart enough or lucky enough to include all the operative factors in your list of direct questions. If (as is entirely likely) you have a mixture of the relevant and the irrelevant you will never know which are the operative ones. From the point of view of a general manager, the attempt to respond to each and every problem detected in a blind test could cause R&D to launch several projects aimed at product improvements that are not really necessary. Also, (3) they can interject bias by careless or misguided wording . . . this being perhaps the least of our worries about direct-question dependency.

Reasons for preference, on the other hand, let the respondent tell you, without prior prompting, what she considers to be the factors governing her decision to choose one product over the other. They also make it possible to compare a series of separate tests, examining the varying levels of response on specific factors. With a total dependence on direct questions you cannot do this because all respondents reply to all questions (regardless of their impact on her preference) and, also, through time, there are very strong temptations to change, or perfect, the direct questions, thus destroying strict comparability. In essence, with direct questions one's analytical scope is seriously abridged, and sometimes even thwarted.

Some researchers suggest obtaining, instead of reasons for preference, favorable and unfavorable voluntary comments on each product, but I feel there are clear and compelling advantages to using reasons for preference rather than *likes and dislikes* on each product. Chief among them are the fact that they are easier to cope with in the interviewing situation. People have a lot of difficulty being negative about most things (especially in some non-English-speaking countries) but you can overcome this by letting them speak comparatively . . . implying weaknesses in one product by stating how the other excels. We have also been bothered by a tendency people have with the likes and dislikes approach—not wanting to say the same thing about both products. This very human urge to say something different (or not to have to repeat oneself) creates artificial response patterns. Also, when you give people two products to try, they make comparisons during the test period and are waiting to talk to you in a comparative mode. It's unwise to disrupt this.

I do, however, like to go a little further than those who strictly adhere to the preference/reasons format, and ask what some call the *advantage-non* questions, that is, "I realize you liked A better than B, but was there any way in which you liked B better than A?" This usually pulls out a few comments, so it is worth the extra time. It also satisfies the R&D guy who may feel—quite correctly, actually—that few consumer preferences are all one-way. (See discussion on open ends versus closed ends, pages 116–20.)

TREATMENT OF REASONS FOR PREFERENCE

One reason for the absence of enthusiasm researchers show for reasons for preference is that the reasons aren't presented in the right way. To be perfectly honest, every time I've been given a blind test report using the paired comparison method, and with reasons for preference included, I have found the writer used the *wrong* base on which to percentage the reasons. This may seem like an awfully petty point, but for want of a nail the kingdom was lost, and it is with such detailed applications that data can reveal insights useful to marketing people.

Here, in a simplified example, is how I usually see it reported:

	Preferred Product A	Preferred Product B
Base—number preferring each	210	90
Reasons for preference:		
Makes more/richer/thicker suds	33%	30%
Cleans better/faster/easier	23	21
Easier to use/pour/etc.	18	16

NOTE: This example has a sample of 300, a preference for A of 70 percent, for B of 30 percent, excluding nonpreferences.

Based on the above display there seems no basis for discovering the underlying source of the overall win for A. Both products have about the same magnitude of responses for each of the three reasons volunteered above. R&D would probably have to conclude that none of these attributes had anything to do with consumer preferences. This conclusion, however, is dead wrong. It is merely an artifact of the manner of presentation.

Think of yourself as the product manager for Product A. You want to know: "If I put that product out on the market, how many people *who try it* will detect and appreciate the sudsing advantage R&D developed?" Note that you wouldn't be asking, as the above treatment assumes, how many *who like* your product will applaud the suds feature. There is a vast difference in the two questions—one that few researchers seem to be cognizant of . . . and it's one reason why nobody ever gets much nourishment from it and why, in a staggering number of companies, reasons for preference have a very tarnished reputation and have been dropped from their litany of standard techniques.

Look now at what happens when the reasons for preference are percentaged on the proper base, i.e., on the total number of people who had a preference—regardless of the product preferred. . . . These are the people who—as best as we can estimate in a blind test situation—simulate the body of consumers who will try your product when it is introduced. (Note: in case you wonder why nonpreferrers are eliminated below, it's because they aren't asked to give reasons for preference.)

	Regarding Product A	Regarding Product B
Base—total who had a preference	300	
Reasons for preference:		
Makes more/richer/thicker suds	23%	9%
Cleans better/faster/easier	16	6
Easier to use/pour/etc.	12	5

Now we can see some important differences. Chief among them is the salutary fact that the sudsing advantage looms large as the principal basis for A's win over competitor B. It is only through this regrettably unfashionable manner of data treatment that reasons for preference can throw any meaningful light on product performance. Yet, simple as it may be to implement, this treatment is the most frequently overlooked one in product testing. And we are all the poorer for it.

REAL MEANING OF BLIND TEST WIN

History's first paired comparison blind test was harder to interpret than any we do today. It's not so much that the methodology itself has changed, but that today we know a lot more about what to expect and how to read the results. Still, controversies over the most innocent looking results can break out. Suppose A beats B 70:30; what does this really mean? Does it say that 70 percent of potential users (all things being equal) will embrace A and reject B? Would we be just as well off if only 55 percent selected A? Is a company correct in insisting on a statistically significant blind test win over competition every time a major formula change is recommended?

Well, obviously there is no definitive answer. The first question can be dismissed as nonsensical unless you test all known products in the category and, somehow, incorporate marketing forces into your test. But the question on how big a win you need is valid. The solution to the riddle can be obtained only through many years of experience. A statistically significant win, in product categories where you find stiff competition, is so hard to merit that shooting for anything beyond that would probably be a fruitless allocation of energies. The 55:45 win is just about all most products ever expect to see. So we are still left with the question, "Is it really necessary to shoot for this? Why shouldn't we be happy with a break-even . . . or maybe even a little loss, like a 45:55. What difference would it make?"

Multicompanied and multiproduct experiences give a pragmatic or functional answer to this: your chances of success are better if you get a win, they decrease markedly at the break-even level, and decline very sharply as you fall below this and get a loss. Going back to my introductory remarks on the overwhelming importance of product quality, your product must be perceived favorably relative to your rival's in order to be granted a good spot in the household pantry, broom closet, or medicine chest. Consumer decisions are usually made at initial trial—or soon after. Market share is built on small margins of success on one product aspect or another. You don't conquer entire target groups . . . you slice off small slivers, and through time, with a succession of successes, in the aggregate, market shares are built up. One small sliver may come from having a slightly bigger chance of pleasing the consumer than your competitor (as testified to in the blind test win), so that on each trial occasion in each home your probability of being victorious is ever so slightly higher than the next guy's. If you go to market with a loss in a blind test, you fail to have the odds in your favor. And, axiomatically, your competitor will have the odds in his favor. A company policy that demands a statistically significant win is a good one for the company that wants to enforce high standards in its marketing activities. It may not always be necessary, but the few exceptions that come along are hard to identify, and anyway they shouldn't be allowed to attenuate the overall corporate discipline represented in such policies.

INTRODUCTION TO DANGERS

Now we are about to get into the guts of the chapter, so a couple of remarks are in order. These will apply not only to this chapter, but also to most subsequent chapters.

There is a host of dangers and risks associated with almost every technique known in the research community. They are all serious, and all have the power to turn golden intentions into dross, but they vary in the exactitude with which their hazard quotients are known.

The big dangers are clear and present hazards of immense importance. But there are other dangers: subtle and lurking dangers of unknown importance, problems and doubts raised in isolated, unelaborated studies. When a company finds that an optional research approach produces results at odds with prior techniques (on which it may have years of trusted experience), it seldom wishes to invest dollars in repeating the technique ad infinitum until it has absolute certainty it does or doesn't work. To do so would be to appear, and rightly so, as a hopelessly romantic academic in pursuit of elusive truths, and not as a serious member of the business community where budgets are limited (and always in danger of being cut) and where all deeds must bear fruits. As a result, though we will report on several of these aborted attempts among a smattering of different techniques, few have been followed through enough times to be able to establish a high level of certitude to our judgments regarding them, nor will they ever be. If any single one is important to a particular reader, they should be explored further, or at least approached gingerly.

Some of these are going to seem like awfully petty points, but—to use an awkward allusion—a weak cotter pin can jeopardize the safety of your car's steering mechanism and endanger your life. Others will seem obvious though you may not have experienced them yourself; and, obvious though *you* may find them, the fact is that they occur with a frequency that would make your hair curl. You occupy a position of honor among the research elite if they are always kept from your door.

DANGER NUMBER 1: Paired Comparison versus Monadic Blind Tests

The research community is emotionally split between monadic and paired comparison blind tests. The choice is critical and will affect the utility value of the results . . . but how do you know if the choice is a rational one, or the backlash of some professional dispute?

The longest-running, loudest, and often most bitter debate in the annals of consumer research centers around the merits of paired comparison testing (A vs. B) and monadic testing (person gets only one product, A or B).

As a matter of fact this issue is so touchy that, like suspicious alley cats circling one another, wary researchers often feel out other newly introduced researchers on where they stand here. I have often been asked on job interviews where I stood on this. A researcher that is beholden to one or the other technique will be suddenly plunged into gossip, fear, and backbiting if a new member of the department with the opposite viewpoint is hired. In the research community this is the strongest single source of prejudice among the players.

First some kind words in support of the monadic design: There are, of course, times when you can use only this format—if you have a truly inventive, first-time-ever product (e.g., an invisibility pill) there would be no parallel product to pit yours against. Or there may be occasions when your product, even though *blind*, may be easy to identify because of its unique shape or some other feature which, in a paired situation, could give you an imbalance—with one product easily identifiable and the other one a total mystery. One would think such bias should be obvious; nonetheless, tests of this ilk are frequently perpetrated by respected practitioners whose public pronouncements against single-product designs have been so vociferous as to have backed them into a permanent paired comparison corner.

But, on the other hand, there are innumerable situational opportunities for safe and sensible executions of the paired comparison method where invective in favor of the monadic is still aroused. "The monadic," you are often told, "is the only natural way to test a product. . . . People don't buy two different brands and use them together. They don't make professed, direct comparisons between brands as a systematic rule. The normal way people use products is one at a time, and they evaluate them on an individual basis within the rough context of past experiences and current expectations.'' And as far as it goes there is a lot of truth in this. However, for some forthcoming practical reasons, I happen to be a mild fan of the paired comparison; and whenever I do a monadic test I keep my fingers crossed, lest the results turn out to be unreadable.

How does one effectively respond to this? For one thing, as hard as we may try, there's no such thing as a natural product test situation. When you are mysteriously selected (''But how did you get my name?'') for a test . . . and asked a preamble of questions about product usage . . . and (if the questionnaire was well conceived) whether you are going to be home for the next week or so . . . and then are given one or more plain white packages that say only, ''Toothpaste, Use First,'' . . . it just isn't the same thing as going out and buying your own toothpaste. Unless you are particularly blasé, you will be more attentive to the product, as you use it, than you would be normally. If it's a familywide test there will be discussions. You will have to chase after one or more of your dissolute kids, getting them to unplug long enough from the Walkman to fulfill your commitment to the young woman who gave you the free toothpaste. If you are the only one that is supposed to use the product, other forms of family confusion will ensue. One of your dissolutes will lose the cap . . . your spouse will squeeze it in the non-Virgo center—revealing illicit encroachment on the sanctity of *your* test environment. The follow-up call-back interview will be late, leaving you devoid of test toothpaste and wondering—as the plaque builds up—if you dare, in the meantime, revert to your regular product. And so on.

No product test can generate normality. Accordingly, it is blatantly academic to let this argument tilt the scale in favor of the monadic design. The enormous blanket of artificiality that cloaks all in-home product tests will be lifted only slightly—probably imperceptibly—by bedding down with monadic modes.

To some, the most cogent argument in favor of the paired comparison method is the *budgetary* one. The monadic costs a lot more. If you want to be expedient about it, you can make that finite research budget work harder, and solve more problems for your company, if you choose the paired comparison approach most of the time—it's more sensitive. This should be self-evident: ask anyone from Chicago to discuss the Bears and the resultant commentary would be decidedly one-dimensional. But ask the same person to compare the Bears to any opponent and the commentary immediately takes on a wider spectrum of observations and evaluations; in fact, it almost becomes rational. It's always easier to compare things than to talk in the absolute. An added benefit in favor of the paired comparison is this: You simply can't compare the emotional impact on management of a 70-30 win to the less dramatic monadic conclusion, which is usually a listing of the results of an array of rating scales, not all of which, unfortunately, will be consonant.

Not many companies ever get to do so many product tests that they have the opportunity to go back into their files and pull out cases where the exact same products were tested both paired and monadically. Some companies will find a few cases of this, but I am talking about dozens. You obviously can't make any scientific judgments about a couple of sporadic tests, but when you get enough cases you should be able to see a pattern. Having a special curiosity about this, over the years I have seen scores of good comparisons, covering many different household, food, beverage, and miscellaneous products. My general observations are:

• Both methods produce the same results, within statistical tolerances.

• To do so at the same level of internal statistical confidence (there is always a catch), the monadic design's sample size must be several times greater than the paired comparison's.

Clearly then, in very practical ways, the monadic pales alongside the two-product test. If, in your company, you customarily get by with, say, a base of 300 interviews for a paired comparison test, in order to detect a win between two products at the same confidence level with a monadic design, you'll need not 300, or even 600, placements, but rather somewhere between 900 to 1200. With products that give consumers particular problems in discrimination (cooking oils and shortening, for example), I've seen concerned mathematicians demonstrate that a total of 3600 monadic interviews would be required to reproduce the sensitivity level provided in a 300-base paired comparison test. So, from a purely pragmatic standpoint, addiction to the monadic drug can be a very expensive habit.

The purely theoretical support for the monadic doesn't give you much nourishment either, once scrutinized. You often hear it said that only a monadic test can predict market results. Happily, there aren't many people around these days that try to make market share predictions based solely on blind tests, but the temptation to do so is frequently not resisted with much vigor in the smaller company. Such strained applications of blind tests are magnified in the monadic through its cunning evocation of glowing optimism for most any product your R&D mavens can whomp up. Since most American consumers are depressingly inarticulate and, as noted above, can't criticize anything in the absolute nearly as well as they can comparatively, open-ended responses on monadics often end up with fewer insights on the product's weaknesses than you need to make actionable improvements. Some people have tried to get around this by creating a mentally paired situation in which the test product is compared to the respondent's *usual brand* ("In what way did you like the product we gave you better than your usual brand?"). Apart from the not inconsiderable probability that many consumers don't have a *usual brand*, the results almost always produce a sizeable victory for the test product . . . that would not be replicated if its identity were revealed. Thus, the validity of using the monadic test to indicate probable market results is highly questionable any way you look at it.

A valid benefit of the monadic is that it can answer the question, "How acceptable is this product?" This is important to know when the product is drastically different from others on the market. *Acceptability*, however, can sometimes be determined by introducing scalar rating devices (a ten-point scale, for example) to give you an absolute rating on each of the two products in a paired test. If you do enough of this, you will have norms that tell you how acceptable a product is.

Some imaginative researchers try to get around the monadic-paired dispute by combining both in a *protomonadic* or a *sequential-single-product* test. You place A . . . go back a few days later and question about it monadically . . . and then place B with the same person. . . . A few days later you return and question on B monadically . . . and then on A vs. B comparatively. (For some companies this is *the* standard way of testing products.) The design is elegant, but some minor problems intrude. One snag is that the first interview casts its influence over the usage of the second product, and, even though you rotate your product sequence, the results are not exactly the same as the simple paired test. Another problem is that such a design characteristically produces *too much* information. One maxim in consumer research is to be Spartan about interview length. The more your interview rambles and folds back on itself (and to most respondents the protomonadic seems terribly repetitive), the more you seem to be encouraging your respondent to say something different. The questions begin to elicit conflicting, equivocal statements which, when edited and reported, give marketing and R&D too many opportunities to vindicate their previous positions. An industrious research analyst can resolve the seeming inconsistencies but, in most companies, decisions will be made about the test product long before he has a chance to do this, or without his even knowing about it.

DANGER NUMBER 2: *Inconsistency of Preference*

There is no such thing as a consistent preference. The issue is a red herring that often intrudes on the soundness of marketing decisions.

At some point in his career it will cross the product manager's mind that blind tests may produce completely random results. Such illuminations usually strike as a report lands on a guy's desk bearing information that, if heeded, will torpedo one of his pet projects. With patently feigned intellectual curiosity he asks: "How do we know that if the same people were given these same two products over and over again that they'd always have the same preference they had before . . . ?"

The researcher's first response could be that he could easily determine the validity of this shopworn attack to the very heart of research. He could, for example, field the old test-repeat-test design, or many other such exotica. But, why bother? It's already been done . . . many times.

Actually, our product manager is quite right. Preferences are *not* consistent. But his case ends there. The aggregate result is almost always consistent. In fact, not only has our product manager failed in his attack; you could say that blind tests are probably the most replicatable of all the research techniques and, hence, one of the most scientific of methodologies.

That given individuals are *inconsistent* preferrers should bother no one. In fact, it would be more surprising if people were consistent. In-home conditions change. . . . They don't wash the same clothes every time, nor do they necessarily have the same type of dirt and stains. Windows may be filthy one time, but merely smudged the next. Hair gets greasy for some people only in the summer and dries out in the winter. Cigarettes taste great after that first cup of morning coffee, but indescribably bad at four o'clock in the afternoon. Some men can only stand to drink beer when they have a football game to watch. When you were a kid you wanted chocolate ice cream one day, strawberry the next.

The issue of inconsistency is just a red herring dragged across the path of objectivity in research and, as an issue, is suitable only for lunchtime banter with junior executives.

DANGER NUMBER 3: Extended Use Tests

Beware of blind tests that leave product with respondents for extralong periods of time: they do not necessarily provide a valid basis for product evaluation. On the other hand, there are some products that can only be tested this way. The trick is to know the difference.

It is not unusual for a product or R&D manager to argue—quite persuasively—that the regular one-week-for-each-product blind test duration your company uses is simply not long enough for consumers to give his *exceptional* new product a *fair* test. Some executives would always prefer to have their products in the home for at least a month. Would it perhaps be better to extend the usage period on most product tests . . . or are there some risks that go along with this?

Blind test results are closely influenced by the lengths of test periods, and even slight changes in this can alter the preference results. I recall an interesting case where we switched from our standard seven-day test to a three-day model in an effort to speed up the reporting time. As slight as this abbreviation seemed, comparison to a seven-day control leg showed that it produced a significant difference in overall preference. Other tests have shown that going in the opposite direction—to a much longer duration—can also make a huge difference.

The pivotal question is why you would want to do it. If there is a strong product performance rationale for doing this then it should be seriously considered, but often such requests for extended testing periods are broached as a gambit by marketing or R&D people who have cold feet about the prospects of their product under normally acceptable testing conditions. Frequently, the extended period (usually four weeks) is a lot longer than the trial period an average consumer gives a product to prove itself. This fact alone renders the issue academic, unless marketing is on record with a promotional plan that will assure this longer trial period taking place in the market. If the product really requires it then it should be seriously considered; but it usually requires such an expensive commitment as to be unrealistic. And if this is the case, then there is clearly little point in conducting an extended use test.

However, some products have to be tested this way. These are products whose performance is time based and whose effectiveness builds up over time. Examples of truly time-dependent products are: bleach, whose repeated use can make garments look progressively whiter; floor-care products, whose shine wears out in time; and hair-care items, which transform hair so gradually the results are visible only after several weeks. Where the consumer can be relied on to give them a reasonably lengthy trial in the market, then blind tests should be arranged to conform with the time-dependent feature. But make sure you test this notion first; it may not be necessary and it may not be safe. And if you have been doing shorter-term tests on the same products for years, it is decidedly imprudent to switch over to the extended use mode without being fully cognizant that the results will probably differ.

As for that product or R&D manager who covertly anticipates that extended use will earn him more favorable ratings, we hasten to inform him that it's usually the other way around. Like fish and houseguests, the longer a product stays around the home, the less enthused the respondent becomes. (In fairness, there are product categories that are exceptions to this rule.)

The consumer's verdict on some products comes alarmingly fast. No amount of forced usage thereafter will change their evaluation. I believe this is true of products like cigarettes: the first couple of drags tell the story—few smokers need more to make a definitive judgment about the product. Thus, it would not make any sense to place a smoker with an entire ten-pack carton to measure the appeal of your new blend . . . unless your sampling program is to consist of cartons rather than the minipacks normally employed.[7] (As a sort of footnote to this, one might logically ask why it would be necessary to give smokers even a full pack, when a simple taste-test of one cigarette might do. Part of the answer is given in Danger Number 2: Inconsistency of Preference, and the rest of the answer is: It is cheaper to do it this way because you are dealing with such an extremely fractionated market; in order to reach your tiny little segment you have to use preselected postal panels. Any other method would cost too much.)

Still there are specific occasions (even with some cigarettes, conceivably) where you absolutely must extend the test period. For example, when you change to a lower-cost blend or formula on your company's big-volume product you may deem it prudent to field an extended use test with regular users to see if they can detect any changes. If they can't, even under this high powered *microscope*, then you might be able to get by without a shipping test, and immediately take the cheaper product national.

One last point: In blind tests the test products are usually used as soon as they get in the home. They are not stored for a while before usage. For some products there is a danger that one week's usage will not be sufficient to reveal what the *aged-in-the-home* product would be like. For some products this should not be overlooked, and an extended use test to show what the product is like near the end of its natural life in the home may be in order on an occasional basis. Examples: ice cream that is great when fresh but turns into guar gum after several weeks in the freezer; old beer that changes flavor; toilet-soap bars that wet-crack; chocolate that *whiskers*.

Most consumers use these products rapidly enough never to see these effects but, on the other hand, with the trend toward smaller households and individualized brand purchases there may be enough people out there who are experiencing these problems in some products to make extended use testing a mandatory addition to your body of techniques.

When you do an extended use test you should give the respondent just enough product to fit her usage patterns and to last her for the duration of the test. You should not load her up with so much product (like several months' supply) to induce her to use it differently than she normally would. In the absolute this could be hard to avoid in any product test, since free product may tend to be used faster than purchased product. The evidence on this is hard to establish since for most products it is difficult to measure volumetric usage for each application and questioning techniques are not very reliable for determining precise information on this. As we've noted already, product tests have many built-in artificialities.

DANGER NUMBER 4: *Product Weight*

A difference in regular market package weights or product densities between your products and competition can become a source of unending trouble in blind tests.

If you want to test your product against competition, and yours, in its market container, weighs twenty ounces and the competition's sixteen ounces, what weights should the respective products have in the test?

This presents a ticklish twofold problem. On the one hand, it can be argued that to test at equal weights is academic since this isn't what the consumer gets when buying the product. The counterargument: this does not matter, since we want to evaluate the product per se, not how much of it they get for their money.

The accompanying problem is how any blind test facing this issue will be interpreted by the people who make decisions based upon it. If it serves them, unprincipled users can easily manipulate the data to their private and nefarious ends.[8] The weight-variable issue affords them an infinite array of opportunities for rationalizing away unfavorable results. For example, if his product loses, the aggressive R&D manager can postulate that, by forcing weight equivalency into the test design you caused his product to lose its impressive economy advantage, which he had "expressly built into the formula to make consumers use it more liberally than the competitive product, and hence obtain superior performance from it." The variations on this theme are limitless. The sharp R&D veteran knows them all and can make mincemeat out of the researcher who thinks the world is all truth and light. Moreover, many of these arguments represent *genuine* concerns and are issues that should be addressed even when one suspects ulterior motives.

Prolonged controversies on this can go round and round, getting you nowhere. They go like this: a test-weight differential may becloud your intent of getting a clear reading on the product formulation per se. This argument says that even though the two products compete with different weights as part of their marketing mix, there are also other ways they compete—such as package graphics, advertising claims, and so on—none of which you would want to intrude on your blind test execution. Therefore, you should not permit a weight differential and should insist on packing both products at the same weights. Unfortunately, though this has considerable merit, it overlooks one important factor that our alert R&D manager pointed out above; namely, the way a product is used will obviously affect its performance and, hence, the way people evaluate it. One can easily see that the more amply filled package will get used with greater flourish and will produce a more cavalier respondent attitude toward diseconomy, and so forth. But things may not always go in favor of the heavier weight. . . .The slack-filled brand might thus be endowed with a hyped quality image that overrules its diseconomy image. You can never be sure what might happen. You may have to do the test both ways (with equal and unequal weights) in order to be sure.

Conceivably, this problem could vary by product type and even within a product category, by the very nature of the attributes that are influenced by weight and density differences. Accordingly, the problem may force you to resort to experimentation (at a low-cost central location facility). You should be able to feel comfortable with your standard testing procedures, but I am always shocked at the number of companies that acknowledge the existence of this problem, discuss it intelligently, but do nothing to solve it. Many of their tests are of questionable validity.

DANGER NUMBER 5: Handling the Non-Preferrer

Gentle treatment of the nonpreferrer just wastes time and money. Most assumptions about them are incorrect.

For some reason, perhaps due to their passive nature, many researchers always allow the respondent in a paired comparison blind test to state whether she prefers Product A, Product B, or has *no preference*. Based on the belief that vast numbers of people are truly nonpreferrers, they feel you may as well give them the alternative and speed up the interview instead of beating around the bush.

The arduous researcher looks at it another way: if more than 10 to 15 percent of respondents *claim* to have no preference, something is terribly wrong. Based on actual field observations, I would certainly endorse this view. I've been present on too many call-backs where lazy, indifferent respondents simply shrugged and refused to commit themselves until pressed to do so by a skillful, aggressive investigator. Four times out of five the indecisive respondent was able not only to state a preference, but to support it subsequently with all kinds of convincing reasons. Making up one's mind is work. Most people instinctively try to avoid any form of mental application. But the preferences are out there, and if you don't go after them you'll be wasting a big portion of your interviews.

Never give a respondent the expressed opportunity to say she has no preference. And when she volunteers it, press her hard for a choice by probes such as: "Did you notice any differences between the two products?" If the answer is affirmative, ask, "Is this enough to make you like one more than the other, or not?" This smokes out most of them. Another probe that also works (sometimes you have to use both): "If you saw both products side by side in a store, both at the same price, which one would you be likely to buy?" This will flush out a few more preferrers.

Contrary to most theories (some of which have far-reaching effects on significance tests), the nonpreferrers, thus handled and transformed into honest citizens, do not necessarily emerge with preferences proportionate to the group that freely offered its preference. The popular assumption that they have to be proportionately the same seldom comes true, and must be based on the amusing notion that those who had a preference exert extrasensory power over the fence-sitters. In actual fact, they usually split 50-50 between the two products.

If you don't force a preference you waste a lot of money. Our actual observations of the no preference respondent have convinced us they are just trying to get off the hook. Forcing them to cough up a preference does not destroy their typicality. And it may be good for them.

DANGER NUMBER 6: *Copy on Blind Test Packages*

Putting copy on a blind test package to flag some marketing benefit that would otherwise be overlooked is sometimes essential. But most attempts at this backfire . . . frequently with surprising results.

Suppose a new product purportedly does something quite unusual, compared to current competitive brands (for example, a cigarette that has all the usual properties—but that also eliminates smoker's breath). Would you not be wasting the whole test if you didn't point out this feature to your respondents? After all, they aren't expecting this benefit, they may not look for it, thus they probably won't notice it. And if this is likely, why do the test . . . especially if the product's intended marketing strategy would call for clearly communicating this unique benefit?

In the real world—especially as all the obvious product advantages were long ago grabbed up and innovators must turn to the unexpected—there are many cases like this.[9] During the period when a benefit is new and unexpected for the consumer, the blind test with on-package copy is the only reasonable way of handling the test. There are, however, some dangers connected with this; some of which you might expect to encounter, others that you might not expect.

First, you should be sure the problem has been aptly defined. The attempt to have copy included in a blind test is a standard ploy in corporate political intrigues. It is not all that difficult for an unscrupulous R&D manager to dream up artificial problems so that copy can be introduced into the design to ensure a win for his new product. Those who are clever enough know of many ways to rig a test, and this is one of the more popular.

Assuming you want to do a paired comparison test, there is the technical danger of creating an imbalance: if you print something like *eliminates smoker's breath* on the test product package, what can you print on the control product? *Regular cigarette* damns with faint praise. But nothing will ever again occur to match the outrageous aberration pulled off by the U.S. Army Quartermaster Corps a few years ago. For some reason, they had concocted a food item they wished to pack in *toothpaste* type tubes. To assess this concept, they labelled some of it *Spacefood* and some of it *Unknown*, and then tested them in a paired comparison *blind test*. When, as all readers have already predicted, Spacefood trounced Unknown, our army announced they had come up with a major contribution for the world of commerce. Rushing into print, they stated their brilliant conclusion . . . that there was a market for Spacefood. Now, in the military tomfoolery is either rewarded or unnoticed, but in the business world it seriously abridges your career.

Modest applications of dissimilar on-pack copy probably won't hurt you all that much, but such tests should be eliminated when you update your blind testing norms since this type of test can produce anomalous results.

As marketing struggles for product differentiation in the midst of diminishing opportunity, and the benefits become more obscure, on-pack copy will become increasingly necessary if many attractive new products are ever to see the light of day. Even in the old days, when the first low-suds detergent was devised, there was no way housewives would have given it a fair trial—being as they were so committed to the obsolete soap-era notion that sudsing denoted cleansing—unless the product were labelled "low suds." If you wanted to test a low-suds toilet soap today you'd probably need to do the same thing—unless you communicate the idea that you have possibly made suds redundant, consumers will not react favorably.

The major weakness of the on-pack copy blind test is not the commonly assumed one of interjecting bias, but quite the opposite: few people will notice what you print on the package. You have to go way beyond this if you want them to pay heed. I recall a series of tests where, first, we tested the products with no mention of a certain unique and normally unnoticed feature, and got no commentary whatever from the respondents about it. To R&D's indignation, we ran the test again . . . this time orally informing respondents about the feature. But only 4 percent of our respondents mentioned it. Then, pushed once again by an understandably exasperated R&D group, we repeated the test . . . this time talking up the feature in copious detail and putting copy on the package *and* on a card inserted in the package. This finally worked—giving us comments on the feature from over 25 percent of the panel. (It still didn't make R&D happy, by the way; all three tests produced the same overall preference . . . but that probably had more to do with their product than with our testing method.)

Another flaw in this is more insidious: if you do make a successful effort at ensuring that your respondents see and comprehend the on-pack copy, they may completely ignore this aspect in their evaluation. Exactly why this happens is pure speculation, but I suspect that people either assume *you* know about the feature and don't feel it makes any sense for them to tell you about it . . . or they accept your premise that this feature actually works and then proceed to look for other things you didn't tell them. I've found that the most effective way around this is to make up a story to tell at time of product placement . . . a story that makes it perfectly clear what the test is all about. For example, in the toilet-bar illustration we would show the two bars of soap to the respondent and say something like, "We've been finding out what women think of these products. . . . Some have told us they liked the bar with the normal suds level—feeling you need suds for it to work; but others said they like the low-suds bar better—feeling that a lot of suds are not necessary. We'd like to leave these bars with you for a couple of weeks to find out which of these women you agree with."

DANGER NUMBER 7: Directed Interest Product Tests

Predirecting the respondent to look for a particular attribute or perform-ance feature in the test products is occasionally done at the expense of objectivity, especially if halo effect is involved.

There are occasions when it is perfectly justified to ask the respondent, at the time of placement, to be on the lookout for some specific performance feature if, under normal use, you would not expect this feature to be especially important to her. (This differs from the preceding Danger in that these factors are *noticeable*.) Packaging improvements are one such area. During the test, the woman's attention will be riveted on the product, *not* the package; and, even though you feel certain the packaging improvement will give you some advantage in the market, and may even make it easier to use the product, she will probably not comment on it in her assessment . . . if you employ *voluntary* reasons for preference. You can, of course, ask a direct question on package preference, but there is always the danger many women will be ill-prepared to respond since they won't have given the package adequate attention during the test period. Accordingly, you would be on safer ground if, at placement time, you told everyone you were especially interested in what they thought of the package. (This naturally assumes this is the major focus of the test and that you were not *also* expecting to get an objective reading on the product.)

You should never do this, however, when the attribute in question generates a valuable halo effect. If you ask people to direct their interest toward the perfume in a shampoo such spotlighting will make it perform in only the most direct manner, thus losing its associative power and totally disrupting its more crucial functioning.

In order to avoid having the respondent focus exclusively on the feature in question, some researchers use the following phraseology: "We'd like you to pay attention to the products' dissolving speed because that is the main difference between them . . . although it is *not the only difference*."

Once deciding that you want to do a directed interest test, make sure the intent of the test is absolutely clear to the respondent. As in the previous Danger, just telling the respondent once in the placement speech won't work, nor will simply adding it in writing on the packages. On two separate occasions, after following what I thought to be very clear procedures, out of sheer curiosity I asked, on the call-back, what it was we had asked the respondents to focus on. In one test only 20 percent remembered; in the other only 45 percent. So if you have to do it, make sure you bombard them with admonitions.

As with most of the departures from the standard blind test, the directed interest test is often conducted by naive research technicians hoodwinked into it by a cunning marketing guy wishing to use the test result for some scheme. Often you find that the directed interest character of the test is not mentioned in the report in these cases, and the data are treated just like in a normal test. All such tests should be clearly labelled *directed interest* and readers should be additionally cautioned that they are not the same as regular blind tests.

DANGER NUMBER 8: Break-evens Accompanied by Attribute Losses

Extreme caution is needed if your product breaks even on overall preference versus competition, but loses on some key attributes. In a marketing sense, this may be more important than the results would suggest.

If your product test nets out with a statistical break-even vs. competition on overall preference you may be persuaded that you are about equal to the competitor, but if this is accompanied by a loss on some critical product or performance trait, you may be in trouble. It depends entirely on what kind of questioning techniques were used.

If the attribute losses were detected'in direct questions, then they probably aren't very crucial . . . since the respondent had to be prodded to mention them. But if they cropped up in the open-ended reasons for preference, then it could be very serious, depending on how pivotal the factor is for your kind of product. If you are testing beer, and the factor happened to be *flavor*, then the problem would be immense; if it were color, it might be relatively minor. With a soap bar a suds loss is always cause for grave concern, but a *shape* loss you might overlook since, for marketing reasons, you might not want to copy competition's shape . . . and these results would not be powerful enough to tell you that shape was going to hurt you much in the market since you did get a break-even on overall preference.

Anomalies between overall preference and specific attributes seldom occur. When they do, it is usually with features that are not very central to your marketing success. But if you find this is occurring with some regularity on factors that your judgment says are vital to market success, then you should closely examine your testing procedures because there is probably something basically wrong with what you are doing . . . or with how you have been judging the market.

DANGER NUMBER 9: *Trying to Disguise Competitive Products*

Choosing to conduct an identified test instead of a blind test—because it would be troublesome to disguise brand identities—may be an unnecessary and unwise choice.

Although eager to test your product against competition, you may be confronted with the nettlesome fact that their product is going to be terribly difficult to disguise. Its brand name may be embossed on its surface—as with most toilet soaps—or it may be imprinted on the product as with cigarettes. Removing the name could mean defacing the product, so the question often becomes: how important is it to always do a *blind test*? Can you get away with an identified test . . . providing you use all the proper controls and so on?

Results of blind tests and identified tests are seldom the same. Few would argue with the premise that, if you wish to get a reading on your product per se vis-à-vis competition, you can't achieve this if you reveal brand identities. In so doing—obviously—you introduce a myriad of miscellaneous influences that have no place in a true product test. Everyone knows a marketed brand is a lot more than its product formulation, and that consumer perceptions will be influenced by knowing the brand they are testing. There may be some value in such a test, but it is *not a product test*.

Some brands, however, are impossible to render *blind*. How, for example, would you mask the identity of Lifesavers, or Dove toilet soap?

But ingenuity sometimes pays off. Glues, spray paints, and special tapes can be effective; but, plainly, whatever you do to mask the competitive product you must also do to your own product to keep everything in balance. Researchers run into this problem, as we said above, testing cigarettes: since every brand has its name printed on the paper, drastic measures are required to disguise identities. You can't just strip out the tobacco and recast it because of the delicate nature of the leaf which degrades very easily. What many cigarette manufacturers do is to wrap a narrow band of special white tape around the competitive cigarette's name. This special paper cannot be removed without totally ruining the cigarette and, once removed, even soaking it in water will not reveal the imprint. Holding it up to a strong light doesn't work either because the tape is heavily patterned on its reverse side. Yet, even though the manufacturer wouldn't put a name on his own test product, he still puts the tape around it, just like on the competitive product. (There is an industry legend that one major cigarette manufacturer thought this either too bothersome, or perhaps an inherent source of bias. They elected to conduct all their blind tests with *blind* people. Come to think of it, maybe that's what they thought a blind test *really* was.)[10]

As with cigarettes, masking the competitive product will often amount to an expediency. The test may never be pure, but it is better than testing your product with full-fledged brand identity. Through experience and by noting how the consumer preferences you establish in your tests follow through in the market, you will be able to develop a body of expertise and a sense of judgment in this. It is not, however, something to take lightly, for the dangers of a wholesale dependence on identified tests are too depressing to contemplate. (See following Danger.)

Still, you are never sure that your respondents cannot tell by the products themselves what brands you are testing. One major toothpaste maker always asks what brands respondents thought they were testing. What they then do with this piece of intelligence is uncertain, since they can't delete all those who guessed correctly because they may represent a key part of the market segment. The data may serve as a good indicator of product uniqueness, however.

While slightly off the subject, I want to register a note of caution: I was reviewing how a major client was managing the task of masking the competitive product for blind test purposes. This was not something that was new to them; they had been doing it the same way for many years . . . using their lab workers to take the competitive product out of its package and then applying their skills to eradicate all traces of brand identity. So far, so good. But what I noticed probably went far toward invalidating all of their past product tests: The workers were tossing out all defective competitive products! And this happened to be a product category where a high rate of imperfection actually existed. Moral: Watch everyone like a junkyard dog.

DANGER NUMBER 10: *Identified Product Tests*

Blind tests and identified tests produce different results. This difference is not always consistent.

The evidence suggests that a product whose market success is highly dependent on *image*, rather than product quality per se, will perform much better in an identified product test than in a blind test. Those products that are not so dependent on their advertising to engineer consumer perceptions will do better in a blind test than in an identified one. We have never seen any cases where the results are similar.

This can confirm what I said earlier, that a blind test is, indeed, an artificial mechanism. At the same time, I am not willing to concede that an identified test is any more the realistic. One thing, however, is clear: translations from one technique to the other cannot be made without acknowledging this difference.

The identified test does have a limited role, but within these limitations it can be very useful. It helps you to understand the extent to which a brand derives its market share position from the product itself vs. its general brand image. It can also be helpful when conducted in conjunction with certain kinds of advertising pretests. (There is more on this in Chapter 5.)

I would still, nonetheless, maintain that the blind test is your premier technique for evaluating new formulas, etc. Its main advantage is its sensitivity: it allows the respondent to concentrate totally on the product . . . thus revealing product traits that may only show up over a very long period of time in market tests with attitude studies. It can also be replicated over the years, whereas identified tests may suffer from variances in brand attitudes as the brand goes through the stages of its life cycle; and variations in the brand's advertising (or in the competitions') can distort the results of an identified test at any point in time. Hence, as a tool for management—which presumably at least likes to feel that it has *some* data from time to time whose foundation does not shift—the identified version is not without serious weaknesses.

Once you have done a few identified tests in a product category, you find that their results are largely predictable. Most of the time they turn out to be little more than a sort of brand-image study which merely duplicates other forms of research you already have on file; at the same time, they usually fail to give you a satisfactory level of sensitivity on the reading of the product under examination.

DANGER NUMBER 11: *Detecting a Halo Effect*

Some blind tests fail absolutely to reveal halo effects, and special designs may be necessary to make these revelations.

This is probably only news to Martians, but in many different kinds of products the perfume—just as an example—that is added to mask the chemical odor will not only smell nice . . . but will impart an added benefit. Detergent perfumes can seduce the user into thinking the brand cleans extra well, or is easier on the hands or fabrics than some other brand. The color of ice cream can easily make the organoleptic perceptions more favorable. Whether intended or not, the halo effect—in most products—is a fact of life.

The bulk of our experience is that the normal kind of blind test, where you pit your product against competition, does not produce sufficient sensitivity to guarantee you a clear measurement of the halo effect of variations in nonperforming factors like perfume or color. The more successful approach is to test your *current* product directly against *itself with an altered* perfume level or different color.

Where you have good reason to believe that the nonperforming associative feature is tightly linked to the brand's marketed image and cannot be successfully divorced from it and tested in a vacuum (such as when the product has a strong advertising presence), you may achieve more reliable results by using an identified product test—either your current vs. modified product, or your modified vs. competition (providing you already know how your current does against competition). This allows the respondent to test the product within the true context, which is how the halo effect may perform in many cases.

Even the strongest advocates of the paired comparison test will sometimes voice favor for the monadic here, conceding that there are times when the old argument that *the monadic is more realistic* is actually worth paying some attention to. In actual experience, I have not always found this to be a very rewarding test design here. Previously (see Danger Number 1: Paired Comparison versus Monadic Blind Tests) I indicated how the monadic can be statistically soporific even under ideal testing conditions, but with halo effect to worry about as well it is excessively obtuse. For example, I've seen perfume-level tests where the monadic could not pick up any measurable difference in acceptability . . . even when the level was raised to a magnitude several times what anyone would seriously recommend going with in the marketplace.

Halo effect can be critical to your product's success and you should take pains to make sure you have carefully thought through your test design before you evaluate it. This may mean you will have to convince management to let you experiment with some of the above techniques before you can offer them the assurance that the consumers' true spectrum of perceptions are being evaluated properly. Today, even in the most forlorn company, marketing people are aware of the many potential manifestations of association-induced perception that their product offers. The question is: do the methods used in product tests give these a realistic evaluation? Serious errors follow those tests that do not.

DANGER NUMBER 12: *Waning Appeal of Innovations in Blind Tests*

Highly encouraging blind tests on very innovative products don't always last long. . . . Repeated several months later, the results may change.

When your product is really new, different, and desirable, premarket blind tests can produce extremely encouraging results. These results may be so much better than anything you ever previously tested that you'd be strongly tempted to get into test market as soon as possible. Some companies, upon receiving such glowing results, omit test marketing and zoom into national distribution right away.

Most seasoned (once stung . . .) marketers know that a blind test result brings no guarantee of market success because of the obvious involvement of the other ingredients of their marketing mix; but the fascinating, and little known, thing here is that, once the product is introduced, even its blind test performance may deteriorate. Once its novelty wears off (this can occur in a period of months, not years), its blind test advantages can fade. There is, therefore, a genuine need to continually follow the progress of the brand, not just with tracking studies in the market, but also in the context of blind tests. Formulation changes and adjustments may be needed more rapidly than you may expect. The preintroductory blind test should not be the last one you do on the product; you should follow it up with subsequent tests after the product has been out for a while. This is a discipline that not many companies follow because of cost considerations or political pressures—especially from R&D. One would always prefer, given one's druthers, to rest on one's laurels and not seek trouble where none currently appears to exist. However, there are sufficient grounds for following such procedures.

DANGER NUMBER 13: *Using Competition's Test Market for Your Blind Test*

When your competitor introduces a truly unique and threatening new product in a test market, R&D's "response" to this should promptly be blind tested against it. But you won't get a true reading if you go anywhere but to the test market for your blind test.

Just as your innovative product will not get the glowing blind test results after it's been on the market for a few months that it got prior to its introduction (see Danger Number 12: Waning Appeal of Innovations in Blind Tests), you must be mindful of the manner in which you probably will be introducing your brand. Unless you are awfully swift, yours will probably follow competition in going national. So, for the sake of realism (the elusive element we keep grasping for in all product tests), your competitor's test market locale is where you should plan to test yours against his in a blind test. It is here that the consumer is more informed about this new type of product, and will be able to give you a more judicious and useful reading. (Naturally, if you think you will be national before him this wouldn't apply.)

Of course this depends on how distinctive the product innovation is, but in my experience the blind test result will differ by whether you do it in the test area or not. The climate created by the competitive product's introductory promotional flurry, plus the ennui that inevitably follows, will have a decided impact on your blind test results. Blind tests are not carried out in the vacuums that some persons assume them to be.

DANGER NUMBER 14: Coding the Blind Test Products

All code letters and numbers introduce bias into blind tests.

Most blind tests are conducted with identifying code letters or numbers to keep the different products sorted out. There is no known code that does not interject some element of bias into the test. Regardless of what code letter/number you use, it will serve as a source of clear bias to some respondents.

Use a letter and they try to guess what it stands for: Does A mean American Brands, American Home Products, Avon; and is B, therefore, Benson & Hedges, Bristol-Myers, Bill Blass? If you test K against M, they assume K to be an earlier version of the test product and that M is a more recent version, ergo, more up-to-date and better.

Similar things happen when you use numbers. The lower numeral is assumed to be a less refined rendition of the product.

This is not just a half-cocked theory. I have seen many carefully conducted tests of this, all of which proved that *all* identifying letters and numerals imposed some level of distortion on the results of the test. The literature, in years gone by, used to be full of such reports as well. Accordingly, it is absolutely inexplicable why researchers continue to use them . . . especially when it is so easy to get rid of them.

Paired comparison tests can be handled in this manner: in the A vs. B leg you label both products in a long code number, such as 91001, in small print; and label, in big print, A, *Use First*, and B, *Use Second*. Then for the alternated leg, B vs. A (you still must balance for order bias, of course) you put a somewhat different small-print code on each product, say 91002, and label B, *Use First*, and A, *Use Second*. The respondent then refers to each product by the Use First/Use Second designations, which keeps them straight in her mind and, on judgment, makes it more natural for her to deal with. You will still have an order bias, but strict alternation of which is used first takes care of that to some extent.

Blind tests are tricky enough without introducing unnecessary elements that can add to their chronic difficulty in smoking out real product preferences.

DANGER NUMBER 15: *Multipurpose Blind Tests*

In trying to get top value for their research dollar many researchers design multipurpose blind tests, i.e., tests where the respondent is asked to use the product for a whole panoply of different functions. Under some circumstances, this can result in seriously distorted results.

When you need to evaluate some unusual in-home application for your product, it would be safer to set aside a special test for this. Don't hook it on to a regular product test in which you are attempting to make a general product evaluation.

The best rule of thumb is that if the respondent doesn't normally use your product for a given purpose, then you should not ask her to do so in a product evaluation test. For example, if the household cleaning product is expressly used for cleaning bathroom tile—but never for woodwork—don't press women to use it for cleaning woodwork if your main point in doing the test is to evaluate the product for its main purpose—cleaning the tile.

Even if the product would be ideally suited to some obscure purpose, the very fact that this is a rather esoteric way of using it could introduce such a severe bias as to wreck the entire test. It could easily force the respondent to focus almost exclusively on this singular application, giving it an inordinate importance sufficient to influence her overall preference. The temptation to save money by doubling up on a blind test's usefulness is strong, but an unwitting or careless yielding to it can result in meaningless data.

DANGER NUMBER 16: *Nonlinear Round-Robin Results*

Round-robin blind tests can backfire if you include too many product attribute variables.

Under many conditions the round-robin design (where several different products are tested, each being paired off with all the others) is the most economical way to test a series of product variations. It helps keep costs down because of its superefficient tests for significance and its hyped-up sensitivity. You can test all your product formula variations, even throw in competitive and regular products for controls, and still come out ahead compared to the costs of a standard blind test. Each cell (A vs. B, A vs. C, B vs. C, etc.) will have a much smaller base than it would normally need, but in the aggregate, the ability to detect significant differences among the products will be easier and sharper.

There is one nagging problem, however. If the products don't line up (i.e., if you fail to get *linearity*) you lose most of the advantages of the round robin and could end up with a series of disconnected, single-cell tests, all on very tiny bases. For example, if you had three products and A beat B, and B beat C, you would have linearity if A also beat C; but this won't always happen, since the respondents can never be certain to be looking at these products in the same way you do.[11] Of course, by the time you found this out, the test would have been completed. If you had a deadline to meet, you'd be in big trouble. So here's what to look for in advance: linearity usually occurs when your products differ on only one factor, such as flavor intensity or sudsing levels. If they differ on several attributes you will achieve linearity only if you are very lucky, so don't take any chances.

Some statisticians claim they have tests of significance for nonlinear results, but this is not good enough. For one thing, they don't all agree on how good these are; and secondly, and more importantly, you will still have to explain the situation to the marketing or R&D folks who have to make decisions on the basis of these results. They will want to scrutinize each cell and the tiny bases you built into the design are now going to be very exasperating for them.

As a piece of incidental information, a series of tests I was once involved in showed that there may be good reason to employ a three-product (per respondent) test design, rather than the two-product format, within the round-robin framework. The three-product approach gave a much better likelihood of establishing a significant preference when sensory fatigue was present . . . and equal results when it was not.

DANGER NUMBER 17: Retrieving Unused Product

Requesting respondents to retain unused test product for retrieval by your interviewer on the call-back may distort the results of your test.

If you work for a security-conscious company you may be tempted to retrieve all leftover blind test product to preclude its falling into competitive hands. Actually, this not only doesn't guarantee that competition won't get it, but it might also cause respondents to use the product differently, i.e., with greater frequency or more liberally than normal.

I was once asked to test the effect this could have on overall preference. I was able to work it into six different tests and was careful to maintain all the necessary controls. In two of the tests the overall preference was significantly altered by the request for retrieval. I'm not saying this would happen in all product categories, but if your company has a habit of doing this you may want to take a close look at the practice.

Pure logic tells you that the appropriate norm would be a test where your respondents were not requested to retain product, since that would be a closer approximation of the manner in which they use the product normally.

Of possible interest to those who don't wish to devote time and effort to experimentation was the finding we made on how effectively women followed our request: Despite making it very clear we were going to pick up unused product, this did not result in any more women having leftovers—or at least they did not admit to it. (This harkens back to Danger Number 7: Directed Interest Product Tests, where we also found that women seldom absorb everything you tell them during the placement interview.)

The weight of evidence says you should not ask people to retain leftover product because (1) it might affect your results, and (2) they won't comply anyway.

DANGER NUMBER 18: *Preference as Predictor of Market Results*

Preference results (overall preference and preference of test product versus usual brand) do not serve as reliable predictors of the consumer's market behavior.

Naturally, once the product has a name, an alluring package, and is propelled into visibility with its advertising, the whole ball game changes, but the question is still often asked regarding blind tests: "How powerful or meaningful are the data generated by asking people if they prefer the test product *or their usual brand*?"

The actual correlation of this information with buying characteristics seems to be rather thin. It does tend to serve as a measure of *strength of preference*, though there are better ways of getting at that (e.g., rating scales). But, even in the test situation, it does not necessarily carry through into action. We have witnessed several tests where people, claiming a preference for the test product over their usual brand, were given a chance to receive (as a token of thanks) free product consisting of their choice of either the test product or their usual brand. The actual choice split evenly between the two products.

To some people the security of a known brand outweighs a preference statement that apparently only reflects a limited spectrum of value judgments, perhaps only regarding the product per se or personal likes and dislikes. Perhaps when the free-gift choice is made, family preferences get considered for the first time.

This serves to point up a chief limitation of any product test; namely, that it cannot serve as a substitute for full-blown in-market testing or adequate simulations thereof.

DANGER NUMBER 19: Perennial Blind Test Winners

Regardless of how well they pan out in blind tests, some products will never be successful in the market.

Sometimes products have certain features that prevent their being used—after purchase—in the same way they were used during a blind test. The fact that blind test product is given to consumers free of charge may sometimes govern this.

For example, concentrated products do not always perform as well in the market as they do in test situations. Imagine the hypothetical case of a superconcentrated sugar with several times the density of regular table sugar. People will be quite willing either to follow your instructions in a blind test or to use the product a little more generously than normal. They didn't pay for it, so what the hell. But when it hits the market the situation changes. For one thing, everyone in marketing knows consumers seldom read package instructions, and since they put out money for it (probably at higher margins than for regular sugar), they are now going to confront an important consideration that generally plays a diminished part in a blind test: the issue of economy, or value for money. Even if the average application costs no more than that with the regular product density, the economy issue can never be fully explored until you get into the test market. For this reason concentrated products often look great in blind tests but flop in test markets. Prell Concentrate, which was one of the rare concentrated success stories, goes out of its way to show how little you have to use in its television commercials.[12]

Each product category could harbor comparable features which must be approached with caution because they are winners with consumers only in blind tests, not out in the real market. Fortunately they are rare, but they do crop up.

DANGER NUMBER 20: Excessive Screening of Respondents

The prescreening of blind test respondents via usage or attitudinal questions can give you a sample that will not be representative.

Sometimes, when testing certain types of products such as low-appeal cake-mix flavors, researchers are tempted to place product only with people who *like that flavor*. To some degree this makes sense; why bother placing coconut-raisin flavor with all cake-mix users when perhaps only 100 out of the 300 total base can even tolerate it? To resolve such a dilemma, some researchers like to screen people for their interest in a new flavor (or whatever attribute would present problems in minority preferences) and then test only among people with an interest.

Unfortunately this can produce unreliable information. Some studies have shown that such screening questions exert moderate biasing influences over the results. Moreover, flavor proclivities are not constant: the same people questioned on different occasions display a sizeable shift in preference which may have no pattern or explanation. With food products, where this problem is most common, an additional snag is that, during any given week, somewhere around 20 percent or more of adult Americans are on a diet (which they don't stick to for long) and this may cause short-term flavor preference distortions.

A better way to do it is to place everyone who you would consider a user of the general product category. If you want to see how well a screening question might help, regardless of what I just said about it, get the *interest* information in a screener questionnaire that is so lengthy that your flavor-interest question is only a small part of it. Make this questionnaire, preferably, self-administered and do not make any reference to it during the placement speech. Check against it in a data processing cross-tab and see if it would have helped any. But *never* bring up the issues normally broached in a screening questionnaire in an oral manner before you leave test product with a respondent.

DANGER NUMBER 21: Concept Testing Prior to Product Test Placement

Combining a product test with a concept evaluation test (obtained at time of placement) could bias the blind test result.

Researchers like to get as much for their money as they can and will often ask women to give their reactions to a concept statement for a new product before giving them some of the product to test.

Anything you say at the time of placement will have a dramatic effect on the respondents . . . much more so than any advertising they will ever see. So what you have done is leave them with a tremendous impression about the product which they will never get in the marketplace. You have thus created a totally artificial situation that can never be replicated anywhere else. Unlike the pure blind test, this will combine two stimuli: the product, which is going to go into the market if successful; and the concept statement and concomitant discussion, which have no duplicate in the market.

If you have not done a concept test long before you had R&D put the new product together, then you are in the wrong business and get very low marks for planning. If, on the other hand, you are trying to incorporate the concept test (or even if you are just reading the concept statement to the respondent) with the blind test so as to replicate the real world, you are deluding yourself.

DANGER NUMBER 22: Telling Respondents What Flavor They Are Testing

People have to know the flavor before they can respond naturally to it.

Research purists have been known to ward off any attempt to print the flavor of a food product on the test package, or even to tell the respondent what the flavor is. "We don't want to bias the test with *advertising copy*," they claim.

This is too absurd to spend a lot of time on. My wife does it to me all the time. I'll get a cream-colored pudding and she will refuse to tell me what the flavor is. I eat it with no visible pleasure, assuming it's her favorite: maple walnut. Then she tells me it was my favorite, lemon, but by then it's too late to enjoy it since it's all gone. Don't do that to your respondents.

DANGER NUMBER 23: Calling a Blind Test a "Test"

If you want to have a successful blind test, don't refer to it as a test in front of the respondent.

Loose lips sink ships, and unless you bite your tongue when you're trying to convince a woman to accept your test product (especially if it's something she will have to eat) you may lose her. She is inclined to be suspicious anyway, but when you start bandying around the word "test" a lot of them get very nervous and see visions of contracting incurable diseases and whatnot. Or her husband comes out of the kitchen, wearing a sleeveless undershirt and holding a can of beer, shouting: "You ain't doin' no test!"

NOTES

1. This sounds like a *major* evaluation test, regardless of the (possibly phoney) time bind. Taste tests are fine in their place, but preparation in a strange kitchen doesn't really equate with making pudding in your own kitchen. Moreover, this eliminates the chance of family involvement which, with such a product, could be an important determinant of brand selection. A researcher may be in no position to overrule product managers who plead urgency, and he may have to do the test this way . . . once. But marketing people should not be encouraged to expect such concessions as a matter of course. In a test of your product against a major competitor, in-home locales must prevail. Client departments should know where the research department stands on this. A chronic state of emergency on matters such as this is a sign of weak planning.

2. He is correct in assuming that taste is the key determinant of product preference in a beverage, but he is wrong in thinking that *that* factor is solely responsible. Color and "mouthfeel" are closely associated with the whole organoleptic impact. To be sure, you cannot get a valid reading if you lock in on only one factor . . . it will be misleading. Also, as in the above illustration, this need for swiftness is out of

place when you are dealing with a deep-rooted problem involving not only product but marketing as well. More judicious testing is in order.

3. Sure, this is okay—providing such tests in the past have not been misleading. You can't test every possible variation in-home . . . it would be both too expensive and too time-consuming. A lot of researchers try to flex their *purist* muscles at such issues, but they usually just drive R&D folks to setting up secret panels. (Many companies have them, and the marketing research departments don't know about them.)

4. In spite of the side issues this is still just a straightforward paired comparison blind test of your product vs. major competition. *Consumer Reports* doesn't know what it is talking about here: most tests show that people don't really like maple syrup anyway, compared to regular table syrups, and we all know consumers never read labels. You might advise product management, however, just to be on the cautious side, to refrain from going national right away, and, instead, given a decent blind test result, to do a shipping test to make sure nothing goes wrong.

5. This is often how it is done. But the comparison of current against new is somewhat academic. The test market is a failure so far; hence, the current formula is not a realistic standard to use. A more actionable test is the new against the best that competition has to offer. If you can't beat them (or at least achieve parity) you are probably wasting your time with the new formula.

6. Without naming names, but in the interest of stressing the importance of this, I would like to relate a story. A friend was research director at a large consumer goods company. Pressed by a zany corporate fad for turning all supervisory and professional people into *managers*, he was forced to delegate everything down to the lowest novices with fresh MBA degrees, in all sections of his department. Management told him to be a *director* and stop fussing with *technique*. Six months out, he found that his people had stopped asking reasons for preference. Forcing himself to overrule the zany fad, he ordered them to reinstate this without delay. Fortunately no major problems ensued. But when he left this company for a better job, reasons for preference were swiftly discarded forever. (Most researchers find them to be too much bother.) This time there were serious repercussions. A major new product, developed under the guidance of a series of blind tests containing only direct questions, was *shown* to have such enormous appeal that the company abandoned its usual policy of test marketing and went national right away. The result was a sheer disaster; they lost well over $50 million out-of-pocket, and the opportunity cost was probably closer to $200 million.

7. "Brown & Williamson . . . took the unprecedented step of distributing coupons for free cartons of *Barclay*." *Wall Street Journal*, December 31, 1981, p. 7: "Marketing—Winners and Losers: Reviewing Some of 1981's Sales Strategies."

8. Researchers would be naive to assume the world awaits their revelations. But the reader, after seeing several indications of grave reservations on the objectivity of the users of research, may wonder at the source of such cynicism. The incentive systems that reward most executives compel some to manipulate data to their own short-term ends. Additionally, research is so often held in such low regard that such embroidery is easily rationalized away.

9. "The pure products of America go crazy—" . . . William Carlos Williams. This quote is from a review of Paul Mariani's *William Carlos Williams: A New World Naked* in *Harper's Magazine*, December 1981, p. 55.

10. Blindfold tests won't work either. It is mandatory to maintain as much naturalness as possible. People have to see what they are using. Smokers have to see the smoke exit the mouth as it is exhaled.

11. This should also serve as a warning to those who like to make assumptions about linearity in assessing new competitive products. If your current product beats competition's new formula, and R&D comes up with an improvement that beats the current, you must not assume you can safely get by without testing the new formula against competition. You must close the triangle. Maxim: you may be logical; consumers seldom are.

12. "Convinced that shoppers willingly would sacrifice convenience for price savings, entrepreneur Wilson Harrell introduced concentrated glass and all-purpose spray cleaners this September. Unlike such higher priced competitors as *Windex*, *Fantastik* and *Formula 409*, Mr. Harrell's cleaners—called *4 + 1*—don't come in spray bottles and need to be diluted with water. He hoped for 10% of the $160 million spray cleaner market. But the product hasn't sold well, say food brokers and supermarkets that handle it; some predict an early demise. 'The consumer tends to talk a lot about economy,' says a distributor, 'but convenience wins in the final analysis.' " *Wall Street Journal*, December 31, 1981, p. 7: "Marketing—Winners & Losers: Reviewing Some of 1981's Sales Strategies."

4 • *Advertising Research: The Persuasion Controversy*

Being unable to muster up courage to begin this chapter, I'll retreat to the wings and just let you read this letter I sent—somewhat galled—to *Advertising Age* a few years ago. They were nice enough to put it in their "Voice of the Advertiser" column, and I trust it speaks for itself. Please take time out to read it while I review my notes from my latest assertiveness-training seminar and get up for writing the rest of the chapter.

To the Editor:*
As reported, the 25th annual Advertising Research Foundation conference sounded like a write-up of the 1954 conference. Clearly, marketing and advertising are rapidly becoming nostalgia professions, with little evidence of true progress.

The same old issues are rehashed annually in a compulsory tribal ritual. Nothing has changed, no one has learned much, and everyone seems hopelessly anachronistic.

Agency execs bristling at creative restraints chide research for failing to measure persuasion (as if they would believe it anyway), revealing an extraordinary ignorance of how advertising actually works that stems all the way back to the 1950s.

Hardly anyone in the business bothers to differentiate between the *copy strategy* (which is the fundamental selling force in advertising) and the *commercial* (which is only the way you communicate and implement the strategy). Once this is accepted it is obvious that recall scores are important. If the strategy is compelling enough, memorable copy will sell the item. Making it memorable is fairly easy, there are only about four things you have to know; but the harder task is getting the strategy right.

It's so simple and clear, yet isolated instances are always being dredged up to disprove it. For example, one conference speaker offers the old chestnut about Life cereal and Mikey, a commercial that has become part of the creative man's mythology. But the whole thing about *Let Mikey Try It* is a widespread popular misconception. Unless my memory has failed totally, the Mikey commercial did not have a low recall score. In fact, it had astoundingly good "flavor" copy point recall. And isn't that almost all you need to get a good trial with a breakfast cereal?

We feel sorry for that agency president who described himself sitting alone in his empty room with only a product and a typewriter, trying to create effective copy, but he should know that the real need today is for strategies that produce a genuine con-

*Reprinted with permission from the November 19, 1979 issue of *Advertising Age*. Copyright, Crain Communications Inc. 1979.

tribution to the client's bottom line (not the agency's). No one needs more campaigns that might only drain cash from the corporate coffers.

We wonder about this executive's decision-making process when he submits that the Burger King *Have It Your Way* campaign succeeded because it made the fast-food chain a place with "lots of fun for the whole family." We thought those commercials, which were damn good by the way, were saying that Burger King was superior to McDonald's hamburger. You could get it any way you wanted, unlike McDonald's where if you wanted a hamburger with just raw onion you had to wait a long time. Surely this is just a simple statement about the product itself. And isn't relative product quality a major factor in the profit equation? (See the Strategic Planning Institute's PIMS Program if you have any doubts about this.)

The fault is not only with agency people who haven't kept up with the enormous economic changes or with agency people who haven't devised the programs that can contribute to the enhancement of the client's economic wealth, or with the rare agency person who merely ends up squandering the client's scarce cash resources on misguided advertising, but also with the entire market research profession because it is so inept at presenting itself and so incapable of addressing the issues of the day that no one listens to it anymore. Do we wonder why the whole marketing profession is so seldom taken seriously in the corporate board rooms and why the financial guys are calling most of the shots today?

If we have misrepresented what transpired we apologize, but we are only going on published reports, since we were unable to attend, being too busy helping our clients fight inflation and developing programs that will prepare them for the 1980s and not a *deus ex machina* return of the 1950s.
Sincerely,
Terry Haller, president
Chicago Research Company[1]

Advertising research arouses fierce emotions. The popular press sees it as a malodorous device to hoodwink a gullible public, corrupt morals, and induce unsuspecting consumers into squandering their rent money on hair sprays and junk foods because it gives advertisers the wherewithal to transmit their sales messages directly to the brain's control center, bypassing Reason's protective shield, and to harvest irrational *wants and needs* below the level of conscious awareness. Society's critics see the research, rather than the advertising per se, as the unprincipled monster that erodes the Puritan Ethic, destroys children's teeth, and wastes energy resources. It is, they argue, the hidden, supersophisticated tools of the researcher that have turned us from a nation of responsible, hardworking, frugal citizens into acquisitive, drug-crazed hedonists.

FLATTERY

Most researchers would be thrilled to find their advertising research had one-tenth this power. *Au contraire,* they profess grave private doubts that *advertising research* really works, or that the money they spend on it can be justified in the company of honest men. Few of them gain respect and appreciation for what little they manage to make of this terrible muddle. They are lambasted by agency creative directors who *bristle* at anything that brings their work under scrutiny and who, undeterred by the notion that anything wielding such large expenditures as a media budget should be justified by something more solid than gut feel, would elect to have all ad research banned by papal edict and its practitioners hung from the yardarm.

Researchers giving presentations to so-called creative people seldom even get their slide projectors set up before the insults and barbs start to fly. Given such an environment, it goes without saying that few researchers eke out much personal satisfaction from their involvement in advertising research . . . if the truth were told.

Every time a researcher speaks before a public gathering on this subject or writes an article for a trade paper, his integrity is called into question. He is termed a *numbers-cruncher* or a *bean-counter* and demeaned for his lack of understanding of the Creative Process and the True Purpose of Advertising. Only the creative person can be expected to:

1. sell the consumer,
2. understand the consumer, and
3. judge the effectiveness of advertising.

Seldom recognized is the fact that, when it comes to consumers, it is the researcher who does most of the talking and listening.

LEO BURNETT

The research clan comes up against some pretty tough resistance here. Few of them are oratorical matches for luminaries like the late Leo Burnett, who once said:

Cold logic can smother a hot idea. In my opinion, research that can adequately and conclusively pretest the long-term selling effectiveness of ideas has not yet been invented. This applies particularly to startling new ideas which to the basically conservative respondent may seem strange and unfamiliar, and which need weight and continuity to make them stick. I have seen many such ideas, which could have become resoundingly successful, killed or diluted by a timid and too-literal interpretation of pretesting results. . . . The work of advertising people is inexact, because any creative process is inexact, and the advertising business, however much it is surrounded with facts and figures, is essentially a creative process.[2]

Few researchers can summon up the necessary verbal electricity to squelch that one. And I guess that's why I have much apprehension about this chapter and the two that follow it. Whatever postulation one sets in motion is going to be ambushed by someone with a vested interest. Numerous research firms earn their bread and butter by testing advertising, some with meritorious techniques, others with ridiculous quackery, and few of them are going to be content with what will seem, as you read it, a very circumspect view of the subject. But, though I be wary and, I trust, prudent, copywriters and creative directors the world over will regard what little that I feel ad research is capable of accomplishing as too much to claim for it, preposterous to behold, and, at the same time, far too restrictive to their work.

MISUNDERSTANDING

So let's go back to that letter at the start of the chapter. I talked about the enormous misunderstanding hunkering at the bottom of this whole unpleasant, backbiting affair. It's a common problem; one that crops up everywhere—not just in the advertising area: people, as a general rule, can always be counted on to confuse strategy with tactical implementation. Once they do this when disputing the value of advertising research, the controversy heats up as effective communication, at the same time, breaks down.

Far be it from me to get any kicks out of trying to undermine Mr. Burnett's position. Not only is this industry giant no longer around for a rebuttal, but he's a Chicagoan—in fact, a fellow Northshorer, with a bond based on income and shared architectural values—but a few things, with all due respect, must be said.

THE ISSUE OF PERSUASION

Look, despite what the Madison and Michigan avenue denizens claim or think, persuasion comes out of the brand's strategy, not its commercial executions, which are merely implementations of its strategy. Until the highrent sectors of the business get to the point where they can incorporate this in their thinking, the task of the advertising researcher will be a troubling source of continual frustration.

How do we measure persuasion? Well, the short answer is we can't. The longer answer is we still must try and may at times come pretty close, though mostly we will run up against a lot of real-world intervening variables:

- effect of other brands and their promotional efforts
- consumer forgetfulness and/or inattentiveness
- economic factors
- trade factors
- affect on individuals from family intervention, etc.

So you have to get to square one . . . where you will see that a commercial or a print ad is just the execution; as such, it is a vehicle for communication. And if communication is to work it has to be memorable—unless you still believe in those turgid 1950s notions about the *subconscious*.

Communication is not all that hard to measure. There was once a magnum advertising industry joint opus called *DAGMAR*, which did not refer to the bovine TV talk-show hostess of the early "Golden Age" we occasionally see on retrospectives, but stood for *Defining Advertising Goals to Measure Advertising Results*. By creating a narrow set of goals it then became easy to go out and gauge the *effectiveness* of advertising. I guess when I define the initial role of an advertising execution to be one of pure communication—leaving the task of persuasion up to the product strategy—I am probably guilty of roughly the same oversimplification, but it is a good place to start, and if, because of technical trepidation, one feels one can't go beyond this, then at least something fruitful will have been accomplished.

Even in my most skeptical moods I find it hard to believe that advertising, despite what else it may be, is not at least communication. If it's not supposed to communicate, then how can it ever hope to persuade? So, we can probably be content with saying that—at the very least—we have to measure a commercial's ability to communicate. Maybe that's not all we have to do, but it is certainly one of the more important assignments in this line of work.

COMMUNICATION SPECTRUM

An added vexation is that not all will agree on what communication is. Or how it works. You can communicate on the articulate level, but you can also do it with nonverbal gestures, music, and so on. Different kinds of communication will, no doubt, require—so the argument goes—different methods of testing.

The articulation variety can, I think, be measured by memory tests. If something were communicated by language and was expected to have any positive effect, then it would have to seep into the mind and be retrievable from the memory cells . . . in some form or other. Nonverbal communication could be retrieved in the same way if it got translated into language in the viewer's mind. If not, then it might come out in the form of attitudinal changes. And if that won't work, then it is probably gone forever . . . and cannot be researched, short of a test market.

That's probably the complete spectrum of communication. It would certainly include the types of advertising that Mr. Burnett and others worry most about when they think about advertising research—the "startling new ideas" and the highly creative treatments that rely more on character and production values than on the spoken word. My own observation is that there are so few of these that it isn't worth getting into a lather about. Most commercials are pretty perfunctory implementations of very simple copy strategies. Simplicity sells. And for the most part they can be researched rather easily with the technique I like best: the day-after recall (DAR) method, which will be discussed in Chapter 6. (Those who can't swallow DARs may want to skip that chapter.)

As for those *other types* of commercials, I think most people would be rather surprised to find that DARs are still very utilitarian. Many of these terribly, terribly creative commercials actually transpire to be perfectly capable of communicating literal messages. But when you do a DAR on them and get a low score you just run into a lot of controversy. People are always willing to accept a high score, but not a low one. They will use any argument that suits the moment, the most common being the *slow-fuse* theory. "The low recall score," they will vigorously argue, "is to be expected—after all, this isn't your usual chopped-liver commercial. . . . This is art! And you dummies can't understand how it's going to work. It's going to take the damn consumers months to get the hang of it, but when they do we'll see lots of action . . . ." If you take them up on this very typical thesis and run the bloody test again three or four months hence, do you know what you'll get? No difference. But that will not faze your detractors. They'll just say it confirms their judgment, that visceral advertising cannot be expected to leave a deposit of *words* in the consumer's mind, especially when the average viewer only has a vocabulary of 1,200 words. What these villains really want is either some kind of test they can control or manipulate interpretively in their own interest (like a focus group, for example), or a six-month test market which at least buys them more time.

Fortunately, today there are better methods that you can bring to bear on these types of problems. One obvious one, though it is not really much different from a test market, is to hook up to a cable/scanner service. That'll give a perfect fix on how well the commercial moves the goods. Definitive, but perhaps on the pricey side (your average agency won't be too ready to volunteer picking up the tab), this approach will call the bluff of any critic of advertising research. Cable/scanners aren't diagnostic unless you overlay some traditional interviewing methods, but for these far-out commercials it is hard to find a traditional interviewing method that satisfies everybody anyway. These techniques are getting too close to being sales research to allow them to be stringently examined in this book, but it is hard to see how anyone, even Mr. Burnett and other agency leaders, could have much trouble buying the verdict of something like this. They may ask for more time to give their slow-fuser time to ignite if the results look negative, but the method is pretty hard to refute if the proper controls are inserted. (Cable/scanners do introduce some political problems, which I will mention in Chapter 8.)

Maybe, though, I'm giving some readers an overly gloomy impression of ad research. I may be deterring a few soon-to-graduate MBAs from entering the field. So, to them I say: Hold on, there's a lot of fun to be had here. While it may seem to the novice that the above are the time-consuming projects faced by the ad research people, they are actually only a small fraction of what must be tackled. In the research department of an agency most of the work is addressed to preproduction issues. Naturally, there is the need to do or buy market studies and to acquire basic information about the product and the consumer's attitudes and usage characteristics, details on competition, and so on; but in every specific campaign there is also a whole raft of petty—but highly amusing—questions that must be answered. Usually the agency is responsible for doing and paying for any preproduction research. Sometimes they share costs with the client. Budgets are quite limited, so you have to be creative. Sometimes politics are involved and it isn't always easy going when the researcher turns up something negative about his agency's work, but agency researchers are people of integrity, and most agencies are aboveboard—feeling that if you are afraid of the results you shouldn't do the research in the first place.

While occasionally the client will pay for and handle the preproduction research, or share responsibilities with the agency, usually clients do not get involved in the research until the commercial is produced. Some agency-client contracts call for the agency to be wholly responsible for any research done on the advertising up to, but not including, the time it goes on the air. In the next chapter I will discuss the former, and in the one after that, the latter. In neither chapter will I cover copy strategy, since it's an offshoot of your business strategy, which is discussed in Chapter 9.

NOTES

1. *Advertising Age*, November 19, 1979, p. 62.
2. Ibid., February 8, 1982, p. M–8: "Leo," by Carl Hixon.

5 • Advertising Pretests: No One Is Ever Happy

A *pretest* is any research you do that tells you if a commercial is any good before it actually goes on the air. There is a broad range of techniques and problems encountered in this. It could start with a concept test where you are searching for either a new way of positioning your product, or perhaps a new product altogether. Some people wouldn't consider that ad research, others would. There are companies that start off all new products this way, even going so far as to shoot commercials and test them before they pass on to R&D the mundane chore of creating the actual product. And, as well, there are many advertising agencies that search for new product ideas on behalf of clients, and they would regard this as the first step in a long chain—all of which they'd designate *pretesting*.

Many agencies automatically send all new copy, whether in a finished commercial or just in a videotaped storyboard, out to a research facility that specializes in testing such early formats. There is also a myriad of little issues that crop every time you plan a new pool of commercials. Are the performers right for the product? Is the music? Would this really be how people use the product? If you say your deodorant is 50 percent more effective, what will viewers think this means? Endless questions. If you like your work to amuse, this is where you can have the most mirth. And despite their contumelious natures, the people you work for are, we must confess, more stimulating than the average automaton of the business world.

If you want to be a *heavy breather* and a *prime mover*, look elsewhere. Few top-level corporate executives will be willing to ascribe more than incidental importance to anything you do in the pretesting phases of advertising development. So, if they're the ones you want to impress, you're probably going to be disappointed.

On the other hand, your chances of getting published are enhanced. Agencies like it when their workers are quoted in the trade press or have articles published in the journals. Few corporations allow this, thinking it too self-serving, or fearful that anything worthwhile discovered in their marketing research department would be equally valuable to competition. Better to keep it secret if they can. (Some, I suspect, feel that nothing substantial could be discovered by their researchers and, therefore, publication could be an embarrassment to their company.)

The dangers involved in pretesting orbit around the various ways respondents are forced into artificial situations. How attentive are they going to be when they watch your commercials at home and how can you replicate this in a studio environment? How rational are they—even at the best of times? Do we give them an opportunity to evaluate advertising executions with a greater level of rationality than they would normally display? Do we transform them into art and entertainment critics, encouraging them to summon forth value systems they normally do not call upon? All pretests are artificial, some more so than others, and some are so artificial as to be grossly misleading.

Another pretesting problem is where to draw the line. Do you test every idea that comes down the pike? Top management seldom swoons with admiration over marketing people who are unwilling to use judgment. There is probably a pyramidical hierarchy of problems and research needs in every campaign that looks something like this:

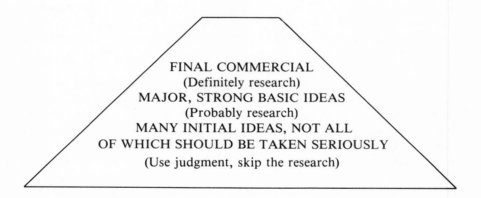

FINAL COMMERCIAL
(Definitely research)
MAJOR, STRONG BASIC IDEAS
(Probably research)
MANY INITIAL IDEAS, NOT ALL
OF WHICH SHOULD BE TAKEN SERIOUSLY
(Use judgment, skip the research)

You have to be careful you aren't swept away by the self-inflating postures of the profession lest you enthusiastically overspend on pretesting and have little remaining for your posttesting, which most certainly would be judged more important in the overall game of business. Indeed, when one listens at the knees of Madison Avenue wordmongers it is easy to imagine the entire economy revolving around them. They see themselves as Sun Kings whose inspired copy buoys up faltering or moribund brands and turns them all into *household words*. They have many engaging stories about products that were going nowhere until they came along to save them. I'm not saying all of this is bull feathers, but their stories are too one-sided to be plausible. And, more often than not, they involve such trivial product categories that they couldn't possibly have the Promothean impact on the economy they fancy for themselves.

I realize that's no reason for refusing to do pretests. *Your* job may happen to depend on *their* ability to peddle trivial products. But it pays, in the long run, to keep everything in perspective. Advertising is not a wide-spectrum antibiotic for all business ills. It is just one part of the marketing mix; and marketing is just one tiny part of the strategic mix. Business strategy will always be a more critical determinant of financial performance than any single tactical component. The supreme strategic factor overshadowing anything an agency can do is *product quality*. Now, I will admit it is a creative challenge to get across a *quality* story in a thirty-second commercial, but other tools are also used to induce trial, so the commercial doesn't have to go it alone. Trial will be the occasion for the big consumer decision—whether a repurchase is in the cards or not—so if you have a limited budget for research it should be obvious where to invest it. Clearly, you don't dissipate it all on the bottom ledge of the pyramid.

There are, however, many useful things that can be done with research before an ad or commercial is ready to debut. But, as usual, the perils are several and various.

DANGER NUMBER 24: The Entertainment Syndrome

Most commercial pretests measure neither communication effectiveness nor persuasiveness. Instead, they merely reflect on the commercial's tendency to entertain.

You invite the women into a studio, sit them down, and tell them they are going to have a chance to view some new commercials and give their opinions about them.[1]

There are many problems associated with the traditional methods of advertising pretesting. One of these is encountered when respondents attempt to play the role of *expert consumer* and proceed to tell you what *they think the market wants.* You can't always blame them for embarking on that helpful mission. One thing consumers think they know a lot about is advertising. They may be childishly naive in assuming that you do not share in this knowledge, but your questions unavoidably supply that impression. And one of the more commendable human traits—the urge to help—intrudes with negative effect to produce exactly what you don't want. She depersonalizes the problem and sets out to speculate on what is right or wrong in the commercial's appeals to some imagined body of consumers she has never studied and which may, in fact, not even exist. You can readily see that the worst fears of the creative director, as expressed in Leo Burnett's critique of ad research, are going to be realized. Those probably viable, admittedly far-out ideas they've labored so hard to develop and fought so bravely to be allowed to show to the recalcitrant, esemplastic client, will likely be severely and unjustifiably penalized simply because our overly helpful respondent suspects they're too dissimilar to what is out there in the market already. Not having previously displayed creative skills more laudatory than constructing a pinecone centerpiece for the Christmas dinner table, she will imagine an *average consumer* who won't like this. "After all, they aren't currently buying products like that," she will think to herself. Or it will strike her that she's never seen it in her neighborhood Sears so it can't be very popular. As most creatives—whatever field they plow—have witnessed since the dawning of civilization, all new ideas are met by an army of self-appointed resistance troops wanting to crush them. The average respondent is an enlisted member of this army. To her, your ads may be great, but in the way the normal pretest is pitched to her, she's going to tell you what *everyone* will think about them.

I think an even more common, more insidious problem when you set out to pretest a commercial is what I call the *entertainment syndrome*. One can never be certain when this phenomenon is present, but I suspect that it is always lurking below the surface and distorts more pretests than we may ever be aware of.

If you're testing three or four different executions and one of them is genuinely humorous, and the others are merely informative, it isn't hard to guess which commercial most folks would prefer coming into their living rooms for the next several months. (Even copywriters find most commercials boring.) When you count up all the commercials the average viewer is exposed to, and acknowledge that most, especially in the fringe time, are cheap, local efforts that make their telephone number the central, oft-repeated sales point ("Call Empire Carpets at 588-2300."), it's not hard to appreciate why any commercial that's a little more entertaining than the usual tiresome fare is going to receive, either openly or tacitly, special consideration from your respondent.

Certainly, some very effective commercials have been funny, exciting, sexually titillating, or in some other way entertaining. But that doesn't say that all entertaining commercials will be effective. In my experience there is more chance the opposite will be true, but whether or not you agree with that I think you can at least sense the danger here. If there is any tendency for human nature to inflict itself on the results of your pretest (as would tend to happen in such subjective situations), then aspects of entertaining presentations may attract greater attention and consideration than you want when charged with measuring a commercial's sales potential.[2]

Anything that detracts from the purity of the communication and from the goal of the commercial—to induce a purchase—can threaten the validity of the pretest. All of these problems impede the basic objective of pretesting, which is to replicate the marketplace as closely as possible. As we can't afford to test market everything and can't even use simulated test markets for all executional variations, then, unless the problem can be solved, we would be better off with pure judgment and skip the research.

For many products, however, there are opportunities to use a much better method to evaluate the probable persuasive power of a test commercial. It is not *perfect*—few techniques are—but it seems to offer a way around most of the objections discussed above and, what's more important, it seems to work. It involves a limited amount of product trial, which may rule it out for some product categories, but with a little imagination it could be rendered suitable even for them. Let's examine the background thinking on this first:

- If you want to simulate the marketplace then, axiomatically, you must have respondents use the product (at least partially or briefly). The respondent must be physically exposed to the product in the context of the advertising. This is necessary because attitudes are shaped by two major forces: (1) the actual physical attributes of the product, and (2) the perceptions that are engineered by its marketing and advertising efforts.
- Advertising pretests must try to incorporate the events of the marketplace that lead up to and include actual product trial.

This is most sharply demonstrated with products that depend a lot on image. Beer, soft drinks (actually anything you drink), cigarettes, etc. are prime examples of this, but to some extent virtually all products have a touch of image working for or against them. Such a dependency makes it mandatory to assure that consumers see the ads before they try the product. You would not expect a marketing effort to succeed well if you didn't start your advertising until after everyone had tried the product (see Chapter 8, Danger Number 80: Timing of Advertising in Test Markets); you want them to see the ads first, because they contain important information or feelings about the product that will shape consumer perceptions. Accordingly, a commercial that is tested without being followed up by some kind of product trial is only half a test. It could be misleading, since it won't connect with the perception-shaping function that it may be capable of delivering and which may (once trial is consummated) be its principal source of strength.

Within this thought structure is the clue to a pretest method overcoming most problems associated with evaluating commercials before they get on the air. It provides a means of testing commercials without making it obvious to your respondent that that's what she's actually doing. What could be better than a test where only the researcher knows what is happening?

There is a wide variety of ways you can do such tests. Naturally you don't need finished commercials. *Ruffs* will do. The key thing is be sure you do not orient the test toward the advertising. Focus on the product. One way I've handled this is to tell the respondents that the client company ("the manufacturer") has come up with a couple of different formulas for its product which we want them to try, to see which they like better. "But before we do that," we go on to explain, "the manufacturer was also thinking of using some new commercials once the winning formula got on the market . . . and so, they made a different commercial for each formula. These commercials," we point out, "are just done in very rough form—so you needn't be concerned about how they look," etc. Then you run the first commercial and, without asking their opinion about it, get them to try the first product. Do likewise for the second commercial and product. Then ask which product variation they liked better—and why. This snares all the commercial-induced perceptions the advertising can impart.

Naturally, both products are supposed to be exactly the same. It goes without saying, of course, that the respondent is led to believe that they were different. In most cases, you will have no trouble convincing them of this.[3]

In most situations this is a superior method for pretesting advertising since (1) it overcomes the interviewing bias associated with the more conventional methods, and (2) it incorporates a real-world test of the advertising's critical faculty for shaping consumer perceptions of the product and for generating those attitudes that lead to repeat purchase. While difficult to administer without the proper background and experience, the technique is, in my opinion, a method that should be employed in place of the traditional methods, where circumstances permit.[4]

DANGER NUMBER 25: Pre and Post Brand Choice in Testing Commercial Effectiveness

Sandwiching exposure to the test commercial between two different opportunities for stating brand choice/preference produces utter nonsense.

The argument is, and several otherwise reputable research firms make a good living this way, that persuasion can be measured by finding out, first, what brand viewers like best (or wish to buy or even receive as a free gift) by forcing them to watch the test commercial, and then getting them to restate their brand preference (sometimes researchers go so far as to announce they just lost the first batch of questionnaires and want everyone to do the brand preference questions over again). Conclusion: people who switch from a competitive brand to the test brand are, ipso facto, motivated by the sales power of your test commercial. Those who switch in the opposite direction are, alas, dissuaded by the commercial.

The more elegant of these practitioners will allow that there is a switching *constant*, i.e., people who always switch regardless of what they are shown; but they know what this quantity is supposed to be and will tell you that it's only the switching level relative to their norms that counts. The norms sometimes vary by product category . . . but they always seem to have on file exactly the right norms for you.

If you believe that a single exposure to a new commercial can convince consumers to switch brands, then there's this swamp land in Florida we should talk about. If, being more realistic, you think a single exposure may be enough to give you a rough indication of the likely success of the commercial, then I've also got news for you.

Switching appears to be *stochastic*, a word you'll be right at home with if you spend a lot of time reading the *Journal of Marketing*. On different occasions the same commercial will get different levels of switching. Even worse, brand switching can occur even when commercials for the product are *not* shown.

Wait, there's more: you can even get a balanced self-cancelling spate of switching, with some respondents leaving you and an equal number coming on board. Result: stasis!

Respondents appear to try to outguess the technique. If you've ever gone to one of these tests you'll notice that the respondents talk a lot among themselves while they're supposed to be filling in their questionnaires. They seem to be comparing notes, and I suspect they are trying to come up with responses that do something other than measure what the test purports to measure. Naturally, this can be minimized with proper supervision and I'm not accusing all of the research services of poor supervision. It is a real problem though, considering that one of the few charms of this approach is that it is inexpensive—the bids are often won by the el cheapos who cut corners, and where else can they cut but on their labor costs . . . ?

The samples they draw are not always satisfactory. This will depend on how they issue the invitations. Some send out postcards inviting people in to view new TV pilots, which must surely attract a nutty segment of the populace. Normally, I don't fret much about sample integrity, but for something like this I would want to be very cautious. I often have the sensation when I go to watch these things that I've dropped in on a meeting of avid PBS viewers hoping to force the commercial networks into having more opera and less tits and ass (T&A).

In one experiment that I conducted with this method we asked people what they liked and disliked about the test commercials. Unfortunately, we were unable to detect any differences in attitudes between those who switched toward our brand and those who switched away from it. Plainly, this does not categorically deny the validity of the switching question because there are many other factors that can induce switching (e.g., sales points, tone of execution, if it seems dishonest or insulting, etc.), but it was surprising, nonetheless. Given the spotlight the technique puts on the test commercial and all the folderol about brand preferences and so forth, I would have guessed that a glimmer of some kind of explanation for the switching would have been visible in the attitude section. The fact that there wasn't left me doubly disappointed with the technique.

Not all of these services position the switching exercise as a chance to win free product; but as some do, to them we must pose the question: How much appeal is there to the average consumer to win a year's supply of cough syrup?

I suspect what really happens is that people sentiently use their postchoice to express some sort of random *animal* approval for the commercial that is not substantiated by any other measurement and not permanent or enduring enough to show up in their attitudes toward the commercial.

These things are so cheap and easy to do it would be hog heaven if they worked. I know that lots of pretty smart people believe they really do. But I have seen them produce too many inexplicable results to have much faith. And I am not persuaded that a single advertisement exposure works in quite that way. At the very most it communicates something and shapes a few perceptions. But I strongly doubt that it disrupts consumer preferences quite that fast; there is too much working on the consumer urging her to maintain her comfortable status quo for the process to be all that slick.

DANGER NUMBER 26: Believability Testing

The obsession with believability measurement results in a concentration on imaginary problems and the possible rejection of good advertising.

Very few highly respected ecospecies of the advertising game spend much time worrying about whether their advertising is believable. One reason for this is that, through the years, they have settled into certain comfortable copy patterns, and tend not to tread very far afield from their well-beaten paths. They stay clear of the implausible to a large extent, sticking to simple, easily comprehended statements that are impervious to challenge by regulatory bodies, and that maintain consistency with a marketing strategy that changes little year after year.

At the same time it is, I think, fairly characteristic of the marketing people who don't get to do a lot of advertising research to want to ask if viewers found the commercial (or to be more specific, its *claims*) credible. If the answer comes back *no*, then they naturally feel compelled to do something about it, which means either reshoot the thing or alter the audio somehow . . . or maybe slap on a couple of supers.

When the unbelievable aspect is minor ("I don't think women look that great after a long plane trip," etc.) this kind of attentiveness to detail won't hurt much, but if the issue in question is basic to the product ("I don't believe a product can do that") then it casts doubt on the entire project, probably generates unnecessary pessimism among the company's more senior executives (who may only hear reports of vague problems and not get into the details), and in essence places the venture in jeopardy.

In truth, incredulity may be a very healthy thing. There may be nothing at all wrong with having a product that is so revolutionary, so exciting, that no one believes it does what you say. If it's cheap, they can (and many will) buy it at little risk, just out of curiosity, to see if it does work. No big deal. If it's expensive, they will probably want to check it out carefully before buying it anyway (as they would even if they did believe you). Advertising will not be the only info input they ever get on the product. After all, they usually buy it from some retail outlet where they study the literature, talk to the sales clerk (admittedly not the most reliable source of information), and—in many cases—get their money back if unsatisfied.[5]

I think that a high believability rating most often accompanies copy that tells the viewer nothing new; that instead just reminds her of something she already knows full well. The credibility rating drops as new information starts to flow. On the other hand, from the tests I have followed, low believability will accompany copy that is arresting and interesting . . . the kind of copy that is associated with unique, exciting new products.

Advertising may be especially effective when it initially generates total disbelief, which quickly translates into burning curiosity because the very features that conjured up the disbelief are also highly desirable. It's like getting a bad dose of cognitive dissonance. The viewer feels the need to resolve this and can easily do so through product trial—if it's inexpensive enough—or by seeking more information if the tariff is high.

Disbelief may be exactly what some brands need to jar consumers out of their comfortable and familiar purchasing patterns and into trying something different. Researching it just raises a lot of red herrings.

DANGER NUMBER 27: Rational versus Emotional Themes in Advertising Pretests

Verbal pretests of possible advertising claims and themes will favor the rational over the emotional almost every time.

Those brands depending on image advertising will have a rough time if you try to test their new copy lines by just letting respondents read them and react via some sort of rating scale. There is nothing much wrong with this approach if you are trying to cull twenty or thirty possible copy lines focusing on product performance and physical characteristics (e.g., "Makes the floors shine more. . . . Makes the floors shine longer. . . . Makes the floors have a deeper shine, etc.") It may miss a few good ones and overrate some weak ones from time to time, but claims built on the foundation of physical properties, in my experience, are usually called correctly in tests of this type. (Of course, these tests are a lot like product concept tests.)

The trouble occurs when you try to get fancy. An emotional appeal cannot be captured in a verbal statement. Lovers of good literature will be shocked at such philistinism, but—in the context of an advertising theme pretest—even Shakespeare would be hard pressed to convey the same feeling that the art director can with lighting, music, and motion. So whenever you try to bring it off in the pretest, without all the production values, it usually backfires and ends up taking second place to the stark-naked product claim. Even then, they are hard to test. We in the industry favor the arty, unusual, witty commercials, but for the average consumer . . . well, they just don't get it. Too much of this type of commercial's ability to communicate and motivate depends on the viewer's ability to draw on vast, complex, built-up stores of implied literary reference, theatrical experience, cinematic exposure, and a broad knowledge of events, all coalesced into thirty seconds. The average viewer cannot manage this. This may sound elitist, but there are profound differences in people extending far beyond the demographic data we are used to.

Cosmetic products probably make greater use of image advertising than does any other kind of item (though I doubt they pull it off with the same efficiency as the beverage and tobacco groups).[6] Take the following lines from perfume advertising and ask yourself how they'd rank if tested comparatively:

- Charlie!
- Sensual but not too far from innocence
- The eight-hour perfume for the twenty-four-hour woman
- Share the fantasy

If the verbal treatment of the advertising idea is not sufficient to convey the feeling, flavor, and mood without a complete execution, then marketing people should use their own judgment and not allow the test to go on. Rational appeals can be weighed and ranked in such tests; emotional appeals defy pretesting. They need the full treatment: lights, camera, action!

DANGER NUMBER 28: Pretesting Print Ads

The headline takes on such an exaggerated emphasis you usually get just a headline test.

Under the normal climate of a pretest, respondents—most of whom are no more facile with the written word than the average high school dropout—will be hard pressed to read the entire piece of copy. For one thing, while it may not necessarily be happening, she may sense the interviewer breathing down her neck with impatience. In some cases only a person with a reading speed of over 1,000 words a minute would be able to get through it all.

We're dealing here with the same consumer who has never read the instructions on a package, who has a kitchen full of expensive hi-tech, labor-saving marvels she can't get full benefit from because she never read their operating manuals, who cannot tune in the UHF stations because she doesn't know how. . . . Or we're dealing with the guy who, in the morning, picks up the paper, reads the weather and a few headlines, and then settles down with the sports page. People don't like to read; it's as simple as that.

The point is that if the ad doesn't convey its principal message via picture and headline you will not get a good test. I recall one test where we tried to determine if a brief paragraph could successfully convey enough information to respondents to get the same rating as a one-page print ad. When women were shown only one ad, or only one paragraph (separate groups, of course) the results were quite different; and our conclusion had to be that the paragraph didn't give the same effect as the full page ad. But when given several of each to evaluate, the results were the same for both approaches. One can only conclude, therefore, that the poor respondent just didn't have time to read the whole ad—and was left with just the headline to go on. Never assume that your test copy will be thoroughly read.

You can sometimes provide the encouragement for a respondent to read your copy more thoroughly by handing her a pencil along with the test ad and instructing her to underline anything in it she finds unclear or wishes to query. Nothing, however, is going to force her to read it if she finds it boring, or if she has trouble with the printed word.

DANGER NUMBER 29: Monadic versus Comparative Ad Pretests

The practice of asking respondents to rank a number of possible advertising themes in order of preference conjures up grossly abnormal patterns of evaluation.

The monadic evaluation (each theme assessed on its own; no reference being made to any other themes) produces different ratings than asking people to compare and rank a list of themes—whether in terms of overall hedonic appeal, uniqueness, importance, to what extent it represents an improvement over current products, or purchase likelihood. All of these mensurations may be great . . . but only if done monadically.

For example, Theme A when tested alone might get the highest rating, but when tested comparatively it can come in last. Hard to believe? Well, I've seen it happen several times in controlled experiments.

But which is the method to accept? I don't think there's much doubt that the single-theme orientation must be regarded as the preferred method. For one thing, it is more closely aligned to the manner in which advertising works. Palpably, viewers will see only one campaign for your brand, not several, during the promotional period. The invitation to compare and rank apparently invokes value systems that viewers don't normally draw on. They are thrust into the undesirable role of art director, consumer adviser, etc.

For the budget watchers who think this would send costs skyrocketing, I can report I've found that, at a single sitting, you can have respondents evaluate three different ad themes, monadically, before mental fatigue sets in. Even when direct comparisons have to be made (for example, when top management irascibly demands to know whether its pet campaign is better than the one the brand group recommends), it's better to either use the monadic parallel approach or, if you can swing it, employ a test involving paired comparison product testing, as described in Danger Number 24: The Entertainment Syndrome. These observations also apply to product concept tests.

DANGER NUMBER 30: Pretesting Advertising for Attitudinal Negatives

It is usually ineffectual to pretest advertising with the aim of detecting subtle attitudinal negatives.

Most advertising is inoffensive, but occasionally dangers of misinterpretation supervene which make cautious advertisers fear a backlash against the brand.

More commonly, questions of taste and potential backlash revolve around subtler issues—whether a particular pitchman is okay, the situations employed too provocative, etc. In my experience, there is no across-the-board guarantee that a pretest can detect potential problems. Generally, respondents will grant you a stamp of approval on just about anything you show them. The more broadcast-ready your test material, the less likely they will be to criticize it, feeling that it is too late (or too unkind) to do anything about it anyway. You can urge them to feel free to speak up, but that doesn't always work on borderline issues where they can go either way. And, as a rule, rough-cuts won't work as well because these won't do justice to the problems everyone is worried about.

A pretest may help dredge up some negatives in an incidental way. One thing they're really good at (because of the high-attention exposure and immediate subsequent concentration on the ad) is determining how much the ad is comprehended. If the respondents can't play back the essentials right after seeing it, it's unlikely they'll ever be able to do so. (Recall or comprehension don't build much once the campaign is on the air for a while; see Chapter 6, Danger Number 43: Do Recall Scores Build through Time?) So, measuring comprehension at this point makes a lot of sense, not so much to assure yourself that the commercial will be understood—since most advertising today is simple enough—but to see if any negatives crop up that intrude on message delivery. In a few isolated cases this may be adequate.

Still, we are faced with a problem that, in our experience, more often develops over time. A commercial can be innocuous at first, but then, as it appears week after week over a period of several months, pressure groups can find fault with it and earn Brownie points by attacking it on an organized basis within their memberships; or more commonly, certain performers in it (your spokesman, maybe) can grate on the nerves. I've seen commercials hum along nicely for months before gradually garnering negatives in their in-market attitude tests. When these grow to a substantial level you may feel compelled to react. Some advertisers feel that whenever a specific complaint ("I can't stand that coffee lady," or "I'm offended by the way it portrays kids as video-game addicts") reaches 10 percent on an open-ended basis, you have a negative that should be addressed. But anything below that is tolerable. Of course, this is just marketing judgment, but successful companies have been able to survive with this philosophy.

DANGER NUMBER 31: Pretesting Advertising Comprehension

Respondents are reluctant to admit they do not understand something. Detecting comprehension problems by going after them directly is less effective than taking an indirect approach.

As I've already acknowledged, most advertising today is pretty simple. Even dull-normal viewers probably grasp the central messages of 99 percent of the commercials they see. But when you are trying to do something a little different, or when you are working up the copy for an entirely new kind of product, you may have cause to question if what you are trying to say will be fathomable to the average viewer.

Some research designs call for exhibiting the copy and asking if there is anything in it "you find hard to understand." As a general rule this won't produce much enlightenment. A lot of people don't want to admit they can't understand something. After all, how stupid would you appear if you said you were mystified by a commercial or a print ad?

At the same time, comprehension is one of the steps in the communication process. But whether a viewer consciously understands or misunderstands your message content is beside the point. Many only think they understand. Sincere in their belief that they've got the message, they are not about to say they don't understand. Comprehension is more properly determined by finding out what message they receive from the test copy. If they've just been exposed to it, there will be very little chance for forgetting, hence the communication process will be captured midstream. If they inaccurately play back the essential aspects of your advertising, then you can probably say some kind of comprehension problem exists.

Once you get on air it will be too late to determine comprehension problems unless you go back to the laboratory. The on-air environment has too many other variables intervening, such as interest level, memory failure, and so on. Immediate recall is the way to explore this.

DANGER NUMBER 32: Far-out Advertising Pretests

Some technically advanced and very engaging techniques bear close scrutiny. Upon close examination they have little going for them.

Recognizing the folly of asking consumers if they think test copy is "effective," many imaginative techniques have been invented over the years that eliminate the need for direct, conscious consumer response. One such is discussed in Danger Number 24: The Entertainment Syndrome, but there are many others that should better be recognized as tributes to man's ingenuity than to his ability to predict advertising effectiveness. There are several of these, and some of the more engaging are discussed below. None is recommended.

Duo-screen

One research tutelary thought if you showed two commercials to a respondent simultaneously and let her decide, by means of a switch, to which one's audio she would listen, you could find out which commercial was more effective. The problem here is in the definition of *effective*. One commercial may have the visual power of attracting her attention because of the situation elements, but the more sober advertising executive would consider that an insufficient reason for choosing one commercial over another. Anyone can, and some do, exploit sensational visuals just to get good recall scores, but the practice seldom produces recall much beyond the situation elements. Unless the copy points, generally most strongly delivered in the audio, come through, the commercial falls short.

Pupil dilation

This was usually employed on print ads and I know of no one developing the method to the point where it could be used for TV commercials, but they may have. The idea was that your pupil dilates when you look at something you like. Since the human body has no control over this, it became a phenomenon rather tempting to measure while people were reading your ads. The equipment was quite elaborate, but essentially it came down to having a camera register what part of the ad the subject looked at and how wide open her pupil was then. Some of the results were quite funny. Proponents of the technique claimed when they tested heterosexuals they got the most positive response with pictures of the opposite sex; with homosexuals the positive occurred with pictures of the same sex. But in one famous, and devastating, example someone showed that men—real men— got the most positive response from looking at a picture of the rear end of a horse. Others challenged the method by claiming that pupil dilation was governed more by available light (camera buffs who know their f-stops will appreciate this) than by visual subject matter. Proponents said they had controlled for light variations. Still other studies found pupil dilation related to increases in mental activity—pleasant or not. The technique never became widely accepted. Even if physiologically sound, it probably sounded too crazy for upper management to accept, so any career-oriented researcher had to be cagey about using it. Understanding it required too much knowledge of human physiology, and, even among those with that knowledge, the method was considered very controversial.

Lie detectors and voice analyzers

The voice analyzer seems to have greater credence than the lie detector, possibly because it has not been around as long. These methods are not used so much to see if your respondent is lying when he expresses an attitude about your ad or product, since few of us really suppose he will do that so often that it becomes a big problem. Rather, these were proffered to detect subconscious feelings that lie below the level of articulation. The trouble with them, aside from some technical issues that I cannot judge, is that they are not diagnostic. Even if you believed what they said, you never know why. This makes it hard to go back to management with a useful recommendation. When you get all your answers from a black box, management doesn't need you around anymore. (That, by the way, is one of the first principles of *me-generation* career planning.)

Foot-pedal video screen

Viewers had to operate a treadle to keep the simulated TV going. Ineffective advertising, proponents argued, would merit a lower level of effort on the treadle than would effective advertising. This requires too great a suspension of disbelief. Clearly, respondents have to see the commercial first before you ask them anything that indicates whether it is effective. Even if you forced them to watch the test commercials first and then put them on the treadle, they'd only put out for the commercials they (1) found useful and informative, or (2) enjoyed. The two together do not add up to *effectiveness*.

There have been many other novel ad research approaches over the years. They are expressive of the concerns we all have with the sheer magnitude of the problem of trying to predict the effectiveness of advertising.

But all these neoteric techniques are up against heavy odds. Any time you have to stake everything on a single exposure to advertising you tread on thin ice. Advertising is just one facet of the overall marketing mix which, in turn, is only a microscopic fraction of the panoply of stimuli and pressures facing the consumer. The prospects of ever being able to duplicate all this in a lab are remote indeed. That doesn't mean we should give up, but neither does it mean we can accept methods that won't stand up to vigorous cross-examination.

The success stories about such techniques as these are often just that—stories. Not that purposeful deception is involved, but often the facts are not judiciously analyzed. Like subliminal advertising—which radio call-in shows accept as the proven intrigues of Big Business—they become part of the popular folklore and are impossible to dislodge with facts and cold logic.

In despair of ever finding an acceptable technique, more and more erstwhile resourceful researchers are turning to cable/scanner panels to assay their ads. While they haven't won over the entire research community (at time of writing only 33 percent of advertisers use them), they apparently are getting close to providing the technology researchers *think* they require for advertising problems (despite the obvious—but usually ignored or undetected—temptations they present to aggressive sales forces). Many, on the other hand, feel that the concomitant loss of diagnostics could, over the years, launch a seriatim at the end of which none of us would be able to develop effective advertising any longer.

NOTES

1. Sometimes our resourceful researcher is more ingenious than this. He may tell the respondent she is going to see the pilot for a new television show, and imply that her assessment of it will decide the fates of famous actors and legions of academy technicians and will be reviewed by network luminaries on both coasts. The entire entertainment industry, she will infer, will be rocked by her decision. Then she settles down as the lights are lowered and is confronted with a half-hour sitcom from the late fifties. And the researcher thinks her so otiose she won't notice, spliced into the film, those strange-looking animatic commercials (for products she's never heard of) or conclude that she's been duped and this is an ad test she's doing, not a program test. If she *is* that stupid, then you've got another kind of problem.

2. As an extension of this thought, a Jesuit, for example, prior to his preoccupation with social injustice and political indifference, might have seen this as the corrupting influence of man's *concupiscence* on his intellect; that man's insatiable lust for the fleshpots of the world distorts his judgment and leads him down the garden path to improper behavior. Experienced advertising researchers would recognize in this the well-known method of hyping awareness by liberal use of near-nude or otherwise provocative models, usually females of ample anatomical proportions. (Though of late, shifting sexual fantasies, coupled with a new view of society and man, have replaced some of the more obvious renditions of this, such as the undraped bosom et al., with new sexual clichés exploiting a newer kind of woman with strangely hirsute eyebrows and flawed complexions.) But even the act of capitalizing on concupiscence has its limits, and seldom do such egregious violations of norms of Christendom produce much more than situation recall; hence the saying, "As ye sow, so shall ye recall."

3. In the days when the Somozas still called the shots in Nicaragua, I tested commercials for a milkshake mix this way in that country. In those times, the sweeping

assumption of marketing experts across all nations south of Mexico, with the possible exception of Brazil, was that the only thing people wanted in a food product was *nutrition*. Every commercial, for any food product whatever, seemed to say something about *ocho vitaminas y minerales*. Our bold premise was that maybe a commercial that spoke about taste would be better. So we made a commercial that lauded the neat flavor of our milkshake product, got a conventional *vitaminas y minerales* one about the same brand from Venezuela (so they wouldn't be biased by having to see one old *local* commercial and one new commercial), and set out to do our nifty little test which, we felt, would revolutionize all South American advertising. Women were invited in, seated, and the office *doméstica*—who'd been asked to prepare two pitchers of *vainilla* milkshake—stood at the ready to serve each beverage at the appointed time. The first commercial was shown and they drank heartily of their vanilla milkshake. Everything was working out great. Then the second commercial was shown and the *doméstica* poured the second milkshake . . . it was pink! I rushed her outside and asked what the hell was going on. She explained that she thought the women would like a little variety so she had made up one pitcher of vanilla and one of strawberry. After her dismissal I heard that she had joined the Sandinists, and the rest is history.

4. I can't see how it would work quite as well if you tried to test a new commercial against an old one. You'd really have to study the details of the situation before deciding. Fortunately, that is seldom at issue. Most marketing executives tire of their current campaigns long before the viewer does and decisions are made to develop new copy which will, in most cases, get on the air regardless of how it performs vs. the current campaign. An old commercial, they think, is worn-out and, while it might test well in an unnatural environment of a laboratory, it doesn't play well in Peoria anymore so there's no point agonizing over it.

I was once asked if a certain cigarette commercial, under review by management, would have a corrosive effect on consumer attitudes. The problem was, you see, the actor in this commercial had a beard. (Readers may be surprised that the question was asked at all, but in the cigarette game the stakes are high and the rewards for being right are stupendous.) I could not think of a decent way of answering apart from using this technique, which even at that I wasn't sure would be sensitive enough to detect such an inconsiderable trifle. But, unable to come up with anything better at the time, I gambled my reputation on it, and survived. It indeed showed that the bearded model presented a problem . . . but not because of his whiskers. Detailed probing revealed that it was his red hair that did it. Apparently (and I think most redheads know this) a sizeable minority of people are really prejudiced against anyone with red hair. As I recall, the figure was over 10 percent.

5. Mail order is a different kettle of fish; you can't examine it and the ten-day free home trial offer is a pain in the ass to most people. Still the very fact that it makes unbelievable claims may, for more people than not, be the very thing that attracts them to a direct-mail offer in the first place. Of course, direct mail is so easy and cheap to test that you don't have to worry for very long about this.

6. The tobacco industry's claim on sophistication in image marketing may have been abridged when it ducked out of television; and with marketing efforts now only at the journeyman level, a huge question mark looms over the horizon as to when the momentum of past creative glories finally sputters out.

6 • *Advertising Research: Posttests*

The biggest task facing the ad researcher is determining if the advertising—as it is ready to appear on TV, in print, or in any other medium—is any good. Being put in the judge and jury role requires more than just running some kind of posttest and reporting the results.

It involves being able to defend the results, fighting tooth and nail to prevent his techniques from being adulterated or abandoned. For many reasons, advertising postresearch invites more flak than any other area of marketing research. For one thing, you have not only your own marketing folks to contend with but also the people from the agency who, needless to say, aren't just going to sit there and watch you shoot down their efforts, and possibly endanger their hold on the account, without putting up a fight. Occasionally, the corporate researcher also has to engage in battle with outside research suppliers who have a personal relationship with someone on the board of directors. This personal bond is stronger than the technical bond—if there is such a thing. All in all, being an advertising researcher when it comes to making that final assessment of a campaign, when it is time to determine if it goes national or not, takes courage and fortitude to withstand the unremitting misery of professional and political strife.

Do not wait for exclamations of approval. Few ad researchers are seen as positive factors in the marketing effort. The better they are at defending their techniques in management meetings against the attacks of injured creative people, the less liked they are. A select few, because of some widely recognized reputation or an extraordinary persona, are looked up to and sought after for their advice. But few reach this plateau, most being viewed by their clients as negative thinkers who have no right to express any opinion at all on the subject of advertising. At most, they are permitted to dispense a few numbers, a recall score, or a persuasion index when called upon, but no one wants to hear about the insights they've been able to acquire from years and years of testing commercials.

The way around this usually heated and unpleasant environment is to develop a system with the logic and consistency of the legal profession. This means you cannot waver from one technique to another for each and every problem—as too many are guilty of doing—but that you must lock in on one or two methods and build up a library of experience you can turn to for special analyses that will answer just about any question put to you by marketing people.

Over the years, I have found two techniques that offer this advantage. One is the familiar day-after recall (DAR) method, and most of this chapter will be about it. If you already use this method you will, I hope, be interested in some of the fascinating things I have discovered about it; these also have a lot to say about how advertising really works. If you can't bring yourself to accept the DAR method, bear with me; there may be something in the chapter that could change your mind.

The other technique is what I call a *campaign communication study*. It's not much more than a DAR that measures the whole campaign (i.e., copy *plus* media) rather than just one commercial. Sadly, few companies wish to devote that much attention to advertising per se and this is not a very popular technique. I feel that anyone who is spending substantial sums on media should make such an investment.

Apart from the controlled panel of cable/scanner services (which, as I have pointed out, I won't expound on except very obliquely, since it gets too close to being *sales research*), I have not found any other techniques that offered the same reliability for posttesting commercials, plus the speed, flexibility, and relative low cost needed by the marketing group.

Accordingly, this chapter will be about the DAR and its extended version, the Campaign Communication Study. Some of the dangers we will explore will only interest people who already believe in these techniques. Other dangers may make some contribution toward religious conversion, although that is not my intention.

DANGER NUMBER 33: *Meaning of Recall*

The exact meaning of related recall in the marketing pantheon is seldom made clear—it's either overemphasized or discounted. One result is that the technique is too often misused.

(See below.)

DANGER NUMBER 34: *Recall as a Measure of Sales Effectiveness*

The argument that recall scores have nothing to do with sales effectiveness is specious and unfounded.

Although you will hear quibbling about anything connected with ad research, few actually disagree that the DAR test can measure how much viewers remember about a commercial. That much is virtually universally accepted. Beyond that, it all becomes raw material to be processed by a powerful imagination.

There are raging battles over what recall means. Is it necessarily a good thing? Does it have anything at all to do with sales effectiveness?—an indication of the persuasiveness of the commercial, its ability to shape attitudes, to induce trial through curiosity if not through enthusiasm, etc., etc., etc.?

Everyone has a pet horror story about the brand with the high recall scores that suffered a colossal sales decline and can cite high-scoring introductory campaigns for brands that never made it. Others have contrary evidence: case after case of strong correlation between related recall and sales success. I recall one brand that had a flat sales curve which, upon using a new campaign that drove its recall scores up three to four times above the average, saw its growth spurt to 33 percent annually. The trouble is, of course, that there are too many variations on how the day-after study is actually conducted. Slight changes in wording of a single question can throw off the results. I do believe high recall and marketing triumphs usually go together, although I am thinking not so much of the *overall* recall score (on which so many commentators seem to concentrate) as on the recall of the *major copy point*.

But, even if recall and success go hand in hand, so what? What does recall really mean? As Don Miller, former chairman of Burke Marketing Research, a leading purveyor of recall tests, said:

The principal rationale of those using the technique is that if a commercial does not communicate anything, it can't sell anything. Thus, the commercial that communicates poorly should be discarded even though a high scoring commercial in itself cannot assure that all other elements of sales success are present.[1]

I find it hard to question this viewpoint. But there are still a few people around who, quaintly, think that man is driven by deep *subconscious* forces he knows nothing about, and that there can be response without awareness. This, they opine, supports their claim for the integrity and value of the amorphous advertisement. But it's all very sketchy and, I believe, comes from people who give no credit whatever to the consumer's native intelligence. You'll often be reminded of some brand of perfume that achieved success by pure image, but often the kind of household penetration that they talk about is very slight compared to the common grocery/drug store item . . . which needs an awareness level up in the 90s and a trial level of over 30 percent in order just to be included in the ball game.

Sometimes they point to commercials that they regard as largely image, overlooking the often glaring fact that they had product description or performance claims (explicit or implicit) in them. Marlboro advertising for example, though most observers would swear it was pure image advertising, conveys a strong "flavor" impression. As Saul Bellow once wrote: "A great deal of intelligence can be invested in ignorance when the need for illusion is deep."

It may never be possible to envelop recall results in a single explanation. There are a number of reasonable theories. One is that inherently interesting or desirable products make it easier for you to get high recall. It means the product concept is good, and that the copy has gainfully exploited it. High recall, then, may be symbolic of forthcoming success. Without a doubt, a recall score can easily be accepted as a measure of the commercial's ability to interest the audience. Carrying this a step further, can it be said that a boring concept is doomed? It is hard to transform a boring product idea into interesting advertising, though it's been done with those bursts of creativity that makes new agencies suddenly acquire new clients.

I think another problem we often run into here is the old one of confusing strategy and execution. The brand with the winning strategy is also the brand which has something to say that will make a commercial memorable.

DAR does measure the ability of the execution to attract attention and be remembered, but if the strategy is flat and meaningless it will have a tough time doing this. It is probably more common to have a poor execution of good strategies—which still get fairly good scores—than to have the reverse: weak strategies which have strong executions that get high scores.

DANGER NUMBER 35: Position in Commercial Break

Detractors claim that DAR scores are subject to all kinds of variables. One is the position of the commercial in a regular network or local commercial segment. It will get a higher recall score, they argue, if it comes first than if it's in the middle or last. This is patently false.

Like all the other attempts to challenge day-after testing, this one relies on the suspicion that there is always something going on that makes it difficult for the viewer to just sit there and watch the commercial. Lead-ins and lead-outs turn them on or off, put them in the mood to be sold, or deter them from receptiveness. Whatever happens before, during, and after the airing of the commercial, they charge, makes it a unique occasion and an unrepresentative test.

I have scrupulously examined the thousands of commercials I have tested over the years, looking at all the ins and outs of the DAR, and commercial environment simply has nothing to do with recall. Oh sure, there might be rare occasions when something shown on TV jars the viewer, such as an assassination bulletin interrupting the show; but most of what goes across the tube is pretty bland, and the viewer has become so inured to even the most outrageous fare that virtually nothing can intrude on the efficiency of the commercial except the execution itself.

But anyway, getting back to the examination of the tests I've conducted, when 30-second commercials were kind of new we used to test them in pairs, and the question was always asked: "Who gets to have their brand on first?'' Since we couldn't please everybody, we had to find out if it made any difference. Our tests showed that it did not. The average related recall score of about fifteen pairs of :30s that we tested in this way was 23 percent for the commercial in first place and 24 percent for that in second place.

Just to see what would happen if the :30 were shown in an isolated position (somewhat academic from the media planning aspect), we tested that too. Isolated gave us 19 percent and back to backs 21 percent, over about seven different tests (different commercials from the ones cited previously). It's a little puzzling that isolated gets the lower score, but the difference is not statistically significant.

Then just to answer someone's question (since we were just pulling back data out of the files) we found about half a dozen cases where our commercial had been lined up with a public service announcement as well as having been tested back to back with a real commercial. Again, no difference.

From the media buyer's point of view these are not too practical, obviously. But the reason we did this analysis was to demonstrate that the DAR testing situation is very robust.

DANGER NUMBER 36: Artificially Elevated Recall Scores

Day-after recall scores are frequently called into doubt because, it is argued, they can easily be jacked up by all kinds of production tricks.

While true, this is so easy to detect that it is not worth worrying about. Methods that are employed to produce high but *phony* scores usually end up generating mostly situation recall and very little copy point recall. Common among these devices at recall hype are those frequently described by creative people over cocktails: "It's easy—I just open up on a huge pair of cans," or one that has only been used in political advertising where Federal Communications Commission (FCC) sanctions don't apply: "The first thing you say is 'Shit!' "

There are, however, methods that can be used to enhance not situation recall, but copy point recall, and there's nothing at all wrong with trying to do that. In fact, that's one of the things the agency *should* be doing. These have little to do research methods, but—very importantly—they do help in analyzing the research results. For the record, some recall boosters that have been successfully exploited in this regard are:

- News Value. A commercial that has genuine news value (e.g., a new toothpaste, with American Dental Association blessing, that eliminates gum disease) will tend to get higher than average recall. On the other hand, it doesn't help to contrive to make mundane messages look like news. And if it doesn't have any bearing on product performance it won't help much either.
- Testimonials. There are a lot of testimonial commercials, especially those that use celebrities, simply because they do get high recall scores. Of course, it helps if the

spokesperson is compatible with the product, like Robert Young was for Sanka, or Jane Russell was for Cross-Your-Heart bras. Role reversal here would not do.

- Humor. Most agencies that like to use humor err by going overboard. Humor delivers high copy recall only when it doesn't detract from the main message. Remember that you are pitching a very broad piece of the population most of the time, which means that you can't allow the commercial to be *too* funny. Some tests along these lines suggest most people respond to humor because they "get the joke," and not actually because they find it funny. With that in mind humor is always a crap shoot. While the agency guys may like Woody Allen, the audience may be more in tune with Shecky Green. If humor can attract viewer attention and hold it while the copy points are being developed, it is doing its job.
- Size of Cast. The fewer the better. Too many characters seem to lend confusion to the commercial.
- Early Brand-Name Mention. Every second that passes by prior to the first mention of the brand name is sheer waste. Viewers have to know what they're watching. A good preacher knows that in his Sunday sermon he must first tell his congregation what he's going to say, then say it, then tell them what he just said. In the same way, a commercial has to start off announcing what brand it's going to be about. Early brand-name mention gives you a 50 percent greater chance of getting a high recall score.
- Number of Brand-Name Mentions. Rule of thumb: two or three times aren't enough; seven or more seems good.
- Showing Product in Use. This is always a good way to support the sales message. (Rough news for breweries.) Any time you use your video to support or reinforce your audio, you've not only managed to produce something better than a radio commercial, but you've also latched onto one of the prime components of strong communication.
- Strong Visuals. Weak, uncertain, passive visual situations don't hold viewer interest.
- Number of Scene Changes. The fewer the better. Rule of thumb: five or less is okay.
- Presence of Kids. I've never seen it make any difference. Even the famous Life cereal commercial, *Let Mikey Try It*, cute as Mikey was,[2] was only an average scoring commercial. Its strength was in its very impressive internal "taste" recall.
- Tone. It should be realistic, direct, and simple. Obscure, heavy, or indirect tone or atmosphere just confuse viewers.
- Supers. You can't use them to patch up a weak commercial. Judgment would say, to anyone who has ever made a presentation using visual aids, that the use of supers has to do something, and it probably does, but it doesn't come through in day-after studies.
- Number of words. Makes little difference. The important thing is to keep the number of ideas in the commercial down to a bare minimum. One idea is really all any 30-second commercial should have; even in the days of the 60-second commercial, those that tried to impart more than one idea suffered.

Caveat: None of the above proves that remarkable exceptions cannot occur.

DANGER NUMBER 37: Replicability of Day-After Recall

In their long history, there have been a few isolated cases of commercials that got a different recall score when retested at a later date, which have spuriously called into question the integrity of the entire technique.

Let's look at the black side of this. If you don't get the same score every time you test a given commercial then, obviously, the technique fails to meet one of the key criteria of any scientific methodology: it isn't reliable; it isn't reporting what it was supposed to. No technique that cannot be repeated is of any value whatever.

Occasionally, the vagary of sampling being what it is, something will go wrong. We all know we should get heads 50 percent of the time we flip a coin, but in some runs we get heads more often. So when you hear of people getting different DAR scores when they retest the same commercial, they probably have a sampling wobble. (Of course, they could also be executing the technique wrong.)

Every time I have been called on to introduce the day-after method in a company, someone eventually comes forth to challenge it. And each time this has resulted in my being asked to retest a commercial that had received a disappointing score. (You're never asked to do it on high-scoring commercials.) Recognizing that something can always go wrong, I've always held my breath when embarking on these *putting your money where your mouth is* episodes, but I've never yet been embarrassed by the results.

Once able to get the technique broadly accepted in a company then, by nature of the fact that I like to test three commercials per interview for consistency, I have ended up retesting lots of commercials over the course of time. This has provided several opportunities to see if the published claims of replicatability are true. I can report that they are. Not only that, but I think that the DAR technique—and this is quite a tribute to it—is probably one of the most dependable techniques known to the marketing research profession. In reliability, it beats most other techniques by a mile.

DANGER NUMBER 38: Specific Recall

Overemphasizing specific recall (as opposed to general recall) places too great a burden on the communication process.

Specific recall is the voluntary mention, by respondents, of any element—whether sales point or situation—that is *only* in the test commercial. *General recall* is something that's in more than one commercial (either yours or competition's). For example, a brand that continually makes a flavor claim would have a generally correct response if the respondent said, "They said it tastes good." However, if in one—and only one—of its commercials it happened to say, "It tastes so good that it'll make your eyes light up and your tummy say 'Howdy,' " and this very line were re-called . . . this would be *specific recall*.

Many creative people and their marketing cohorts feel, rightly I think, that effective communication necessitates strong, vivid, and highly memorable specifics. And they like to use the level of specific recall as a gauge of the efficiency of a test commercial. Some researchers automatically include a breakout of specific recall in their reports; a few analytically overemphasize it. It is, admittedly, a good indicator of communication strength, but so is—in another kind of way—general recall. Penalizing a commercial or an entire campaign because it gets across only general recall is imprudent because it loses sight of the intent of the copy strategy which, in almost all cases, is geared to getting across a very general notion (like "good flavor").

Needless to say, while a surfeit of specific recall is admirable and does indicate that you have an arresting attention-getting execution, unless this assists in getting equally high (or at least high enough) levels of copy point playback, you don't have a commercial that is doing its job. Many commercials that achieve high levels of specific recall do so only among the situation elements.

The same is true of incorrects, to a lesser extent perhaps. While it is unusual for a brand to have more than one major copy point, a brand that has and omits one of them in a given commercial need not suffer remorse when it garners some mention of it in the incorrects. Though the viewers may have mistaken the intent of the commercial, as long as they made a mistake that could still be regarded as favorable to the brand some worthwhile communication has taken place. It's not exactly what you were shooting for, but it is not the evil implied by the word *incorrect*.

The objective of advertising is, at least in large part, to communicate. The more vivid the communication, the more efficient the commercial may be judged. And whether the recall is highly specific can be a sign of the success it has had in being vivid and rich, and all advertisers should strive for this. But in actual practice it is seldom achievable and commercials should not be rejected because they are unable to generate a high level of specifics when they are still giving you healthy amounts of correct general recall.

DANGER NUMBER 39: Common Problems in DARs

Simple acts of carelessness in the conduct of a DAR interview can invalidate the entire test and produce dangerously misleading results. They also give the technique a bad name.

The DAR interview was developed with blood and sweat over a period of thirty-odd years. It contains many elegant refinements dedicated to assuring consistency and—good news to agency executives—the highest possible recall. Specifically, the wording of each question is geared to producing reliable readings on the *test* commercial and minimal memory seepage from other commercials. Accordingly, it is foolhardy to allow investigators or anyone connected with the study to alter the wording of a DAR question or probe. But carelessness in the field work is the research supervisor's burden. Even the heavy breathers should pause long enough to read about this. It's a source of a lot of grief and screw-ups . . . as petty as it may sound.

One common act of negligence is dropping the phrase "last night." The question is supposed to be, "What did they say about Burger King in last night's commercial?" The phrase, "last night," is also in all subsequent probes. When it's dropped, as interviewers are sorely tempted to do because it's not the way they normally speak, you begin to get unwanted responses about Burger King's past advertising. The average respondent's mind is always on the brink of shifting gears. It takes hardly anything to get them to wander off the topic. By accidently chucking the "last night" phrase you suddenly have them talking about the entire history of the brand's advertising, thus artificially adding several percentage points to your recall score. In some foreign languages, the expression "last night" has a less definitive meaning than in English. Don't ask me why. In Quebec, for example, where they allege to speak French, I found that you had to say "last night *only*" ("*hier soir* seulement") in order to get the same effect. Otherwise you got outrageously inflated recall. In one test to determine the normal *bogus* level of recall—how much recall you pick up if the commercial was not actually shown but the interviewing conducted as if it had been—saying simply "*hier soir*" gave us a 28 percent recall, but when we added the word "*seulement*" this dropped, on a subsequent test, to 5 percent, which is the normal bogus level. My judgment is that you would have the same situation in Spanish and Portuguese, but I've never had enough loose cash in the budget to test it.

Even when your investigators faithfully follow your exact wording, you can sometimes hear respondents saying things like, "Burger King usually shows. . . . " At this point the investigator should stress that he or she only wants to hear about the commercial shown last night. When respondents don't announce such intentions you're up the creek.

Some interviewers have to be reminded to record every word the respondent utters. The verbatims will play a big role in the analysis and any attempt to get by with a précis can throw things off. When we have to go by what the respondent actually said in order to judge the *richness* of recall, we can't make do with what the interviewer thought she meant.

Tabulation is another problem area. Someone has to decide which of the verbatims are related. This is one of the few times in marketing research when you print the actual open-ends in the report, so you can't hide behind an edited computer printout. You are naked and there are rules to keep you honest, but somehow these rules don't always filter down to where they have to be applied. It's a supervision problem, of course, but more so than other lapses with the tabulating group, this one can make you look bad.

Tabulators and coders should also be closely supervised to make sure they pick up everything that is said in the verbatim—no matter how perverse or slight it may seem. Okay, I know . . . another *motherhood* statement. But in one company the data processing chief told me his girls (sic) would no longer handle our questionnaires because they had profanity in them. Words like *damn* and *bullshit*. Even worse, in Brazil, I couldn't understand why one of those revolutionary food commercials with the "tastes good" claim that I was proselytizing wasn't producing any "taste" recall. Everybody tried to tell me it was because my judgment was wrong—that Brazilian shoppers weren't interested in taste. I got riled up enough to do a Watergate-style investigation. Tracking it all the way down to the raw questionnaires, I found lots of "taste" mentions. Quizzing the coders, I learned that they had elected to ignore the "taste" comments because *they knew they weren't important*. Sometimes the poor researcher just can't win.

DANGER NUMBER 40: The Folklore of Day-After Complaints

A lengthy spate of popular, untutored charges leveled against the recall method needlessly weakens one's faith in a highly reliable technique.

There are too many plebeian objections to the DAR method for me to tackle them all here. Some are dealt with in other Dangers. The more popular ones are addressed below.

Product usage bias. This one says that if you are a sales prospect for the product, your recall scores will be much higher than if you were not in the market for it. I will owe that this is probably true to some extent for print ads, but when it comes to TV the effect of this is slight. For example, back in the halcyon days when cigarette commercials were still being broadcast, I was never able to see any significant differences in recall between smokers and nonsmokers. There are many other examples suggesting product propensity has little (i.e., something—but not much) to do with recall. You do not have to be a product user, or even a potential user, to be interested enough in the message to pay attention and stash it away in your memory cells. Accepting this objection to the DAR technique is *tantamount* to claiming that people easily forget unpleasant experiences. Our taverns are full of people who belie this. Commercially, the danger of subscribing to this objection is that it sets up arbitrary norms for given product categories, thus opening up a dreadful can of worms. One consequence may be setting your sights too low with products that have had, historically, low DAR scores. The agency or the product manager would argue, fairly convincingly, that this is par for the category, and that they should not be expected to be able to produce commercials that approach the average for all products. Going back to the cigarette business again for half a minute, this was true in the mid-sixties. They got DAR scores that averaged only about one-half of what other consumer products were getting, and the marketing executives I dealt with had been thoroughly convinced by their agency that cigarettes constituted a low-interest category and that it would be impossible to develop copy that would score as high as soap, for example, which, for some unknown reason, they considered a high-interest category. This, of course, was a lot of crock. With extra effort and a bit more thought and analysis, once the commitment was made commercials were produced that scored as high as and higher than soap commercials.

Memory skills vary by program/magazine. This one claims that a commercial may get a higher score on one program (such as ''60 Minutes,'' with its alleged brainy audience) than on another show (the average hot tub/car chase drama). Well, the fact is that this is utter nonsense. No reputable study has ever proven this age-old contention, though many have tried. Since the proper execution of the DAR method restricts the obtaining of recall only to viewers in the *commercial audience*, it is hard to believe that this distorted view has persisted for so long. Audiences do vary demographically, but the skews are seldom that great to be able to upset recall scores perceptively. Some of the tests that people cite to prove this charge are based on *program audience* data—which is not a valid way of treating the matter. It's just sloppy analysis.

Value systems control viewer perceptions. This argument says that viewers will only allow themselves to perceive (i.e., pay attention to and absorb) things that their value system allows them to be interested in. Hence, recall scores can be distorted by this. This objection is not one you often hear in the world of marketing, but it crops up in academic discussions. I believe the practical person would just shrug this one off. If the value system of the viewer precludes his grasping the commercial message, then so be it. There isn't much you can do about it. And it is probably wrong anyway (see above).

Commercial position. Some say it is better to be near the middle of a show, or at the end, because that gives you higher recall. This in fact is true when you base your results on program audience (see above), but it is a media consideration and the findings on this are actually very complex and vary by program and time slot. Early evening shows, for example, have a lower commercial audience to program audience ratio than do prime time shows (presumably because families are scurrying around getting dinner ready and shouting at one another). When this is used to disqualify the DAR method, however, it is not valid. As mentioned previously, DARs use the commercial audience base. When examined this way, position in the show makes no difference. Hence, you can use any commercial position to test a commercial, providing you ask coherent program and commercial prompts to establish commercial audience presence. All these problems were worked out years ago.

Length of time brand has been on market. They usually try to convince you that the longer the brand has been around, the higher it scores, or vice versa. The facts are that the *new* brand, in its introductory commercials, will get the highest scores of its life cycle, all other things being equal. Introductory commercials, no doubt due to their inherent news value, will on average, score about one-third more than regular commercials. So don't be happy if your introductory efforts get DARs equal to your corporate average.

Some cities naturally score higher than others. This is probably a result of small bases, though I have no information that would disprove this allegation. The prudent researcher would never use just one city to test a commercial. The limited data available on this phenomenon doesn't suggest that there is such a thing as a consistently low-scoring city. Neither can it be said that some cities favor one particular brand or that scores correlate with local market shares. Still, the fact that this phenomenon is observed rather frequently, albeit on small bases, could suggest exercising caution using cable/scanners or simulated test markets in one city alone. If related recall is an indication of the probable success of a brand (as I think the evidence usually shows) then a test carried out in a low recall-yielding locality would be misleading.

DANGER NUMBER 41: Problems with Sloppy DAR Executions

A lot of research firms assume they know how to do day-after recall studies, but few actually do. Those that lack the necessary sophistication are guilty of a plethora of errors, all of which invalidate their results.

Day-after recall study results—in those companies where the technique is honored—are used with immense intensity and earnestness. The system cannot tolerate even the tiniest relaxation of technical standards. But the dilettantes, in haste or ignorance, often let the side down with careless executions.

Sloppy program audience definition. Some fail to provide a solid guarantee that the respondent really saw the test program. "Did you watch the last fifteen minutes of 'Hill Street Blues' " is too loose . . . to give one of the many examples of faulty wording I have come across on frequent occasions. For one thing, somatized and satiated by viewing overdose, some viewers actually don't know what programs they are watching, and the availability of multichannels via cable now makes the problem even worse. More kindly, a viewer can leave the room for a minute to answer the telephone and return unaware that her kids have switched to another program. All kinds of things go wrong. Inarguably, without painstaking program prompts you inevitably include a lot of respondents that shouldn't be there.

Sloppy commercial audience definitions. Most amateur renditions of the DAR will omit this altogether. This is even worse than screwing up on the program audience definition. Anyone remotely connected with advertising knows that not everyone who watches a show will be present for all of its commercials and that this ratio can vary from beginning to end, by type of show, and (as mentioned previously) by day part. You can't afford any inconsistencies in a DAR study. Sloppy commercial audience definition can introduce enormous artificialities in scores.

Sloppily going for same night recall. I don't think many firms do this anymore, but you never know when it'll make a comeback. It's a neat way to hype recall scores; they're obviously going to be higher an hour or so after people see the show than they will be the next day. The industry standard, however, is day after . . . because it is considered more actionable in that it reflects what aspects of a commercial are retained by a consumer during her first real opportunity to buy the product. Would this apply to Denny's, and other late night eateries? Yes, there is strength in numbers—in all of us subscribing to the same standards.

Sloppy treatment of verbatims. You shouldn't have more than one or two verbatims per test that force you to use pure judgment in classification. The following are related: correct specific elements only, correct specifics plus incorrect specifics, correct specifics plus incorrect generals, correct generals plus incorrect generals, and correct generals by themselves. Unrelated are: specific incorrects alone, specific incorrects plus correct or incorrect generals. The only argument you should ever have is in deciding when something is specific.

DANGER NUMBER 42: Recall Drop-off

Day-after recall must be just that. Delaying the interview—even for one day—lowers your scores.

Day-after recall is called that for very good reason, but still there are some researchers who feel they can make up quotas of interviews, or do the entire study, two days after exposure.

Though tests show that day-after recall is higher than two-day-after recall, some researchers, reluctant to interview on a Sunday (not because of ancient blue laws, but because of overtime/holiday charges), try to make do by delaying interviewing until Monday.

Declines in recall are quite rapid over the first few days following exposure. Immediate recall (i.e., from interviews conducted right after exposure) are, of course, the highest you can ever get, often producing scores in the high 80s or low 90s. By the following day you'll be down into the 20s. Two days out, you'll be in the low teens. (The average score in a two-day-after test will be 40 percent less than a day-after test in the case of television commercials, and 30 percent less for print.) Naturally, this will vary for certain types of executions and product categories, but across the board it says that day-after exposure is the proper timing for the test if you want a timing procedure that taps the most productive point in the ad's influence over purchasing.

DANGER NUMBER 43: Do Recall Scores Build through Time?

Common lament: "A commercial's recall scores build up—from a low, unsatisfactory level to very high levels—simply by being on the air for a few months. You can't judge a commercial by a DAR conducted early in its life. We should wait six months at least before doing the test."

Agencies are very clever at capitalizing on this line of thought. They like to push the *slow fuse* theory. "This commercial," they will urge you to believe, "is so different that the target audience is going to have to get used to it. At first they won't believe it, okay? And they won't be able to understand it, okay? But through repeat exposures, okay?—they'll come to love it, okay? Then you're going to see a record breaker for your company. . . . These recall scores are going to climb. Okay? But first we gotta be patient. Okay?"

Okay, indeed! But, to be charitable, I wouldn't want to say it's never happened; people have told me of such cases—though they've never been able to come up with many details.

Actually, quite the opposite is true. It is not unusual to see an average commercial suffer a decline of about one-third in its recall score over a six-month period, or to see a very strong commercial's scores get somewhat better. But weak commercials, as a common rule, get even worse through time. Commercials should be tested early in their life; most researchers, for this and some obscure technical reasons, like to pick them up on their first day of exposure. (Technically, this makes it easier to delineate commercial audience presence via the commercial prompt, and to classify verbatims by reference to the specifics. Aren't you sorry you asked?)

The declining score is more plausible intellectually. After all, why would a commercial that attracted and held so little attention the first time a person saw it suddenly, or even gradually, begin to do better later? It doesn't make any sense. Those that start off weak are bound to get worse, not better.

However, I'll admit this much: the viewer's comprehension of specific phrases can improve drastically over time.

DANGER NUMBER 44: Effect of Past Advertising on Recall Scores

The belief that past advertising (strong or weak) influences DAR scores is incorrect. Recall tests are killed by claims that the brand's past will come home to haunt and distort the test.

Recall method detractors often argue that a brand with very strong (in terms of copy and media) advertising will almost always get high recall on its new commercial as a residual effect of past glories and that, therefore, it's pointless to do any DARs because the results would be meaningless. Conversely, if a brand has had a history of weak advertising it will not be able to benefit from this effect and, therefore, it's unfair to subject its new advertising to a recall study. Cynics would note that the latter argument is heard most often.

Both arguments belie the amazingly rigorous and intricate lengths to which the DAR method goes to ensure that only recall of the test commercial is picked up in the test. But without regurgitating the details of the technique, one can easily demolish these arguments by citing any number of actual case histories.

That a brand would never experience any variation in its recall scores is, as most researchers making lavish use of the DAR technique know, certainly not the case. Even brands chalking up a track record of above average commercials over the years have been known to come out with pools that score even higher than in the past and, conversely, they occasionally come a cropper. Hence the famous saying, "What have you done for me lately?"

Among the many examples I have looked at was one that was most convincing and interesting because it had to do with a brand whose annual ad budget, in terms of today's dollars, was over $100 million. Its recall studies over the years produced a broad range of related recall scores, all the way from 8 percent to 51 percent. The scores were sporadic: sometimes high, sometimes low—they did not progress in a straight upward trend. This brand had a very well known slogan, whose recall (which dissidents would say should have been constant) bounced around a lot—ranging from 0 percent to 23 percent, again with no trend. Sometimes it was able to get across very specific copy points and sometimes not—the range for this was from 0 percent to 38 percent, with no trend.

The big point here is that—apart from that bogus recall level you always get—people don't fake their recall just because they happen to know what your brand has been saying in years gone by.

Another quick piece of evidence which almost any research department can dig out of its files, that would put this objection to bed is a comparison of TV and print recall scores. Unless there is something very strange indeed going on, almost any brand will experience higher recall scores for its TV commercials than for its print ads. If past advertising intruded on these tests, as the detractors insist, there would be only minimal difference.

Most of the commonplace objections to the DAR method, like the prevailing attacks on many other noble research methods, have an unfortunate appeal to the typical nonanalytical, top-of-the-mind fast trackers who call many of the shots in the business world. The objections all sound entirely plausible. But when you do the analysis—as few ever have time or inclination to do—you find otherwise. Clare Boothe Luce once said that she tended more often to side with the pessimists of this world than with the optimists, explaining that she felt the pessimists more often had the better information. In like manner, I'd say I was a skeptic, because when I hear something critical of a standard technique, I find that it is seldom based on careful analysis.

DANGER NUMBER 45: Counting Old Copy Lines as Correct in DARs

Counting a verbatim unrelated because it contains a past campaign's slogan or copy line not present in the test commercial is too strenuous and may give a distorted impression of the efficiency of the commercial.

This is not exactly the research world's most pressing issue, but it serves, if nothing else, to establish the philosophical framework in which DAR studies are to be analyzed.

Let's say we're testing a McDonald's commercial that doesn't contain the phrase "You deserve a break today." Let's also assume this phrase has been so thoroughly communicated over the years it's become part of the consumer's vernacular. Now, what do we do if a respondent in our DAR study says this is what the commercial said? (If we do nothing else about this problem, can we not marvel how such a relatively obscure branch of modern civilization can create such profound intellectual puzzles?)

Strictly speaking, the respondent is wrong, but in a sense McDonald's is always telling us *we need a break*—that's the whole point of a fast-food outlet. In a general way, it is hard to imagine this as an improper interpretation of any McDonald's advertising. There is a grave danger that a new commercial will be falsely penalized when it conjures up perfectly valid, and still strategically consonant, sales points that—merely because they were not articulated in the script—must be discounted by following the letter of the DAR law.

Consumers often will think that new commercials still convey the *thought* of old, well-established slogans, etc. When Winston cigarettes occasionally dropped the "tastes good like a cigarette should" line from its TV announcements they continued to receive slogan recall, provided the commercial strongly implied a "taste" claim but not when other factors were stressed. Any brand with a slogan skeleton in its closet may experience a wide range of gratuitous slogan playback; thus, I believe, indicating that it is genuinely believed by the respondent to be what the commercial implied. (Otherwise there'd be no range—just a constant.)

The research supervisor should not stick to the letter of the law governing the classification of verbatims, but to the spirit. The usual law says that incorrect recall can make some verbatims *unrelated*, but how do you regard recall of the old slogan? If it is still an accurate—no matter how quaint—rendition of the copy strategy, then it should be regarded as a *general correct*. Doing otherwise would be disallowing the role advertising plays in forming the spoken language that enters into the shaping of brand attitudes; to wit, the frequency with which we observe that impromptu favorable attitudes are almost perfectly worded playbacks of certain campaigns.

That ad researchers would even take the time to worry about such issues should be reassuring to the layperson. It is a small, isolated demonstration of the hard work backing up each DAR report that most people never see.

DANGER NUMBER 46: *Effect of Double Exposure on DAR Scores*

Viewers exposed to two commercials for the same brand in the same night don't give better sales point recall than viewers with only one exposure. The practice of multiple spotting (usually done only in local markets) in the same show is a terrible waste of media dollars.

I risk retaliation from all of Chicago's UHF stations for choosing to reveal this, but the march of science must continue.

In the course of conducting on-air tests one cannot *always* have the test evening purged of all subject brand advertising (but for the test commercial) though one does try. I have examined about five or six serendipitous cases where the commercial audience base was established for an *accidentally* aired second commercial, thus permitting recall to be obtained from respondents exposed to both commercials. Furthermore, we had enough interviews to break out the folks who saw just one of the two commercials. In none of these cases, by the way, was the double exposure to the *same* commercial, but to two *different* commercials for the same brand. (I apologize for such a long-winded setup for what is, basically, a pretty simple conclusion.)

In all cases the overall related recall was higher (by about 40 percent) among the doubly exposed folks, but—and this is the key finding—internal recall (copy points and situation elements) was virtually identical with the one-exposure group of viewers. It made no difference whether the commercials were placed back to back or appeared in different programs.

Psychology fans will immediately recognize in this the much beloved process of *adaption*, which is where a stimulus loses a wallop with continued repetition—like your average used-car-dealer ads on the late late show.

One possible useful implication of this is that, since overall recall goes up, it could be a way of getting fast general awareness for a new brand. Then call it a wrap once the brand is successfully introduced. But if the delivery of sales points is your main goal, it would seem that the point of diminishing returns is quickly reached in a media plan. Just keep in mind that those results are for the commercial audience base, and that showing the same commercial (or different commercials for one brand) twice or thrice on the same night doesn't necessarily produce multiple exposures.

DANGER NUMBER 47: *Predicting Recall Scores*

There is no cheap method—short of a complicated form of analysis only trained experts can do—of predicting related recall scores.

Some firms like to tout their methods for predicting recall scores, but common sense says that if they really worked the big research houses specializing in DARs would be defunct. I suppose now and again they have predicted scores accurately enough, but unless they do it across the board, under controlled experiments, it's not good enough to qualify for serious scientific recognition.

I've worked on techniques, using captive audiences, that could sort out the good commercials from the weak but that were totally unreliable for predicting the magnitude of copy point recall, which is what really counts at the checkout counter. Without that ability, I'm not sure what use they are.

Considering the high cost of commercial production (while animatics give you the same scores as finished commercials, a lot of marketing executives still shy away from testing copy this way) and media, it's penny-wise and pound-foolish to fuss over investing a few bucks in good ad research . . . unless you can be 100 percent certain that the fast and dirty technique will yield precisely the same result as your on-air test.

There is one way to predict recall scores, though I'm not sure many readers would actually want to do it. It puts you too far out on a limb. My company once offered it as a service but we had few takers, probably because it appears to be based too much on judgment. Recognizing it'll never become a cherished member of the Research Methodology Hall of Fame, I believe, however, that describing it is still useful, for it covers valuable terrain that is applicable in writing the analysis in a DAR report. Since research summaries seldom receive Pulitzers, anything that can make them more uplifting and readable should be met with open arms.

My method is also useful to people building mathematical models of advertising performance, since it permits introducing their data in smaller lumps—one way, albeit a small one, of minimizing error. Moreover, one of the chief difficulties of model building is in translating the qualitative into the quantitative, and my method allows you to do just that.

Of course, you have to swallow the premise upon which I base it, and that may not be a palatable experience to one and all. It certainly requires one to accept the inherent value of the DAR technique, for one thing, and then go on to accept the *basis of recall*. The initial premise that advertising is essentially—though not necessarily exclusively—*communication* must be conceded. But, once acknowledged, different marketing strategies, each with its own copy strategy and idiosyncratic executions, can be woven into a model without incurring a research charge.

Prior to perfecting this technique, I performed an extensive analysis on several hundred day-after studies to see what factors—uncontroversially visible to the eyeball—seemed to pop out in the high-scoring commercials, and which linked up with the low-scoring losers. Some of the executional traits found here have already been discussed (see Danger Number 36: Artificially Elevated Recall Scores), but they aren't helpful in forecasting recall scores. Fortunately we also know of some deeper strategic characteristics of communication efficiency: audiovisual sync, empathy, interest level, and clarity.

Audiovisual sync is the degree to which the picture complements and supports the sound. You would think that commercials would all be okay on this factor, but, in fact, it is surprising how many are just like radio commercials—they've got pictures that do nothing to reinforce their sales message.

Empathy is a double-barreled item. On the one hand it has to do with how well the commercial *talked* to the viewer. On the other it concerns the extent to which its internal parts hung together.

Interest level is simply that—how interesting the commercial is. This has to do with its subject matter, its situations, etc.

Clarity is really a question of ease and simplicity.

Commercial executions that do well on all of these will get very high related recall scores. Sometimes a commercial will earn its high score by doing great on some of the factors, but not so hot on others. But, in all cases, some combination of these four factors will explain the resultant DAR score.

If you do a lot of related recall tests you can develop a sense of judgment about these factors. I wouldn't recommend it for someone fresh out of college with only five or six DARs under the belt, but after a few years of playing around with recall studies one cannot help but develop a feel for them. If you make a conscious effort to look at each test in terms of these four factors, you will eventually find it not too difficult to predict how strong each will be in a forthcoming recall study. Test yourself on this a few times before going public with it (unless you've already sent your resume out).

Here's how the quantification process is done: If you grant that excellent 30-second commercials get scores of around 40 percent (the average is only around 20 percent), then visualize a balanced *excellent* commercial having equal parts of the four factors so that you could assign each an index value of 10. Their sum is thus the 40 (percent) in the recall score. Now, this is just something to use as a *mental target*. You can then view any test commercial and try to assign each of the factors a value, keeping in mind that when you give one of them a 10, it means you are awarding it a score equivalent to that of an *excellent* commercial. But if you're very, very enthusiastic you can give a factor more than 10; after all, a :30 *can* get a score of more than

40 percent. To make a long story short, do this for each factor, add up the numbers, and that's your predicted recall score.

Until you try it you probably won't have too much faith in it. I think it is worth doing if you want to make a more useful contribution to your company's advertising efforts via the analytical insights it gives. I'm not too optimistic that it's got much of a future as a purely predictive device because no one will believe you anyway. Even if they did, they wouldn't want to bare themselves to upper management as justifying their hefty media budgets based on your guesswork, no matter how good. That's known as being *naked as a jaybird*. But a researcher can easily conquer the curse of Cassandra with a carefully orchestrated program which should include frequent public appearances, writing a weekly column for the *Wall Street Journal* (be pithy), regularly guesting on the "Today" show, etc.

So many DAR reports are transmitted on a take it or leave it basis. Often the analysis is just a bunch of numbers no one reads. Instead they prefer to go straight to the tables. All most readers want is the overall score, the internals, and some indication of how rich the verbatims are. Most advertising and marketing executives prefer to chuck the researcher's summary and write their own. My approach gives them something to ponder. They may want to challenge it, but that's fine because it will finally provide the basis for a dialogue and hoist the researcher into advertising's mainstream, where he belongs.

DANGER NUMBER 48: Recall Scores of Commercials in Color

The added expense of going to color did not result in better day-after scores.

Ho hum . . . who cares? This is out of the distant past. But—there is an object lesson here. Something that says a lot about how we make business decisions these days.

For young or forgetful readers who now assume color TV has always been around, it should be stated that, even in the glory days of ad agency creative *boutiques*—the Seminal Sixties—household color TV penetration was far from universal. And the question then being asked was: does it really pay to shoot your commercials in color?

In those days the published studies always favored the use of color but, to the skeptical researcher, the research behind them was never very convincing.

At the time, day-after studies did not show any difference in scores between color set owners and black-and-white set owners. Recognizing that maybe these two groups were not exactly identical demographically, one assumed that, if anything, the color set owners would give better recall because they were probably more ardent TV fans (i.e., the higher incomes that allowed them to buy a color TV came from their being better educated, ergo, smarter) and had better memories. These sweeping assumptions were all unfounded, but the point was there were no theories saying that the black-and-white set owners should give higher DAR scores.

Apart from all the theory, the plain truth was that color set owners were not more receptive commercial viewers when the basis of the measurement was the day-after technique.

Most of the 1960s research that shilled for color was terribly faulty, but few ad titans noticed. Then, as now, technical quibbles were hard to explain to the lay person. Invariably, instead of doing recall studies, the networks showed that people watching commercials in color got *better vibes* than people seeing them in black and white. Ideally, in order to smooth out the demographic/psychographic factors that influenced this, they should have shown the same commercial again in black and white over the color sets, and, just to follow proven scientific procedures, done the same with a color commercial over the black-and-white sets. Technical matters precluded this, don't you see.

Regardless, perhaps, few advertising moguls would have passed up the opportunity to go to color. Color offers production values that black and white cannot, and there is more to advertising than just recall scores, if one must be frank about it.

But the sinister thing here is that everyone plainly rushed into color, accepting all the technical limitations offered by the networks, so that now we are saddled with a color transmission system that is an aesthetic embarrassment (and a less than optimum sales tool) compared to the European varieties, for example. We have trained our consumers to accept it—they all think it's great, with its gaudy, smeary, color reproduction and constantly line-ridden picture—and for the next several years we are stuck with a system that cannot always optimumly display our products. The washed out, blue-and-orange tones of the budget priced Cinecolor, used in the 1940s by B-filmmakers like Republic, mainly for cheap Saturday matinee westerns, were never half as good as Technicolor for the movie industry, but the United States seems to be one of the few countries where the TV industry felt that Cinecolor was good enough for them.

A more careful, more judicious use of research back then might have helped stave off the rush to color until the technology improved. As an allegory, this is applicable to many other aspects of doing business in the United States over the past couple of decades. We rush to be first but end up being second best. We could avoid this with better research and better analysis.

DANGER NUMBER 49: Using Laboratory Methods to Evaluate Commercials

Nothing can replace normal viewing conditions. No lab test can simulate conditions in the average home when a commercial comes over the air.

While some laboratory methods can be modestly helpful in the developmental phases of new advertising formulation, they never succeed in duplicating all of the variables occurring in the home that can impede the commercial's ability to deliver its assigned message intact.

Many different studies could be cited to demonstrate this, but one in particular should suffice to illustrate the point. Like much of the classic navelgazing in the advertising world, this one goes back to the late sixties when the Corinthian Broadcasting Co. commissioned a firm, then called Daniel Yankelovich, Inc., to evaluate the effect of *length* on the communication value of TV commercials. While some of us harken back to the sixties with nostalgia for miscellaneous reasons, to ad folk it will be remembered as the decade when the 30-second commercial began to shove out the :60. Today we would salivate if given a chance to buy a minute of network time with the low cost per thousands of the 1960s, but the question as to which is the better communication buy is now completely academic. In those days, however, minds were not yet made up.

Our interest, though, is a technical one. The study that Corinthian commissioned, and the resulting critique that the Advertising Research Foundation (ARF) dumped on it, brings up some important points about the use of laboratory research that are still valid today.

To synopsize—and I hope I don't do any of the players a grave disservice—Yankelovich exposed groups of people to four commercials (each for a different brand); each commercial was available in both a 30-second and 60-second version, only one of which, naturally, was shown to a given group. Several pre- and postexposure measurements were taken, using both self-administered questionnaires and focus groups. The ARF was invited to review the study. (It had been the practice to get their blessing on anything that would be used for promotional purposes in the trade; I suppose they figured that the ARF imprimatur legitimatized a study.)

Anyway, the ARF was merciless. Incredulous that the Yankelovich study uncovered no important differences in effectiveness between the :30s and :60s, they asked if the technique Yankelovich used really was sensitive enough to detect differences of this sort. The ARF thought not. They said that the *forced viewing* of the laboratory setting was the big problem. Introspectively, the ARF mused that if the lab magnified differences then the failure of the study to discover any differences meant there were none; but if forced viewing, on the other hand, minimized differences, then the failure of the study to find any was simply an artifact of the technique. The ARF then opined that forcing the viewers' attention on the commercials would raise the communication level (and perhaps even attitude levels) for *all* the commercials tested and would, ergo, tend to minimize the differences between the two formats. Then the ARF noted what many advertisers already knew from their own studies, that on-air recall studies (they cited a study published by Gallup and Robinson) showed real differences in recall between :30s and :60s. The usual difference was that the :30 got about two-thirds the recall score of the :60.

Yankelovich was given a chance for a rebuttal and things got a little bit heated. They accused the ARF of implying that they were guilty of methodological "naivete," which, they charged, was one of ARF's "less appealing tactics." They also said that the ARF had left out a lot of things that the study had actually discovered. Principally, Yankelovich said, the study did find fairly large differences in test results, but that they were *not* due to commercial length, but rather to the nature of the commercial *message* itself. In addressing the issue of laboratory environment, Yankelovich pointed out that, indeed it was true, the laboratory did magnify differences. This was a well-known fact, they said, and for this very reason the finding that length of commercial made no difference is most significant. Yankelovich then asked: if this kind of project was not suitable for the lab, then what kind would be?

Both sides, at least superficially, seemed to have formidable arguments. With hindsight, however, I think most advertisers would concede that the :30 format got lower scores than the :60 but that the cost:benefit ratio was in its favor, and :30s became the standard. As a footnote to history, it is hard now to believe that the average consumer brand could find enough to say about itself to occupy a whole minute. Perhaps modern cinematic experiences have made today's audiences quicker. On the late show we see that when Burt Lancaster got a call from Lizabeth Scott inviting him to view her act at the club, the director felt compelled to show Burt leaving his cheap residential hotel, hailing a cab, cutting through evening traffic, paying the cabbie, entering the club, checking his hat with a quip to the hatcheck gal, etc., etc. Today, right after the phone call, the director would cut to Scott's act without even a fade.

In the end analysis, I think the ARF was absolutely right. But part of the problem was in defining the purpose of the project. I think Yankelovich may have seen it as mainly a task of measuring that nebulous *je ne sais quoi* called *effectiveness*. In fact, this is what they stated as their purpose in the report. And the ARF clearly saw it as a project for measuring communication. If you go the effectiveness route, you are in a *never-never land*, but if you choose the communication route, you almost automatically lock into something like a day-after test, and will have to confess that the only way you can tackle it is with in-home viewing conditions. You certainly wouldn't use a focus group, although they may be useful for examining other kinds of problems—such as the nature and quality of communication.

Well, maybe it's unfair to go back so far in history and dig up something that is better-off forgotten. But these sorts of things still happen, and it is best to be wary of studies that draw on laboratory findings that can't be supported by in-home tests. No one yet has been able to duplicate the scrum and fantod of the average family room and it's not about to happen.

DANGER NUMBER 50: Campaign Communication Studies

The neglect of a systematic ongoing tracking of a campaign's communication effectiveness can cause false calls on wear-out, over- or underspending on media, and all varieties of other errors in judgment.

There are important endeavors in ad research that go beyond the individual tests of a commercial. They encompass the entire campaign. In the broader scheme of things campaign measurement may be most vital in helping to judge whether the goals of given copy and media strategies have been met. Yet this is probably the most neglected area of communications assessment.

It is customary to concentrate on tests that help in the chore of developing copy, of making it as intrusive and persuasive as one can, and these, in the main, employ recall measurements, attitudinal scaling, intent to buy questions, and so on, all as the individual commercial can deliver. But certain limitations prevail. It is only the exceptional commercial that can, upon just one exposure, do everything the whole campaign is meant to do. And too, these tests fail to position the test commercial in the real world context of the complete mix of media and competitive activities. *One-shot* testing has big deficiencies. The consumer, in order to realistically react to your advertising, needs time to process a lot of different bits of information, to relieve whatever cognitive dissonance these may generate, and to permit mental synergism to take place. We know of studies in retesting DARs that the weak commercial will not build through time, indeed it usually declines; while the stronger commercial may build in awareness—ergo, in effectiveness. Wear-out is always a potential problem at some point in time. Sampling may come along to revitalize (or kill) a consumer's interest in a brand. A media plan may or may not deliver good reach-and-frequency. While it would be nice to let factory shipments or sales audits tell us if a campaign is working, we cannot isolate our advertising from all the other variables that induce purchases, so we are left with the requirement of some form of research that gives us a glimpse of what the campaign, per se, is doing for us. Is it a good investment, or isn't it?

The cleanest research is research that reliably does what you want it to, and in the case of ad research this usually means keeping your objective modest; i.e., concentrating on advertising's primordial role of communicating a brand's marketing strategy and product platform. In assessing a campaign, we need to know what the consumer thinks we are saying and how well she understands it. Our copy strategy is designed to sell, to persuade, to establish a certain uniqueness about the brand, and our media strategy to reach the target market with a desired frequency. Our method of assessing the whole campaign has to determine if it is getting across the right points to accomplish this, and to determine when wear-out begins.

Attempting to be erudite, some call this *cammetrics*—the measurement of campaigns—but it's really just an advertising awareness study. A key part of it is establishing the level of *correct* awareness of your advertising: after the respondents have been exhaustively probed on what they can remember of everything the brand has ever said or demonstrated in its advertisements across all media, the questionnaires are appraised to determine if the verbatims are relevant to the brand's actual past advertising (a lot harder to do here than in a DAR study since some brands have lengthy histories).

The norms will vary depending on product and company, but a gross, untutored average would be somewhere in the area of a 35 percent correct awareness level. But that doesn't tell the whole story. If your brand is only getting 35 percent with a $20 million ad budget and competition does the same with half that expenditure, you have a situation in which you are probably guilty of considerable communication inefficiency. You would also be greatly disturbed, I should think, if your level of incorrect awareness was higher than your level of correct awareness. Both of these cases may serve to suggest that budget increases—the automatic pursuit of most marketing persons—are not needed, but that the answer is in better executions, etc.

Occasionally a day-after study may tell you that certain copy points recall very well, but the campaign study may indicate that they fail to establish themselves over the entire span of the campaign's duration, thus indicating what needs to be remedied in your next flock of commercials. Declines in given copy awareness could indicate wear-out. Comprehension problems can also be smoked out: do they get better or worse through time?

Many researchers like to include attitudinal measurements on these studies, but we feel that that tends to overload the interview and in the end does justice to neither the advertising awareness nor the attitude sections. Both sections require too much detailed probing. Also, some research executives like to turn these into *real* tracking studies, with the interviewing going on every day for the life of the campaign. I have no problem with that, though I personally think that they tend to get rather tedious to management and turn into wallpaper after a while. If you only do them once or twice a year, they may be read with a greater sense of urgency, unless you are dealing with a test market for a new brand where management is in the clutches of high anxiety and wants bulletins almost daily on anything that is happening.

What is amazing is how few companies want to bother with campaign studies. They will do several research projects leading up to the production of a pool of commercials, including, sometimes, DARs on each commercial in the pool; but when they release it to the airwaves, they seem to lose all interest. Considering the enormous amounts of cash they put into media, this doesn't make a hell of a lot of sense.

DANGER NUMBER 51: Brand Preference and Intent to Buy as Methods for Determining Advertising Effectiveness

Relying on buying intention ratings of viewers as a measurement of commercial effectiveness is ill advised.

Recall levels aren't always supported by equivalent intent-to-buy ratings. If you think the latter is crucial, then there is the danger that you might be persuaded to minimize the recall results. But how does one put the two separate measurements in balance?

If you analyze this across several different comparative studies you may find, as I have, that intent to buy is high only when something *new* and *important* about the brand is presented in the commercial. As I see it, this has an intuitive appeal—it's hard to see why old information, which was also not important, would beget any elevation in buying intent. If so, what chance does any brand have once its life cycle gets beyond the introductory period? Facing up to marketing realities, if the brand has been a success it's not going to change its strategy just to have something *new* and *important* to say in its advertising. Still, it needs the continual support of some form of advertising—hopefully, commercials that get high recall scores—but unless it changes its copy strategy it's going to have low likelihood-of-purchasing ratings. Sounds like Catch 22? It would be lunacy to change a successful strategy just to get a higher intent-to-buy rating. In the interest of sanity, the only plausible course is to ignore the latter and go for the high recall. A Vulcan, carrying the logic to its conclusion, would recommend avoiding intent-to-buy ratings altogether since they can play no critical role in the intelligent marketing man's scheme of things.

More broadly, some researchers think that the resistance many consumers have to switching their professed preferences around every time they spot a new commercial is a natural attempt to avoid disturbing their normal habits; thus, it may have very little to do with a judgmental rejection of the brand's copy platform.

This may be more true in some countries than others. I've talked with my fellows in the United Kingdom, who think this rigidity occurs more intensely there than in the United States because there is a greater respect for tradition.

Intent to buy is, of course, a kind of attitude rating. (I trust that no reader really thinks that when the respondent says she is "definitely going to buy" the brand, she really will.) It is therefore worth pointing out that some researchers have discovered that advertising can successfully bring about sales increases *without* a concomitant improvement in brand attitudes. The reasoning here is that people are usually exposed to a brand by several means—not just advertising—and their attitudes may be formed before the commercials are seen. (Note: we are discussing postmeasurements, not pretests here.) Conceivably, the advertising can activate purchases among prospects who are already generally favorable toward the brand. Such would not show up in buying-intent ratings obtained in conjunction with DARs.

Lastly, buying intent is probably tainted by the *entertainment syndrome* effect. *Fun* commercials get the reward of the high buying likelihood rating from respondents who like to assure having these, rather than sterner fare, on the TV shows they watch.

Buying intent, as with many seemingly innocent research queries, is not as guileless as many assume. There's more to it than meets the eye.

DANGER NUMBER 52: Determining Wear-Out by Attitude Scaling

Any method purporting to determine when a commercial has reached its wear-out point by using attitudinal rating devices is sheer poppycock.

Some services purport to be able to tell you when you should yank your commercial off the air (and presumably replace it with something new) by offering a service using attitudinal rating scales to determine how much viewers like or dislike your commercial. Normative data helps importantly in this determination, they will tell you; and, of course, it helps in selling their service as well, since, for many research buyers, copious norms mask a multitude of technical sins.

While most readers will, no doubt, regard this as a terribly unsophisticated view of the advertising process (and now-retired Ted Bates copywriters are probably chuckling to themselves as they bask in the Florida sun), there are people who blindly subscribe to this notion.

The consumer's rating on how well she likes a given commercial is little more than a measure of its ability to provide entertainment or, at the very least, innocuous background noise. Neither equates with effectiveness. If your recall scores are good, why should you care what people think? Your commercials aren't there to amuse, but to move the goods.

Still, there is no point irritating people when you don't have to. The proper way to handle this is to solicit open-end responses; i.e., find out what people voluntarily tell you they like or don't like about your commercials. Then study the responses to see if there is some *specific negative* that is growing larger over time. When it reaches a certain threshold—some say this will be at the 10 percent level—you should start to worry. But not before.

DANGER NUMBER 53: Media Weight Tests

The practice of using measurements of cumulative advertising recall, attitude changes, or even product sales, to evaluate "small" changes in media spending is usually unproductive.

Increases in cumulative advertising recall (see Danger Number 50: Campaign Communication Studies) occur mainly through improvements in the copy and not in the media plan. Small increases in media weight—barring a dramatic sharpening in the way the media is targeted—do not usually register. This is also true when you use attitude change or product sales as the measurement. None of these factors will change enough to be able to measure them with precision without either a doubling or halving of media spending.

Judgment tends to go against this, however. Given all the theory—plus one's own intuition—you'd think that there should be a smooth curve depicting the effectiveness of different spending levels. Nonetheless, I've not come across anything in actual practice that proves there is. According to the research I have seen on this (and there's been quite a bit of it over the years), consumers are quite insensitive to subtle media spending changes and respond only to very dramatic increases or decreases.

This would tend to bring into some doubt the typical mathematical model that puts a straight-line value on media expenditures. The true effect is exponential, and the shape of the curve probably varies by circumstances.

DANGER NUMBER 54: Editorial Environment

The contention that editorial environment influences print day-after recall scores not only inaccurately calls into question a lot of perfectly valid advertising research, but—even worse—it introduces faulty thinking and waste into the media plan.

There are lots of studies that show how particular periodicals exert jumbo-size influence over the *effectiveness* of the ads appearing in them. As far as I know, none of these have employed a technique as pure as the DAR method. I will concede that editorial environment probably means something, but it's impossible to measure, short of a test market. When it comes to day-after scores, you will seldom be able to reproduce these effects. So—for the media space buyer—it comes down to this: why pay a premium when all books permit your ads to communicate equally?

I recall one test about a dozen years ago involving two periodicals whose formats were extremely different, thus making it a good case to draw on: *TV Guide* and *Look*. Most readers will be familiar enough with *TV Guide* . . . small page size and somewhat peculiar color reproduction. *Look* was the size of today's *Life* magazine and had excellent color quality. Here's what the test showed: in nine tests of back-cover ads, *TV Guide* produced an average DAR score of 9.5 percent, while *Look* gave us 11.4 percent . . . not a significant difference. Also, the average back-cover recall score over a wider range of magazines, including *Ebony*, was 11.0 percent. For inside ads ditto results: *TV Guide* 6.0 percent; *Look* 5.6 percent.

In another test conducted a few years before that, using *Life, McCalls,* and Sunday supplements as the vehicles and involving four different brands, there was no difference in recall scores by magazine or by position in the book—except for the back cover, which always produced higher scores (one-fifth higher than inside), or adjacency to a pop-up coupon (also one-fifth better).

It's easy to concoct studies that shill for any given magazine. Readers will be glad to tell you they'd believe ads in the *Wall Street Journal* more easily than those in the *National Enquirer,* but almost everything the most serious ad research has told us over the years says this is irrelevant. People are notoriously lax in their ability to trace the source of their ad recollections.

DANGER NUMBER 55: Readership Scores

Readership is a meaningless concept.

Some research services provide print advertisers with a fairly inexpensive service where their ads are measured and evaluated according to how many magazine readers (as they flip through a magazine they have previously read) claim to have *noticed* and *read* them.

It's kind of an old-fashioned technique, but people still use it. In its more elegant circles, the advertising craft has advanced well beyond measly concerns over whether people read the copy. That is seldom the *big* issue. Barring the more ticklish problem of sales effectiveness, the real question should be: Does the ad communicate anything, and if it does, what?

It helps very little if everyone reads your ad but fails to get anything positive from it. Day-after studies tell you what the ad's message delivery power is and are useful diagnostically; claims of noting and reading are of nil diagnostic value.

On judgment, the technique probably suffers by being inextricably dependent on the visual aspects of an ad: illustrations and layout.

It is abjectly appalling how such superficial techniques persist over the years. Over twenty years ago, Marder and Davis showed that you could obtain readership claims on ads that respondents could not possibly have seen and concluded that "the numbers generated by aided reports of exposure to ad elements are substantially *useless* as factual reports of prior experience."[3] Other researchers claimed that the nonexposed scores could range all the way from 6 percent to 81 percent for different ads. I, myself, in using the method, got different scores on the same ad when it was retested in subsequent editions of the same magazine. In one case that I recall, the advertisement scored 43 percent in the first test and 88 percent in the second. And even if you believe in the slow-fuse theory, the time lapse wasn't great enough to allow for it.

The technique is a phony. If results can't be replicated, and if bogus ads spliced into the test magazine can get up to 81 percent claimed readership, then the technique simply can't be trusted. The rule book says that all methods must be replicatable.

DANGER NUMBER 56: Believability in Print Ads

The issue of believability, in itself of questionable soundness, in the case of print ads raises special doubts and dangers.

Though we have already denounced the practice of asking people if they *believe* given test advertising material, the custom will likely continue. With print, it is an even shakier practice.

While editorial environment has no bearing on copy recall (see Danger Number 54: Editorial Environment), we suspect that it artificially influences claims of credibility. It would be hard to assume otherwise. For example, a piece of copy appearing in the *Atlantic Monthly* would project a higher believability factor under direct questioning than the same copy in the *National Enquirer*. If you still must get a fix on believability, do it outside of editorial environment.

DANGER NUMBER 57: Print Recall and Interest in Product

Direct comparisons of print recall and TV commercial recall scores is jeopardized by the self-filtering of the audience.

Although one should never attempt to regard one percentage point of print recall as the same thing as one percentage point of TV recall, the implicit allusion to such comparisons in marketing documents is not infrequent.

The tendency for the users of a given product to give you higher recall is vastly greater in print than in TV (where it is virtually nonexistent). Television recall scores are less affected by a person's interest in the product category because viewing is more automatic and uncontrolled. Print is more selective; a person can easily avoid reading an advertisement that isn't about a product category he has some interest in. This same person would give at least passive attention to a TV commercial for the same product. Hence, recall scores of print ads cannot be directly equated to TV commercials scores since there is an element of *selectivity* in the print test base that doesn't pertain in TV tests nearly as much.

There are many other reasons why the two vehicles shouldn't be compared directly: TV's ability to evoke feelings, to stir the imagination, etc., are considered superior to print's, and so forth. These don't show up too clearly in recall studies. But for those that prefer less ephemeral reasons, the *self-distillation* of the base should suffice.

DANGER NUMBER 58: Print Recall and Cheating Levels

Respondent cheating has been detected on print recall studies.

All *memory tests* will elicit *cheating* by respondents who mistake the purpose of the test and strive to provide you with data they may think you need. In the midst of an interview some will ask their kids to prompt them on the content of a commercial. Vigilant investigators are required to discourage this.

Print day-after studies, however, open wide the door to another kind of cheating. Unbeknownst to the investigator, the respondent can easily reach for the magazine where the test ad appeared, open it to the right page, and simply read it off—giving perfect verbatim recall. The fact that you don't very often get perfect recall suggests few people actually do this. How serious is it?

Being suspicious of anything that moves, I once looked into this. After we got recall, we asked our respondents if they had the magazine handy, and then, if they "just happened to have it open to the test ad at the present time?" I should add that—to the extent it was possible—we tried to make them believe there was nothing wrong with having done this by prefacing it with some kind of mollifying statement. On one test 4 percent of readers had the book open to the test ad. In another test the number was 8 percent. I must confess that I don't really know what to make of this. The fact that the print recall technique produces a very wide range of scores makes me want to feel that cheating is not all that serious.

On the other hand, print recall scores aren't usually all that high that you can feel comfortable with that kind of inflation. The bogus level of recall is bad enough. (In print it is 2 percent vs. TV's 5 percent, under controlled conditions.) I'm at a loss to know what conclusion to draw on this one. If your scores are averaging around 10 percent, an 8 percent cheating level hurts. Does it vary by magazine; would weekly periodicals suffer the same degree of cheating as monthly magazines? Does it vary by product category? Do demographics affect it? Sorry, I don't have any of the answers, and I'm leaving readers with a problem I have no solution for.

NOTES

1. *Television/Radio Age*, May 31, 1971, p. 38.
2. There was never any truth to the mysterious rumor that little Mikey was killed when he swallowed some Pop Rocks and his stomach exploded.
3. *Public Opinion Quarterly* 25, 1961, pp. 467–68.

7 • *Production Aspects: Jejune but Pivotal*

Tiresome to some, lifeblood to others, the production aspects of the research game present more problems than some are aware of and most like to think about.

Production consists of things like interviewing, coding, tabulation, data processing, statistical analysis, and anything else that goes into the task of giving shape and dimension to the conceptual and cerebral heft of marketing research. Staffed generally by the lower-paid members of the profession, the production contingent receives only sporadic and brief attention from researchdom's managerial hierarchy . . . often with dire results.

That time-honored expression, garbage-in-garbage-out, applies here and, with a vengeance, comes back to haunt and plague those fast-tracking research executives that superciliously choose not to ascribe to research production its due importance. Shaped more by whim and anecdotal lessons than by scientific management, interviewing techniques have never been rigidly standardized (perhaps because they never can be) and every practitioner appears to have his or her own likes and dislikes. The research supplier must take pains to govern the labor cost of each project, which largely consists of the interviewing burden. Thus, as a businessperson there is no compelling incentive to induce one to search for more dependable questioning methods unless they produce significant cost savings. The added value that better but more costly interviewing would give the service would be lost on most clients, who are more concerned with bottom-line assessments and who may have neither the time nor inclination to get into the nitty-gritty deeply enough to understand the advantage of what is being offered.

Field supervisors, an intrepid and energetic lot, have idiosyncrasies that are sometimes too murky to fathom but which lead some organizations headlong into interviewing habits and procedures that may not necessarily contribute very solidly to the attainment of marketing truths. Many of these are based on the need to keep their investigators happy, not to irritate respondents, and so forth. Professional associations heroically purporting to speak for the entire trade periodically attempt to establish standards, but by and large there is so little intellectual and scientific clout to what they do, and, even when intuitively good, they are communicated with such a negligible sense of urgency that for the average professional researcher to ignore their admonitions and violate their norms merit the same severity of moral sanction as being drummed out of the Book of the Month Club.

Different research organizations do the same things and yet get different results. Or so it would appear. This maddeningly makes it impossible to foster any serious movement for professional standards. The fact that this is an illusion, that the differences are due to the many inconsistencies in execution, is beyond the normal powers of observation and analysis, and the individual researcher's net impression is that what he or she does is somehow protected by craft gods, and is superior to what the next person does. It is a profession, much like a cargo cult, in which there is much hope. It is also a discipline lacking in scientific conduct.

Are you worried about the cheating? Yes, some interviewers still do cheat. Less often than some lay people suspect; more often than some researchers like to think. But why pick on marketing research and why should this be any surprise? Cheating occurs in all professions, in all branches of business. Controls are usually installed to limit interviewer cheating to far below statistical tolerances, making it tolerable. Low-frequency cheating is harmless, but faulty questionnaires can never be considered such, and therein lies a far bigger problem. At best, we get competent, though not excellent, interviewers who usually stick to the questionnaire we design and who can follow up on respondent inconsistencies and ambiguities; but when the questionnaire is badly cast, when the sequence of questioning generates its own damning bias, what can the interviewer do? He or she will never be invited to change it. And the field supervisor, so inured to bad questionnaires, has probably long ago given up on ever getting anywhere by his or her complaints.

Coding, tabulation, and the whole data processing scene offer scary additional opportunities for error, many of which can never be detected. The lowly coder is often the only soul who actually reads the finished questionnaires. Failure to assure that the coder is familiar with the background of the product, or of the study, may accidentally result in misinterpretation and miscoding of comments. And the true meaning of this information is then lost forever.

Some of these, to be sure, are mainly management problems and, in theory, can be solved by any number of approaches, although in actual practice management skills usually fail to alter human nature for more than a few weeks at a stretch, and the problems usually return then only to be ignored lest the manager be an admitted failure. If these are the problems for the administrators, there are still enough dangers emanating from the production aspects of marketing research that are also capable of challenging and exciting our imaginations. So it is to the dangers that we now turn.

DANGER NUMBER 59: Open Ends versus Closed Ends

Sloth and profit seeking, not reasoned argument, may be the real allure of closed-end questioning. Result: you may get only half an answer or, even worse, totally deceptive responses.

I'm sure, as a student, every reader preferred the *closed-end* or multiple-choice exam over the essay type or *open-end* exam. It was easier to study for, easier to pass. You could even take a chance and guess at the answers. But as parents and employers we can also see its drawbacks; students now are ill prepared by an educational system that evaluates them almost entirely by closed-end testing. They can't organize their thoughts and they can't write clearly.

A similar dichotomy exists in marketing research. The vast majority of studies take only the closed-end approach. Its advocates argue that it is more efficient than open-ended questioning and produces results with the same, or even better, utility value; and they are in the majority among the members of the research community. Nonetheless, there is a strong and vocal minority that believes the majority is dead wrong, and I happen to share their sentiments. Here's the story.

Open ends have never been popular with researchers. With or without computers and optical scanners you still have to struggle through the interviewers' frequently illegible handwriting and then, once you decipher that, you have to distill hundreds of stray comments down to a manageable number, deciding which goes where and inevitably ending up mediating arguments between the coders and their supervisor. And if you are doing a continuous tracking study or a pre-and-post study, you have to take pains that all the coding is done with impeccable consistency. Frankly, it is no fun, it certainly isn't easy, and if your research firm is fighting to submit the low bid there's no way you'll win if you go heavy on open ends. It's labor intensive, a chore to control and supervise, and to most researchers a real nightmare they'd rather avoid.

Also we have the problem of analysis. Only those who are thoroughly experienced in it ever get much out of it. The researcher who prefers to let the computer do the grunt work, who feels that only the multivariate analysis of his or her particular religious persuasion harbors the ultimate truths, cannot cope with open ends where each and every respondent has not been forced to speak on every issue, for one loses so much statistical power that coefficients begin to waver and flicker and take on copious error auras. Blame it on the computer, like everything else, if you want, but the open end as a way of life in the research trade is dying, if not already dead, and with its passing we have, I think, extinguished a fine and prized source of illumination that was once a wellspring of insights and marketing direction. And we aren't left with much of a replacement as we all gravitate to the tribal huddle of the closed end. Quite candidly, I, for one, cannot even pretend to understand the consumer unless I hear it from her in her own words. I want to know what she has to say about a product, or whatever, rather than how she responds to a set of questions someone else thought up. I want straight talk. I trust her to tell me what's on her mind. But I'm not sure I trust the researcher because—even though he or she may know the trade

and the product well—things change over time or, by the power of marketing and economic forces, new issues may crop up that he or she is not aware
of. Even if everything that could possibly impinge on the way the product is
perceived is listed, when the consumer answers all the questions, I won't
know which are vital to her and which are not. I don't rate my Seville very
favorably on gas mileage . . . but I don't really care because the subway is
more convenient for me and I only drive the thing 1,000 miles a year; so
what interest would General Motors have in my opinion of the Seville's
mileage? Yet I'm sure the average researcher would put that attribute at the
top of his list, and might omit my favorite feature on the car—the real
leather upholstery—which may sound overly frivolous, but, apart from
Jane Fonda, aren't all consumers frivolous, and doesn't the open-end approach allow for frivolity?

Who can inform me better than the consumer? On what basis should I
turn to a research technician for an understanding of the product, of how it
performs in the home, of what benefits it delivers, when the user herself can
tell me all I need to know that affects her actions. If she doesn't have the
wherewithal to tell me this, then how does she think about the product at
all? The point is she doesn't—or at least not deeply—since her thoughts are
words and if the words don't exist because certain organoleptic/mechanical
concepts are alien to her, then they do not govern her actions.

Many years ago women chose their laundry detergent brands simply because they got the clothes clean. Then, in the 1950s they began to get interested in whitening power. And in the early 1960s they went for brightening.
All of this was first detected in the open ends of attitude studies. As these
two comments grew and grew it got to the point where no self-respecting
soap company could deny their shareholders the rewards of capitalizing on
these new performance needs. If the closed-end attributes had been bound
in brass in the 1940s I doubt this would have been discovered as quickly, or
that the wheels of marketing innovation would have been as truly aligned.

The urge to do things at lower cost is strong. It is not enough to say this
may be unwise or that you may occasionally miss an opportunity, because
in many Geneenean companies the horizon is only the next fiscal quarter.
But for those who wish to be serious about the quality of their marketing research, or for the chief executive who would like to feel he could trust the
judgments of his officers, the following arguments in favor of the open-end
approach should be carefully weighed:

- The consumer has to tell you what's good and bad about your product and not be
  limited to a checklist of attributes provided by you. For example, if you blind test
  your product vs. competition, lose on overall preference, and then proceed to ask
  a series of closed ends on various key attributes ("Which flavor did you like better? . . . Which mixing instructions were easier? . . ."), you will seldom be able

to identify the true representation of factors that consumers perceive as having a direct bearing on their preference. This practice, accordingly, robs you of insights into segmentation strategies and product differentiation opportunities, and of the ability to construct effective marketing plans. Only open-end reasons for preference ("In what way was A better than B?") can help you here.

- Even with years of testing experience on the same kind of products, the practice of prelisting your attributes can be dangerous. You may think you know how people will respond to open-end questions, but locking into a frozen set of closed-end probes leaves you wide open to the danger of failing to isolate product/formula characteristics that influence consumer perceptions. And you might be measuring things with zero influence over consumer assessments of a particular test product. Attempts to get around this by introducing secondary scales to gauge the importance of each attribute you list sometimes appear to help, but the resulting analytical mayhem yields unreliable information. The successful marketing strategist needs to know exactly how his products are perceived and why they are evaluated in such and such a way. A commitment to the closed-end approach is little more than guesswork.

- Experiments with the closed-end approach have produced strange results. I have witnessed blind test interviews where, after answering multiple-choice direct questions on innumerable product attributes, respondents tried to go back and change their overall preference. I shudder to think what this could do to you on a self-administered (mail) questionnaire.

- Over the many years that I have been concerned about this issue I have gotten a very clear impression that the companies that rely on the open-end approach generally have greater success in the marketplace. In informal discussions with researchers from different companies with common product categories I have gathered that those that base most of their product decisions on open-end research enjoy bigger market shares. Market share superiority emanates from superior strategies, which in turn come from better marketing research.

It would seem only reasonably judicious to question closely the researcher who proposes exclusively closed-end modes. Question him deeply. You may find at the root of his conviction, not experience, not a well-formed postulation, but cant, habit, and a sinister computer orientation where the system runs the man. Above all you may find an inward-thinking technocrat, not a person well suited to the solving of marketing problems, nor one flexible enough for the rapid changes that contrapose the world of business.

DANGER NUMBER 60: Clearing Up Open Ends

You can save field time by dropping the requirement that interviewers ask respondents to explain their ambiguous or incomplete open-end comments, but in the process you will lose vast mountains of information.

The average interview can be looked at as a process of disambiguity. Many, if not most, of the open-end comments have to be *cleared up*. The skilled investigator does this automatically. Unfortunately, it does take a lot of time and probably doubles the length of the interview. Because it is so hard on the budget, I once tried to find out what I really lost if I asked my interviewers just to accept whatever the respondent said. I asked our investigator to do this on every second interview and to do the other half the regular *clearing up* way. The results convinced me we could not drop the clearing up procedures despite the expense. We learned that approximately 15 percent of all comments became unclassifiable; i.e., we just could not tell what they meant. Things like "easier to cook with," and "easier to use" may satisfy the superficial researcher, but to the R&D manager who is charged with knowing how to improve the product to make it competitive this sort of vagueness gives no direction whatever. Also, since the process of clearing up tends to encourage the respondent to give even more comments as the additional probing jogs her memory, we discovered that the total number of comments declined quite a bit. In the "control" part of the study we had an average of 1.57 comments per woman; in the "test" part where we had dropped the clearing up process we had only 1.43. Now, some researchers would be willing to live with this, but I would not. I feel you must do everything you can to bleed as much information as possible out of the respondent.

DANGER NUMBER 61: Direct Questions (DQs) as Supplements to Open Ends

Elaborate use of DQs as supplements to open ends is a wasteful practice that can lead to sloppy analysis.

Only through open-end responses, I submit, can you really find out how important a product feature is to the consumer. Open-end responses are the only means you have of determining what spectrum of attributes consumers perceive as having a bearing on their brand choices, etc. On the other hand, the more skeptical researchers feel you have to ask each respondent point blank about all of a product's key features in order to learn how they feel. Also, those who are incapable of understanding any data without the crutch of a multivariate analysis are forced to travel this route.

While I feel that this practice can lure research report readers into believing that all the bases have been covered, I believe it actually is misleading, inasmuch as it forces the respondent to speak to issues about the product that may not be remotely relevant to her. Nonetheless, it is hard to convince people you can survive on open-ended questions alone and expect to get answers to all their specific product attribute questions. The issue then becomes: what do you lose and what do you gain by adding DQs on specific attributes to an interview whose central thrust is open-ended?

Since product testing is where you usually run into the controversy this is where to concentrate our analysis. In theory, the response to a DQ can be one of three things:

1. It may be a mere rationalization of the respondent's overall preference: those who prefer A over B will automatically say that, ergo, A is better on everything, even on factors that have never before been considered.

2. It may have no bearing on overall preference; e.g., in answer to your DQ a respondent may say A is a better-smelling lipstick than B, but odor still may have nothing whatever to do with her brand choices.

3. It may be very critical to the determination of overall preference, but the respondent might not have mentioned it in the open ends because of embarrassment or because she thought it was too foolish, too unimportant to bring up. (This profound philosophical issue used to perplex people in the soap industry. Many soapers felt that for a lot of products they made, such as liquid dishwashing detergents, "ease on hands" had these ephemeral or frivolous properties. Today, however, it is argued that the sweep of history has removed all shame, that the *be good to yourself* movement has allowed consumers to view everything they want in a product as some kind of entitlement that they would vociferously demand if denied.)

In one exercise I calculated correlation coefficients for the consumer evaluations of different attributes as given in voluntary reasons for preference vs. the overall preference, and then did the same thing for an array of comparable DQ responses within the same studies. The principle here was that while any response that is independently correlated to overall preference can't exert any influence over it (nor is it safe to say a positive correlation does either), if there is any logic at all to the interviewing patterns within a product testing situation you should achieve the same magnitude of coefficients for both open ends and DQs if they essentially measure the same thing. (If DQs measure the same thing, you don't need them.)

The results showed that the coefficients were, indeed, just about the same. For example, with a floor-care product, "cleaning" reasons in the open ends had a 0.75 coefficient vs. overall preference, and in the DQ a 0.80. All the other attributes were as close.

Other analyses, using a greater variety of products, showed the same thing: the attribute preference displayed in reasons for preference tells you the same thing as the DQ over 80 percent of the time. In the remaining 20 percent, only very seldom does it give the opposite answer; usually it's just a matter of a diminished spread between the two products.

Consider this practical problem: What do you do if the DQ says that the new, experimental perfume for your leading shampoo brand is strongly preferred over the current perfume, but the reasons for preference don't show much of a spread between them? Oh, one more point: assume the experimental perfume would slice about five percentage points off the brand's gross margin. Now, what do you recommend? It's arguable, of course, but the prudent course is to give the open ends a lot more weight in your marketing decisions. Don't use the experimental perfume.

It obviously won't screw up the interview if you ask DQs after you complete the open ends, but time is money, and they do take away from the opportunity to ask other questions that may be more important. Generally speaking, I maintain that most DQs are a waste of time—because they give you the same answers as the open ends—and a danger—because they serve as a temptation to the lay user to read unwarranted implications into the test. DQs should be posed only for aspects of the product that would not normally be mentioned voluntarily.

Of course, if the researcher has sold lay management on the necessity for elaborate multiple regression analyses—which only he can understand—he's stuck with DQs, which is too bad because it probably means he's giving the open ends short shrift, from which marketing will suffer.

DANGER NUMBER 62: Statistical Significance

Researchers often make unrealistic grabs for analytical certainty, insisting on decision safety levels far higher than in any other areas of the business. Unless you know what they are doing here you may unwittingly be robbed of several worthwhile business opportunities.

When one talks statistical tests of significance most people within hearing range zonk off on you. Actually, it can be quite interesting . . . mainly because it is an area where the inmates have taken over the asylum.

Marketing people regard the researcher's use of a 95 percent confidence interval as an absolute axiom of his science. This handicaps your freedom to provide actionable information and to make a concrete contribution to the strategic planning effort of a profit center.

Statistical precision is important. But problem solving is more important. Statistical analysis must serve, not rule, the decision-making process. Here are a few comments on the issue:

- A 95 percent level of certainty is usually a wasteful restriction. Most business decisions, even the really big ones involving divestitures and acquisitions, are made with a lot lower probability of success. Why should research data be subjected to such a rigorous test when hardly any other activity of the enterprise is?

- An 80 percent confidence level is ample in most cases. The use of an 80 percent certainty criterion can save you approximately 35 percent of the cost of doing research through smaller samples, or it can provide you with a greater number of usable conclusions. Hence, you can get more mileage out of your research budget and still operate within a probability field superior to most other decision areas in your company. I once successfully introduced an 80 percent criterion in a major company with no ill effects. Management doesn't want to fuss with a lot of numbers, and if the researcher sets the standard they will usually go along with it if it is reasonable. To most managers even an 80 percent level of certainty is a luxury.

- A preoccupation with statistical analysis can lead to dubious research designs. We have seen researchers who will do almost anything to garner enhanced statistical precision even if it means reinterviewing the same people over and over again or totally abandoning open-ended questions (as noted previously).

- Statistical significance should not be confused with marketing significance. I know of a major consumer company that refers solely to the 95 percent blind test win as *significant*, and that has conditioned its top management to accept only that order of win for market introduction. This may be an expedient measure, or even a very good discipline, but it tends to confuse a statement about probability (vis-à-vis the null hypothesis) with a marketing factor (the magnitude of the win). The former can be an artifact of sample size, while the latter is dependent on product quality. Management should always be provided with a clearer picture of the research data they are given to use.

There is nothing in the business world that says you have to be 95 percent certain in any decision-making situation. Usually, the pursuit of a better ROI is so difficult (and in fact quite anxiety-provoking) that such a luxury is not permitted. Each decision must carry its own criteria. It is the researcher's job to know what these criteria are and not mislead or restrict management in its attempt to make sound business decisions. The discovery of good marketing strategies is hard enough without setting up artificial roadblocks.

DANGER NUMBER 63: Focus Group Moderators and Strategy

Few focus group moderators know enough about the product, strategic options, or marketing feasibilities to ask useful impromptu questions. The consequent superficial results can lead to equally superficial marketing decisions.

Focus groups, as most folks see them, are those unstructured sessions, involving eight to twelve people, plus a moderator, where various hypotheses about products, commercials, consumer problems, etc., are explored in considerable depth. The focus group method is the most popular of all the qualitative techniques.

There are some really good focus group moderators whom even traditionally hard-to-please agency creative people love. Their sessions are great for copy ideas, their reports read well, their recommendations are made with both feet on the ground, and their presentations are an embarrassment to no one. They are, alas, few in number and would be equally successful in the creative area or in marketing management. They are not typical research people, so some would say.

Most focus group moderators seem to have recently arrived here from Mars. Endowed with a background in psychology or some other system of beliefs, they place much emphasis on the act of interviewing and the remarkable human interactions they think so rewarding. They slough over the planning and analytical processes that precede and follow their focus group sessions. Every stultified notion dropping from the mouths of respondents is warmly greeted as a new revelation and relayed with dispatch to bored marketing managers. No sensible appreciation for marketing feasibility seems to accompany their preparation; marketing to them is an amorphous mass. Nor do they understand strategy. The sobering upshot is that they cannot pursue conceptual leads as well as our ideal moderator, who instinctively knows what is interesting to marketing people and what is not.

Without this useful appreciation for what makes marketing tick, the traditional focus group moderator needs a TV newsman's earphone hookup to the clients sitting behind the two-way mirror in the lounge, so that the clients can bark questions at her as she misses all the promising leads. The only really useful way to achieve germinal information in a focus group is for the moderator to come prepared. Unfortunately, few ever do.

The solution is to find someone who knows advertising, marketing, and strategy well enough to ask meaningful and provocative questions. This person doesn't have to have a research background. In fact, few researchers—as good as they may be—have enough of a feel for what is required here. You could say conducting a focus group has little to do with research at all, except for the ability to frame questions in the right way and to maintain objectivity.

DANGER NUMBER 64: Focus Group Moderators Too Gullible

What you hear and see in a focus group interview is often an artifact of group dynamics and not necessarily reflective of real attitudes. Some of it, if left unchallenged, can be grossly misleading.

The group dynamics of the focus group are often served up as the method's key success factor, and this is probably true. Group interaction spurs thought and brings more ideas out on the table, giving you a chance to ventilate more hypotheses and a greater variety of feelings. But there is another side to it which is not so good. It can also generate phoney statements and self-serving posturing on behalf of some respondents.

This is not a serious problem if the group moderator is strong in leadership qualities and has a special antenna to detect the blowhard and the spotlight seeker among her attendees. Unfortunately, few moderators have the strength of personality to do much about this. Most tend to be naïfs who are only too willing to swallow whatever the respondents say, perhaps out of secret relief that they are talking at all. Accompanying this weakness is often an inordinate desire to be appreciated . . . that irrepressible love of mankind that got the moderator into the people interviewing line in the first place.

The best moderators will have no truck with the "I love people" refrain. A moderator is not the same thing as a friend. The moderator is there to make sure the group covers the ground laid out in the outline approved by the client, and to make absolutely sure that what the group has to say is said *with conviction*, not just as something to fill up the tape. This requires the ability to challenge the respondents, to see how tenaciously stated attitudes are held, to see how much background knowledge they have about a subject, and to see how flexible their vocabulary becomes when they are jarred away from familiar complaints and praises onto paths that they may not have explored before about the product and related matters under discussion. By pushing them, by displaying skepticism about their sincerity, by letting them know they're going to have to work for their fifteen- to thirty-dollar stipends, the moderator gets them to break new ground. The resulting tape and analysis thusly are able to answer more questions and cover more issues than the client thought he had any right to expect, and supply insights normally thought unattainable.

The focus group is the place to stimulate thinking, not just to accept a casual, cocktail-party dollop of small talk. It's the only occasion in the world of marketing research where anyone gets a chance to do this. Tougher moderating means that less of what you get from the group will be hot air, and that comments will come in on a higher plane and with greater seminal value than those you get from the garden party focus group.

This still doesn't make the focus group a source of definitive answers, but you do intend to validate it all with quantitative research, don't you?

DANGER NUMBER 65: *Long Interviews*

Excessively long interviews are the bane of the field director, but there are more critical reasons for keeping interviews brief.

Any man on the street could opine that interview length can affect the quality of data you get. With a standard sort of Usage and Attitude (U&A) study involving only one open-end attitude section, you get a lot more comments than you would if you added another attitude section. Expanding from one to two open-ended sections renders the respondent terse ("No, I just like the taste. . . . Just the taste. Nothing else.") and less cooperative. But the probable reason for the dwindling cooperation is not the interview length per se, but the boredom it induces. If you employ a variety of different types of questions, giving the interview a nice change of pace, you might keep it interesting enough for the respondents to stay on your side for endurance tests of thirty to forty minutes, or even more. Unfortunately, this may not always be practical. By sheer force of will and misleading statements ("I've just got a few more questions left") you might be able to get most of your subjects to hang on to the end, but their responses will become wearied, their answers not as conscientiously considered as in briefer interviews. There are few subjects that average people know enough about or feel deeply enough about to keep their interest up for long, and the commonplace subject of the marketing research survey is not exactly brimming over with gripping issues. At least not enough to sustain one's interest for more than twenty minutes or so.

Sometimes you are better off splitting an interview in two and using parallel matched samples, rather than trying to coax reluctant respondents through excessively lengthy interviews. Nobody likes a bore except other bores and extremely withdrawn introverts. If these are all you still have with you halfway through the interview, you end up with a sample devoid of the movers and shakers, the heavy breathers, the tastemakers. Though it may look good on paper, your sample will consist of society's drones. Ergo, your marketing plans will be skewed toward them. *Sic semper* the world of plastic.

DANGER NUMBER 66: Interviewing the Same People Again

"Memorable" interviews can affect attitudes. It is unwise to interview the same people twice on the same topic.

There was a time when it was fashionable to run a pre-and-post study using the same respondents. It gave the ultimate in statistical exactitude and meant you could follow purchases through time and see how the marketing efforts brought about brand switching, etc. There have been many studies of the consequences of doing this. Some date all the way back to the 1930s. The archeology on this practice is quite extensive.

The gist of the investigation is that if you stick only to quantitative information (purchases, usage habits, etc.) there won't be any detectable bias associated with reinterviewing the same folks a few months later. But if you branch off into the qualitative (attitudes, etc.), the second interview won't produce the same results as going to a fresh sample would.

There is one exception to this: If the qualitative is obtained in a laboriously closed-end manner, such as in a brand image study, no bias results. But when you force the respondent to think at length about one brand and expound extemporaneously on it, a profound effect on her behavior and attitudes may follow. Whether this reflects a genuine shift or merely a desire to please your interviewer, whom she assumes to be working for the brand identified in the premier interview, cannot be ascertained. Whatever the cause, it appears that attitudes are always more favorable the second time around . . . than when you go to a fresh sample.

DANGER NUMBER 67: Central Location Tests (CLTs)

Concerns about the nonrepresentative samples obtained in CLT facilities are often little more than academic nonsense.

Few research studies employ truly random samples. That would be too costly. But random dialing comes pretty close, and most interviews are done by phone so that in most cases the prescribed norms of the sampling experts are almost met.

But does it really matter all that much? Obviously, some types of sampling procedures won't even come close to giving you a representative sample. Intercepts at the posh Northbrook Mall on Chicagoland's Northshore certainly wouldn't yield the same results as Loop intercepts. Neither would equate with a national probability sample.

But what about the most common way most of us go to get our *fast and dirty* research done . . . the central location panel? By that I mean the deal where we rent a hall and invite respondents in for interviewing. If you jam in ten or twelve different tests, all brief, and organize it right, you can handle over a hundred people a day and achieve commendably low per-interview costs. Some companies use church groups and their basements, others use CLTs to answer all but the most high priority questions. The issue is this: since we know this doesn't give us a random sample, are we kidding ourselves by accepting the results?

Well, the answer is yes and no. In obvious areas, such as brand attitudes and so forth, you will not get the same results. But if you limit these CLTs to what they are really good at, such as quick little taste tests, premium evaluations, show tests, and so on, you will, according to the experimental work I have seen, get the same answer as if you had gone door-to-door or telephoned in a selection of cities. This was true 80 percent of the time. In the other 20 percent of cases only minor differences which should not alarm anyone occurred. For one thing, they were usually within normal tolerances; for another, in no case would the resultant decision have produced a marketing disaster.[1]

I don't think this is the evidence the charlatans were waiting for to allow them to toss the commonly accepted rigors of sampling out the window, thus bringing back the Literary Digest Poll and making QUBE seem respectable, but it says this: with certain limited kinds of tests, the kind that make up the bulk of most research department's assignments, sampling meticulousness is not really worth the cost. It comes down to the fact that people are people, and for a lot of the objective kinds of tests we all have to do, anyone will suffice. The ability to incorporate this into your thinking would immediately magnify the power of your marketing research department (MRD) budget. In prudence, you should test it first to see if it applies to your particular product line.

DANGER NUMBER 68: The Bias against Telephone and Mail Surveys

A small coterie of avidly finicky researchers has a blind spot that precludes telephone surveys (sometimes) and mail surveys (frequently) from their information-gathering nets. In both cases, this culminates in an unnecessary drain on the marketing research budget.

Telephone interviewing has been around for decades, and today is almost robotized, but I can recall when it was still considered risky by some highly respected interviewing houses. It was not because they felt you couldn't get a decent sample—even in those days telephone incidence was very high—but that they felt people wouldn't level with them over the phone. Largely, these sentiments have long since disappeared.

For one thing, experimental studies through the years showed that, for most of the most commonplace types of research problems (attitude studies, blind tests, etc.), there is no difference in results between telephone and personal interviews. Contributing to the gradual but steady breakdown in shibboleths against telephone interviews is the fact that almost every product category—including those that were supposed to be ultrapersonal and embarrassing—and almost every private problem as well, have been surveyed, probed, and assessed quite nicely by phone. While we must still await the arrival of the universal household incidence of videophones in order to be able to use visual aids, such as would be needed for a package graphics test, just about every other objection to the phone method has been demolished.[2]

In fact, I suspect it is the telephone's faceless anonymity that has even made it easier to ask certain types of touchy questions, like income and political affiliation. Nonetheless, there are still some old die-hards that refuse to use the telephone for anything more than the most perfunctory information gathering, ruling out anything of a qualitative or diagnostic nature. They have their reasons for this, but I think they would find that most of their objections should have evaporated over the years. They could be enjoying significant cost savings that they are now missing out on. Oddly, some of them, bent on eyeball-to-eyeball confrontations while eschewing the phone method, have no qualms about street intercepts at 42nd Street and Broadway (for interviewing purposes, that is).

Luckily, the phoneophobes are a rare breed, but the antimailists are much more numerous. Since the U.S. Postal Service has not yet managed to get its prices up to where mail interviews are no longer competitive with oral interviews, postal techniques are still worthy of consideration.

The usual objection is that people who take the trouble to answer a mailout must be very different from the rest of the population, who probably are accurately categorized as *functionally illiterate*. Additionally, it is understandably suspected that these non-letter-writers probably don't have pencils or pens in their homes, can't remember to mail anything back, misplace anything you send them, and cannot be counted on to follow simple instructions. Those that do respond to a mail survey must, therefore, be smarter, better organized, and plainly unrepresentative of most zodiacal points; thus, they are not equally prone to our advertising inducements and must, consequently, be atypical consumers.

There are some stray bits of evidence that support this rather cynical view. In the past, members of formal mail testing panels were known to subscribe to more magazines, thus supporting the suspicion they were more literate. To the concerned marketing executive this also suggested that they were exposed to more print advertising, which could have made their habits and feelings different from the great unwashed TV audience. Indeed, other examinations suggested they did more home-oriented things like baking cakes and pies and little gingerbread men. And, through the years, others have even leveled charges that they watched more television than average folks. All in all, this led some companies to ban mail panels for testing advertising copy or media plans.

But most of these objections are relatively minor compared to all the other worries researchers have. And you can get around many of them by balancing the mail panel to eliminate the problems you believe make them atypical. More importantly, rapid changes in family structures (more single adult households, more working women, the economic struggle just to stay above water, etc.) have made some of these objections sound rather quaint and have presented new problems in assembling respondents by mail to represent your market segment. In its favor, however, is the reality that personal interviewing is also facing many of the same problems. In both cases the answer is that with bigger budgets you can get the samples you need. Cash inducements work wonders.

All we should really be worried about is this: do mail surveys work? What does the investigative track record show? The record is not immaculate, but then again, it is not all that bad. Take paired comparison blind tests for example. In every examination I have seen, the overall preference came out the same as in the personalized method. The open-ended reasons for preference, while sparser and (since they couldn't be cleared up) blunter, gave just about the same conclusions.

One problem connected with even the paired comparison mail blind test is its tendency to fetch a higher rate of nonpreferences. (We discussed the nonpreference problem in Danger Number 5: Handling the Non-Preferer.) The problem may exist only for those intrepid souls that push hard for a preference in their personal interviews, since they can't obviously push hard in writing. For those who submissively buckle under to the respondent's initial noncommittal posture, the problem may not exist; their nonpreference rates are egregiously high no matter how they do it.

Evidence on the monadic product test by the postal method has not, on the other hand, been so good. You don't get the same response pattern . . . but this is probably due to the monadic's lower sensitivity. In doing a monadic by mail, you will find that the open ends will be largely favorable. The unfavorable comments appear to dwindle down to only a few, possibly because the freedom to be negative takes a little prodding, and some indication of its acceptability from a live interviewer. In one test situation of mail monadic vs. personal monadic, in the former the ratio of favorable to unfavorable comments was 5:1, but in the latter it was a more healthy 2:1. Some product performance areas were also evaluated differently in the two techniques, though most came out the same. Researchers who like to put all their eggs in the closed-end basket may have better luck at getting their postal monadic to equate with personally conducted ones, but their luck may be a result of the artlessness of the closed-end method per se, and hence the whole thing would be delusory.

One theory says that if you are a fan of the open end you cannot put any direct questions on a mail questionnaire because, obviously, this would expose your correspondent to all kinds of notions about the various product characteristics you are interested in. She would see this before she answered the open-end part, she might go back and change her answers if she later thought she hadn't filled up the page enough, etc. I must confess to having some sympathy for this theory. But the facts do not support me. It is not true. The experimental work shows that direct questions do not appreciably influence the open end comments. Maybe it would if you were using the same panel too frequently on the same type of product, but otherwise it would seem that the respondent to a mail questionnaire has little *pride of authorship* and does not feel obligated to double back and fabricate her open-ended answers to incorporate new elements that only your closed-ended questions would have made her think of. After all, I guess few of them feel like they're writing an exam that they will be graded on. So they're a lot more relaxed than research purists imagine. (Or is it that cognitive dissonance doesn't bother them?)

Obviously there are some kinds of products that cannot be tested by mail. By the same token, some almost have to be. Cigarettes, for example, can't feasibly be tested any other way because the market is so segmented that it would cost a small fortune just finding the right kinds of smokers. How many phone calls would you have to make to find three hundred 120 mm ultralight menthol cork-tipped cigarette smokers?

Properly executed, the mail test is almost as good as the personal method, but you give up some fine points. Unless you are logistically locked in, the mail method should be used with discretion, and probably not for major product evaluation tests on important brands. In other words, it should be seen as a supplement to regular testing, but an important supplement.

Executionally, it is not always necessary to use a research house that specializes in mail panels, though they have become so cost efficient that in many cases the headache of launching your own mailroom activity wouldn't be worth it. But, in case you haven't tried it yourself and would like to consider it, it may be useful to know that if you use *old* respondents previously contacted by phone or personally, especially those to whom you gave test product, you can get very high response rates with relative ease. You already have a lot of demographic data on these folks, and they are already known to be cooperative. Of course, the more you use them in this fashion the higher your response rate gets as you distill out the uninterested parties. You might anticipate a response rate of between 40 and 85 percent even without first asking them if they want to do it (i.e., by just sending them blind test product cold).

DANGER NUMBER 69: Phrasing the Question

It is common knowledge that a questionnaire must be free of bias and ambiguity that could invalidate the whole study. Most researchers can avoid commonsense blunders, but few ever rise to the plateau where they can guarantee a questionnaire, plus instructions to the interviewers, that are totally unbiased.

Contrary to popular belief, normal conversational habits and patterns don't suffice in interview designs. Normal conversations are not good examples of clear communication. Yet most researchers seldom realize this or come to appreciate the thin ice they tread when they assume the average respondent will be able to interpret the meaning of their slovenly phrased questions. The complaint department on this one could fill several pages, but it is the principle that is more important. To convey that principle, here is one example:

The research alumni of a famous midwestern consumer goods company, so the story goes, share a recurring nightmare where their boss calls them on the carpet for sabotaging a test market by forgetting to include the phrase *or not* in a study.

Why would they have these strange dreams, any sensible person would ask; what makes putting *or not* at the end of a question loom so large in their lives? Why do the folks that work for this one company (name on request) feel that survey results can be invalidated by the omission of a phrase many researchers consider an affectation?

In yes-or-no questions most respondents have a strong impulse to give you a *yes* answer. Now, intelligent readers are going to think this is a lot of nonsense, so here are a few reasons why this happens:

- Once they've agreed to be interviewed, respondents are curious about what you're going to ask them. A lot of the initial screening questions in an interview are dichotomous; too many negative answers could—they think to themselves—terminate the interview before it gets very far. To satisfy their curiosity they have to keep the questions coming by feeding you positive responses.

- For some types of questions many interviewees are simply incapable of giving a negative response unless it is absolutely clear that it will be acceptable. The positive one is generally thought to be the *right one*. Both possibilities have to be clearly presented. "Do you ever use the Yellow Pages?" would produce a far greater number of affirmative answers than the more proper "Do you ever use the Yellow Pages, or not?"

- Questions that drop the *or not* produce inaccurate information. It is not unusual in actual experiments to have the *or-not*-suffixed query produce 20 to 30 points fewer affirmative answers than the same query without the suffix. Comparisons to independent data sources, such as purchase diary panels, characteristically reveal that the *or not* question produces the more reliable information.

- The pull toward the positive response is even more extreme among certain language groups. Hispanics, for example, are notorious yea-sayers. Unfortunately, they will try to tell you that *or not* is also a lot more awkward to say in Spanish ("*o no*") than it is in English. In fact I don't know of any foreign language where the purists enjoy using the phrase. That's too damn bad, but it is still a vital point and if you want reliable information from foreign consumers you must instruct the field personnel in these basic facts of life. Most foreign tongues, with the exceptions of ancient Greek and Latin and modern German, are too loose to produce the kind of ultraprecision we need in marketing research interviewing without major transfusions of American English syntax. In the less developed countries (LDC's) there will be a big split in the vernacular between those who have virtually no education (the consumers) and those with a college education (the researchers). The latter will insist on phrasing their questions in some classical or literary version of the language more suitable to eighteenth century drawing rooms than to the mud huts their respondents usually live in. Needless to say most denizens of the Third World have only passing familiarity with the polished phrases of the Enlightenment. We can thank our lucky stars, those of us who work in the United States, that we do not have this problem. (This is because the educated in the United States are not all that literate.)

The *or not* issue is just one of the many examples where interview design has to go several steps beyond the level of ordinary common sense. There are many other types of interviewing bias to worry about. Asking, for example, "Can you tell me anything about the commercial . . . ?" will produce considerably lower recall than the more imperative "Tell me about the commercial. . . ." Good questionnaire construction consists of many such elements learned over the years, and it is absolutely shocking how many studies go to the field every day with structural faults big enough to invalidate entire projects. This is the real nightmare . . . for everyone in marketing.

Even when you write an impeccable, airtight questionnaire you still have to worry about its implementation. Housewives will rapidly shift gears and start talking about extraneous matters without the neophyte interviewer ever realizing it. This is very dangerous since it is often undetected. It frequently happens in focus groups with a moderator who is unfamiliar with the subject matter and too preoccupied with attempting to follow his or her own questioning guide to notice that a side comment has sent the group off talking about some entirely new subject. I'm sure the reader has seen this take place in business meetings where no one listens to what is being said since they are too anxious to make their own points. In structured interviews it happens often—even when the questionnaire is followed faithfully, but more often when the interviewer sloppily elects to drop certain pivotal phrases. For example, in a Campaign Communication Study they should ask, "and what else did Pepsi-Cola say in its advertising," but, because they assume the respondent has been following the flow of the interview, instead they just ask, "What else?" And this soon deteriorates into what Coca-Cola and Diet Rite said in their advertising. It can sneak up on you before you know it.

Unless clients are willing to pay more to the interviewing services, the absolute quality of their work cannot improve. Training takes time and money, and the appeal of highly competent investigators is usually outweighed by the accompanying higher costs when bids are compared.

One reason why so much interviewing is faulty is that most interviewers are now trained on telephone interviews, instead of face-to-face with respondents, as was the case many years ago. Nothing can replace the experience of seeing the female customer in her own home, with the confusion, the kids running wild, the doubts crossing her mind as indicated by the quizzical look after hearing an awkward question. Only in her home can the interviewer have the opportunity of, after talking about Gleem for ten minutes as the toothpaste the family "always uses," seeing the housewife step into the bathroom and bring out the Colgate, which she then confesses was what she meant when she told you Gleem was her brand. The value of the face-to-face confrontation in removing all ambiguity and doubt, which only the most perceptive investigator can detect over the phone, leaves the truly professional interviewer with instincts that last a lifetime. Some field houses still provide this type of training but, generally, it has been lost, throwing in doubt most interviewing done today.[3]

Even with the perfect questionnaire one can have difficulties producing a stream of veracity. Everyone knows that when the housewife says she never pays any attention to advertising, her cupboards will be filled with heavily promoted brands.

People don't always permit themselves to tell the truth, but it is hard to know when this happens. For example, in Latin America, just about every housewife you talk to will tell you that every food product she buys is chosen because of its vitamin and mineral content, but more subtle and believable tests show that, as everyone in the food business probably knows, her selections are really made on the basis of flavor. Years ago, when the

Puritan Ethic had greater control over our tastes, this kind of rationalization was more extreme than it is now. Men are worse than women in this regard. They let their machismo intrude on their basic honesty in many cases . . . few male smokers, for example, would confess to any health concerns (other than being occasionally a little short of breath after doing the mile). One must be careful not to believe everything in a survey and to know, for your product category, just where it may be impossible to get at the truth. Ultimately, the good researcher serves his client by knowing when to flush out comments that are more reflective of human ego needs than of genuine attitudes and behavior.

NOTES

1. I am obviously not making comparisons to national probability samples. In fact, I would be awfully surprised to hear of anyone doing these types of *spot* tests using such samples. In most cases, it would be physically impossible.

2. One important element of consumer evaluation that cannot be produced over the phone like it can be in the field is socioeconomic classification. Your marketing needs will determine whether or not this is important, but the phone data, naturally, is limited to verbalizations on topics such as income, occupation, material possessions, education, etc. This may be serviceable data, but it neglects to treat the question of taste. Taste can be vital for a whole host of products, especially those with snob appeal like wine, cosmetics, clothing, cars, books, magazines, restaurants, and so on. When you ponder the fact, as I do often, that Chicago transit workers earn seven times as much as the average American author, then, clearly, income is a very misleading indicator of consumer tastes. "Money is not the measure of man," said Captain Ahab.

Procter & Gamble, at a time when the door-to-door interview was more predominant than it is now, had a highly refined method of classification that was dependent only on visual observations. Based on the accoutrements of the house and the grooming of its inhabitants, families were put into one of five possible classifications, each with subdivisions. At the zenith was A. It was virtually nonexistent. The Vanderbilt mansion (as seen in the Peter Sellers film *Being There*) would be an A. At the bottom of the scale was E . . . the worst of what the big city slum had to offer. Most people were either D (Archie Bunker) or C (Ann in "One Day at a Time"), but a high D was hard to tell from a low C. When in doubt, P&G investigators used little tricks. A high D could become a low C if they had lined drapes in their living room. (Now that drapes are passé, they'd probably have to check out the miniblinds.) Neatness also counted. Unshaved legs would bar a housewife's entry in the C category (which would necessitate modification in parts of Europe). The worst insult you could level at a P&G field girl [sic] would be to call her D. Being human, they also used this method to exact revenge on uncooperative women; a snooty B housewife would be downgraded to a low B by offended investigators. All the field girls wanted to be Bs when they finally settled down.

The benefit to marketing was incalculable. For one thing, it helped in deciding issues of taste in TV commercials . . . something that income information cannot do (unless you are willing to accept the concept that money, ipso facto, guarantees taste, just as it has done in Las Vegas).

Years later, I noticed the same system being used by a research firm in Puerto Rico. But there the draperies had been usurped by the refrigerator. If you didn't have one, you were a D. If you had one in the kitchen you were a B. But if it was in your living room you were a C. Sounds fair.

3. There is no truth to the theory that these problems are not encountered when you interview men, that their minds are all like steel traps, facts are at their finger-tips, and the dangling pronoun alien to their speech; the words of which fall like the prose of Hemingway from their lips as naturally and effortlessly as fallin' off a log and as beautiful as a bucket of lemon pies in a bed of daisies.

8 • *Miscellaneous Is More Fun*

Ask any researcher—if you can get his guard down so he won't just lip-sync the *official* answer—what kind of project he likes to work on best and he'll tell you package research, name research, things like that. Small things. Not the momentous thirty-six-month brand tracking study; not the elaborate, serial product tests; not the ten-county new product test market with its multiplicity of synchronized studies in advertising awareness and attitude measurement—but the easy little things that sum themselves up on one page. They take a lot less production work than the former, of course, but they still involve the same amount of human interaction—which some researchers simply refuse to shun. They are, to be absolutely frank about it, more fun . . . mainly because they contain few hidden traps, fewer chances to make an absolute ass of oneself by forgetting to order an all-important mathematical deus ex machina as it goes to the computer center (too late after it comes back, old chap). They are so easy that if you did make such a mistake, you could probably take the whole mess of raw questionnaires home with you that night, reprocess them by hand, and still catch the guest host's monologue on the "Tonight" show.

And for those who enjoy life on this planet for its many opportunities to help their fellow inhabitants, they bond the researcher to a broader spectrum of characters: package design artists, premium salesmen (who present you with cheap, but welcome, plastic trinkets every time they come to see you), people from the demimonde of the merchandising department ("Not quite marketing, old boy," a toffee-nosed marketing V.P. from England once told me) who have coupons and free samples to test, and all the other wonderful folks who brought you the modern world of trade and commerce.

Lastly, these client types have fewer dealings with marketing researchers than with marketing product managers and R&D supervisors. The lack of familiarity has prevented the breeding of contempt, and they tend to marvel at the researcher's slick bag of tricks and think of the *tricksters* as *very smart geniuses*. So it can be real joy to work with them, and a balm to the bruised egos researchers suffer as one of their industrial hazards.

That should not give the researcher carte blanche to abuse the *innocenti* and palm off techniques that fail to stand up to the same rigorous intellectual scrutiny that the less-enamored marketing cohort has been known to enlist in his dealings with research. Indeed, there are dangers to be avoided here as elsewhere. They who tolerate you deserve no worse treatment than they who maltreat you. Unfortunately, these dangers have received less attention than those in previous chapters from the inquiring-mind sector of the research profession. The techniques in question, perhaps because they have an air of frivolity or because they are the kinds of assignments given to junior members of the department, have not been subjected to the same barrage of validation studies as the ostensibly more substantive areas of marketing research. I was at first tempted to skip this whole chapter because of that, but relented upon realizing that very little if anything has been written on most of these dangers; and that if one were to wait for all the required validation work to be done, it would mean delaying comment forever. We have therefore elected to press on.

DANGER NUMBER 70: Brand and Corporate Image Studies

1. The alleged image thus obtained may be merely an artifact of the research design.

2. There are few cases where an image study has propelled a business into new directions tactically or strategically. They are, more often, either ignored or manipulated to prove a priori conclusions.

In marketing, the last refuge of the scoundrel is often the brand image study. As the Bible is to the unprincipled, the image study is to the self-serving, fast-track marketer. It offers him or her any answer he or she cares to contrive.

Where research is abusively employed more for political purposes than for its search for facts, battles between marketing and research are inevitable—even before the image study begins—as the former struggles to include attributes he knows he can *win* with, and as the latter digs in his heels trying to maintain objectivity. The invincibly eloquent marketer can usually connive to have it his way through those clever arguments (punctuated with hints of inside knowledge) the researcher has no match for. If he really knows what he's doing, the brand manager can end up with several attributes that, whether rated positive or negative, he can subsequently manipulate to justify any marketing scheme he has up his sleeve. For example, phrases like "for conservative people" can be interpreted in any way he likes. He can—and will—scheme to have the attribute phrases sound remarkably similar to his *own* ad copy, thus hyping the ratings on those traits. He can even connive to control the list of competitive brands included in the study; he can introduce selected minor or unimportant brands to bleed off the favorable ratings that would normally go to his major competitors, thus making his own brand appear stronger by comparison. Or he may, claiming saintly objectivity, split major competitors into segmented parts (Brand A Regular and Brand A Extra strength) with the plausible argument that this is how consumers view it. As valid as his arguments may be, they are not necessarily conducive to a smoothly functioning and easily interpretable study. It would be comforting to think that all this is just silly speculation; that none of this ever really happens, but career planning exigencies mandate successful profit center performance, and objectivity is easily sacrificed when circumstances provide the temptation.

But even in the absence of such skulduggery, and when bolstered by the best factor analysis available, the image profile emanating from all this is, nonetheless, only as plumb as the attributes employed. When possible, qualitative research is used to give leads on what characteristics govern consumers' brand evaluations, but there is more to it than just this. Brands do not simply jostle each other in narrow little microcosms, but are subject to a broad panoply of forces beyond the control of a single brand. For example, the competitive relationship of Brand A to Brand B may change favorably following months of forceful advertising, but during the same period the whole product category could come to be viewed differently (due, for example, to an energy crisis, or some such event) by the consuming public. Hence, no real gain will have been made. The brand image study is put together in a way that can never completely encompass everything, and its very brevity and physical limitation, coupled with the illusion of sweeping universality, may cause profound misinterpretations.

Its wholesale acceptance can be highly hazardous. Usually, a lot less thought than one might wish goes into the planning phase. The attribute phrases, which are its essence, are frequently drawn up by a relatively junior research technician who will attempt to have his work reviewed by his superiors and later by marketing. Amazingly, as vital as it is, his original list of attributes is seldom questioned. Hardly anyone ever takes the effort to make a major contribution to its development. Accordingly, the efforts of one person—who cannot possibly possess the inspired insight to span the entire spectrum of critical factors impinging on marketing success—form the basis for a study that will then be alleged to represent a trustworthy and comprehensive perceptual map of the consumer's ideation of the market. That so momentous an assignment is usually given such short shrift by senior people—who could probably make a truly useful contribution—is, I suppose, understandable. No harried executive has the time or motivation to spend several hours composing attribute lists when pressing issues of seemingly greater moment must take priority. In fact, most image studies are dead long before they start. What goes into the field is a set of half-baked attribute parameters out of which, after due analysis, you may be expected to decide the fate of a major piece of your business.

Actually, few things in research are duller—or less actionable—than your run-of-the-mill brand image study. In a company that regularly does loads of research, it generally reveals very little. Where each product has its own product manager plus three or four assistants, all of whom are tuning into desk-tube data flows, such research is déjà-vu. It works better, I feel, in companies where little research of any kind is done. At least there they can create more excitement; and if they serve as an entree to further (and sounder) research projects, then they might be tolerated. But seldom do you ever see them used as major shapers of new marketing strategies.

There are worse things than errant *brand* image studies. Image studies are a real menace when they are instigated to determine the *corporate* image for financial relations purposes. The notion that a dozen pat attribute phrases can provide any insight into why Wall Street won't do handsprings over your company borders on the demented. One can only cringe to think of the research technocrat pontificating on what simplistic factors constitute the intellectual pantheon in which your company must somehow struggle for recognition from investors and analysts. (This is discussed more thoroughly in Chapter 10.)

DANGER NUMBER 71: Attitude Studies

The most overlooked, most abused technique in the research lexicon is the attitude study. Most companies avoid them altogether, except during emergencies. The few that use them fail to maximize their usefulness.

The most important thing to any brand group (that intends to be around for the next few quarters) is its *consumer franchise* and what it thinks of the brand. . . . Or is it? So seldom do I come across companies that have acquired the good habit of doing systematic attitude studies that I really wonder if all the slogging it took to build up that franchise means anything to them at all.

Attitude studies mostly seem to be reserved for *ad hoc* purposes. When on the verge of doing something risky on the brand, marketing managers will sport themselves to a test market wherein they'll order up a tracking study or pre-and-post Usage and Attitude (U&A) studies; but they hardly ever settle on a consistent technique—each occasion apparently demanding a custom-made study—thus losing, absolutely, any usefulness in studying the past in order to plan better for the future. Their files are ungenerous. When you go through the files of a highly disciplined company that has made the commitment to attitude study standardization, you find a wealth of data that helps you interpret current studies. This virtually magnifies the power of your insights severalfold. In the undisciplined company, even after they have done the *ad hoc* research, the conclusions are still a matter of judgment and subjectivity.

These wayward corporations will spend a lot on product tests (a disproportionate share of the budget), another small fortune on advertising, afterwards send the brand out on the market like kicking the young bird out of the nest, and promptly lose all interest.

None of the research preceding the launch helps to maintain the viability of your investment, which should be a major concern—even down among the marketing troops—as long as the brand exists. With no systematic application of standardized U&A studies, on all key brands, a company will be caught with drooping drawers the first time it runs into trouble. The first time its brand group will be alerted to a problem on an incipiently faltering brand will be when their SAMI data goes sour. U&A studies would have detected the trouble well before that, and the company would have had a chance to patch up the situation before it got too far down the road to ruin. It's an old marketing axiom that the best (some say *only*) time for remedial action is before a share decline begins, not after it has started to nose-dive. Marketing momentum is hard to stop. It's a lot easier and cheaper to nip problems like that in the bud.

I don't see why a U&A study has to be as complicated as most people like to make them, or as expensive. Here are some comments on how I think they should be done:

Experience Section. Begin with an unaided brand usage question—i.e., find out what brands (in your product category, naturally) were used in the past four weeks/three months. These voluntary mentions are worth more than involuntary ones because they tell you something about brand identification and strength. But you also want to ask if your brand has ever been used, and if so, when last. Recency of usage is a good thing to know. Most product managers like to know where they stand here and, over time, what the trend is. The same line of questioning is put against purchasing—because not all users will have actually bought your brand (samples, old boy). It doesn't hurt to also ask if they have the brand on hand. The analysis of this section can reveal a lot about a brand's marketing problems, about its strategic position on the market matrix, and it provides you with the raw data to use to break out the interviews when it comes time to analyze the attitudinal data.

Attitude Rating Scale. Everyone has their own favorite attitude rating scale. Some will glamorize them with impressive names, the most licentious being *hedonic scaling.* I like a ten-point combined verbal/numerical scale myself. Despite all the baloney that has been written about rating scales over the past several years, I don't think it really matters what you use if it gives you a fair degree of discrimination and if you use it consistently.

Attitude Comments. Use the open-ended approach; get both favorable and unfavorable comments. Keep probing until the respondent runs out of comments ("What do you like about shopping at K-Mart?" "What else do you like about shopping at K-Mart?"). Ask this over and over until the interviewee says no more, then strike once more with your *coup de grace*:

"Is there anything else you like about shopping at K-Mart, or not?" Results can be broken out by current vs. lapsed users to show what problems the fallen-away consumers had with the brand. Major attitude groupings (all comments about price, for example) should be *unduplicated* as well as shown in detail for maximum effect.

I've probably worn out my welcome on the subject of open ends, but here are a couple of extra reasons why they're good here: they provide you with vital analytical data like the ratio of total favorable to total unfavorable comments, and a summary of responses showing how many made *only* favorable comments (they're really on your side), unfavorable comments only (enemies), and a mixture of fav and unfav (you have to work them over a bit). These give you a real feel for consumer sentiment and may even provide the brandman with the added clout he needs to convince management to give him funds for product improvement programs, etc.

When should attitude studies be conducted? Every year for most brands. And on a pre-and-post basis in tests of formula changes, advertising changes, or other major marketing upheavals. They help assure you against being oblivious to gradual, subtle consumer attitudinal deterioration in face of unannounced product changes necessitated by use of cheaper ingredients or packaging materials you had hoped to slip by the customer. Mimicking the oft voiced warning of Lana Turner, the consumer might well say: "Don't take me for granted, you big lug."

DANGER NUMBER 72: The Problem with Closed-End Attitudes

Closed-end attitudes are one-dimensional. They lack scope. They may be misleading.

Once again I am drawn into singing the praises of the open end. I like them everywhere. Attitude studies included (as mentioned in Danger Number 71: Attitude Studies) because here they play a special role. They alone can introduce you to fast-breaking attitudinal problems *as they happen* and keep you up to date on what people are thinking about your brand. When you get locked into a frozen set of closed-end attributes or product performance features, you get locked in—what more can I say?

Side-tracking for a minute, there is another problem about U&A studies, regardless of how you do them: they give you a false impression of security. If attitudes are okay, then all is right with the world, *you think*. It's impossible to rate and evaluate everything, and things out of your purview can shift and affect the performance of your brand, but *not necessarily the attitudes*. To illustrate the point, comparative consumer attitudes toward Ford and Chevrolet can remain in constant balance, while they improve overall for Datsun and Toyota year after year. The old-fashioned adding machine probably maintained a good attitude profile long after the pocket calculator had begun to make inroads.

Many moons ago everyone thought they could measure everything pertinent to the product and predict where market shares were going. By just tracking attitudes and awareness over long periods of time for all top brands in a category the whole mystery of the universe would unravel. The ARF's infamous DAGMAR program was one such manifestation of this extravagant notion.

The trouble with all this was that are too many variables imploding on the marketplace that affect the product's fortunes. Attitudes toward the brand and its competitors just aren't the whole picture.

This does not mean it is not worthwhile to do proper U&A studies on your key products (and on competition if you have the money in your budget for this) because—limited though they may be—if you appreciate their limitations you can use them wisely to keep tabs on the market. Attitudes do have some power over a brand's destiny, and attitude studies do reflect—if only partially—the forces acting on it. If you allow yourself to be in the dark on this, you will be quickly outwitted and outmaneuvered by competitors who make a point of obtaining this form of intelligence.

These studies—to get back to our opening premise—will serve you best if you put your major analytical emphasis on the open ends and give short shrift to the canned closed-end features, as these will be too sterile to help you keep the brand out of trouble.

DANGER NUMBER 73: Determining the Importance of Attributes

Respondent rationalization, ignorance, and ego defensiveness limit the researcher's competence in assessing the importance of product attributes.

The open-ended approach assumes that people will implicitly signal that given product features are important to them, by the mere token that they mention them when telling what they like and don't like about a product. In *most* instances this is a safe assumption. But there are a few categories where psychological factors bar any attempt to reveal the relative importance of product characteristics.

Indeed, in some cases the consumer herself is not aware of these relationships. In other cases they can suddenly change. One day *cost economy* will be the crucial determinant of brand selection, the next day it becomes *convenience*. In the latter case, ample samples and timeliness will probably take care of the problem; but in the former, the respondent's lack of awareness of importance is something that is a real challenge to the researcher.

Some fools rush in where analyticals fear to tread, and just ask respondents flat out to tell them how important a given feature is. Many multivariate designs innocently incorporate this approach in their formulas. But to the researcher who wishes to be able to stand by his studies—to have them hold up in the court of business accountability—this is seldom a very satisfactory solution.

In all candor, this is one of the more embarrassing shortcomings of marketing research. Some researchers won't even talk about it openly, feeling that once they admit they can't tell marketing clients what's important in the product, they relinquish a major part of their usefulness. But whether admitted by researchers or not, the more knowledgeable lay people have already thought deeply enough about their customers to appreciate their irrationalities in brand selection and are reluctant to accept research that purports to have mysterious ways of getting around this. The acceptance of importance claims made by interviewees honors them with more ability to employ the necessary logic than they usually display in the marketplace. Consider these potentially difficult areas: packaging for generic products, battery life for transistor radios, mildness vs. cleaning power in shampoos, health aspects vs. organoleptic aspects in cigarettes, style vs. durability in clothes, and so on. Halo effect attributes can never be safely assessed by direct questioning methods, and this can cover more territory than one might suspect. What, for example, is the halo effect of good gas mileage on the comfort impression of an automobile?

It is generally better to use some kind of indirect approach. The sensation transfer method can be applied to many problems of this type. The less you actually force consumers to decide between two attributes (who may bring with them psychological overtones), the less you risk having them spew forth with abnormal and uncustomary reasoning patterns.

Luckily, by default, the problem is becoming less burdensome to marketing. One thing that has softened its damage is the unending spate of brand proliferation cast forth from the universal discovery—and exploitation—of *market segmentation*. Much to the chagrin of economists and corporate planners, who see in it the seeds of fiscal ruin, it has been growing in intensity since the late sixties. But it has been a boon to the marketing research profession because, in a great number of product categories, you don't have to establish that *Attribute A* is more critical than *Attribute B* when both can probably lay claim to some market segment.

In this perspective, everything about a product has its takers and our problem is summarily relegated to a lower order of seriousness, where it merely hobbles your chances of determining how big the segment is. Although multivariate syllabi abound that one can devote to such a task, the cold fact is that the new product failure rate—which is either still at the same high it has been for two decades or is much worse, depending on whom you want to believe—clearly indicates that this is not being done very smoothly.

DANGER NUMBER 74: Dual-Brand Attitude Studies

The ban on studies asking attributes about two different (competing) brands from the same respondent is unfounded.

It is now and again argued—but only among that tiny band of researchers that actually do attitude studies on a regular basis—that if you attempt to get a respondent to give you open-end attitudes for two competing brands she will either (a) feel compelled to say something different about brand number two, even though she may not feel differently about it, or (b) feel the need to say roughly the same thing about it in order to be *fair*.

I am unable to persuade myself that consumers really have these personal commitments to household products, but enough of my colleagues have expressed qualms about this that I have, upon occasion, taken pains in dual-brand attitude studies to break out the results by brand asked first, to see if differences actually do occur.

The only difference I've seen is what you'd ascribe to fatigue. That is, the second brand covered receives fewer comments. This is readily understandable to anyone who has tried to conduct an interview in which more than one open-end section—of any type—appeared. Respondents either run out of gas or just lose interest.

Provided you are insistent on strict brand rotation, the attitudinal readings will not be affected by the dual-brand design. This presents an opportunity. We all know that it's hard to get people to express negative attitudes about a brand. We usually learn that a brand has an attitudinal problem by inference, i.e., by the sparsity of the positive comments it garners. But, with some ingenuity, you can increase the sensitivity of open ends in obtaining negatives by approaching the problem much in the manner of a paired comparison blind test. By getting respondents to compare your brand attitudinally with its chief competitor ("In what way is X better than Y?"), you allow a much greater torrent of invective to pour out. There are several reasons why this is so. One is that, like any paired situation in research, people find it easier to think in the comparative than in the absolute.[1] Another is that the normally kindly housewife can criticize a brand with comparative comments that don't sound as harsh as the more direct outright single-brand approach.

Naturally, you have to make sure you balance for usage characteristics (especially recency of experience with the brands), but once having taken care of all the obvious housekeeping details, this approach can intensify the degree to which you can illuminate problems on faltering brands, which some researchers feel is one of the more difficult tasks they face.

DANGER NUMBER 75: Awareness of Change in Product or Package

Flatly asking if any recent product changes were noted will invariably yield affirmative responses regardless of the facts.

Question: If you changed your formula slightly, put the new version on the market and waited six months or so, would it then be okay to ask people if they had noticed any changes in it? If, for example, 25 percent said they had, would the change be significant or not? To make it more complicated, if you had not wanted this product change to be noticeable, could you live with the 25 percent?

Answer: Unless you asked the same question before you made the change, and did the same study in a control market as you did in your test city, you won't really know what you have. People are always imagining one thing or another and many consumers notice changes where none have in fact occurred. First you have to establish the bogus level.

DANGER NUMBER 76: Reinterviewing the Same People

Respondents are easily influenced by being interviewed. Follow-up interviews with the same respondents may be ill advised.

Reinterviewing the same people seldom works out as planned. It is a total failure in Usage and Attitude studies where one brand is spotlighted with considerable intensity. Poststudy attitudes will be very different here from what you'd get if you went for a fresh sample of people.

Reinterviewing is probably okay on multifaceted studies where no single brand is highlighted. In tests on brand image studies, for example, no differences were observed between the results given by reinterviewed respondents and fresh respondents.

DANGER NUMBER 77: Making Market Predictions

Research, a crystal ball is not.

Unlike most folks, marketing people are so used to working on future plans that they don't always realize that most research is actually dedicated to solving problems somewhere in the future. Product tests, advertising pretests, test markets, etc. all look forward rather than backward. It gets taken for granted.

Most research projects, though, encompass only a small piece of any pie. It is clearly impossible to quantify and calibrate every single thing that will affect the consumer's future purchases. No one can even pretend to know what these are. At best research helps us feel confident that the elements we can control are executed in the best possible fashion. But we can never control everything.

Test markets aren't always right, but even if they were they do not really forecast. All they really do is give you a chance, on a bigger scale, to repeat something sometime in the future.

Anyone following the recent legerdemain of economic forecasters (of whom Harry Truman said something like, "If they were laid end-to-end, I wouldn't be surprised.") will not be exactly buoyant about the reliability of crystal ball gazing.

But these harsh realities don't get the poor researcher off the hook; people are always stomping into his office and demanding he get off his duff and find out what will happen if such-and-such occurs. Then when the poor soul calls it wrong, name-calling orgies follow. It's a no-win situation. So, with only discouragement to offer, let us review some of the methods that have been tried.

The Market Test. These, including the simulated test market (STM), are too expensive to be used to answer all prediction requests befalling the average researcher. Even when elaborately done, they can suffer badly from poor sampling. The STM may err by not accurately calling the type of consumer—the market segment—that would be lured by the inducements in question; and the old-fashioned test market may unwittingly stray into the wrong geographic area. All take place several months before national expansion, allowing plenty of time for competition to muster its forces and prepare for combat; or in these frantic times, let sweeping economic changes—absent in the test—encroach on your national incursion. The latter is growing more serious. External factors now bear down heavily on attitudes, changing them with relative ease. Our populace, like an overstuffed chair that bears only the imprint of the last person to sit in it (to borrow from Sam Johnson), is shunted by the news media from hedonistic optimism to stoic pessimism, from mindless escapism to sheer despair, after exposure to quicky, 90-second news items. Still, the market test is the only thing we have that puts all forces in natural balance.

Product Tests. I still meet people who think that the results of a blind test are the harbingers of future market share glories. The experienced researcher will have seen too many tests with glowing results that failed to carry through into the marketplace. Tests that give favorable results are fine. We need them, we want them, without them the marketing effort would probably stumble, but they should *never* be read out of context. Obviously, the product isn't everything. There's also the name, the package, the advertising, the trade and the competition. And that's just the beginning of a big gestalt.

Scalar Devices. Concepts testing above a certain magic level (seven or more on a ten-point scale, for example) usually do well in the market. But this predictive value is not guaranteed because execution has a lot to do with ultimate success. Some minority preference products, like flanker flavors for a line of cake mixes, can be successfully pretested with monadic product tests. Some rating scales are better at forecasts than others. When you go to the more direct scales, such as the *willingness to buy* scale, you usually get an exaggerated or overly favorable result, and it is safer to just stick to the overall rating device and avoid trying to get the respondent to predict her behavior. When you ask her to predict something you invite her to indulge in a mental process embodying too many rationalizations. As supporting evidence, note how consumers seldom seem competent at forecasting how many times during a given period they will buy certain products . . . their volume estimates are crazy. (See Danger Number 78: Ability of Consumers to Remember Purchases.)

Simulated conditions are always artificial; they totally neglect certain elements of the marketing mix and overstress others. Sometimes, if you know of a good sales researcher, you can go to him and he'll give you a better forecast (just using the seat of his pants) than any STM. These are rare individuals, but I've known sales research geniuses who consistently come within two-tenths of a percentage point on predicting the end of Year One market shares for new brands.

For your interest here are two cases of forecasting failure:

Refrigerator Ownership. This may be old hat to some readers, but someone recently reminded me that in the 1920s a survey asked people if they thought they'd ever buy an *electric* refrigerator. Hell no, said 90 percent, who felt the icebox was good enough.

TV Program Ratings. I was once implicated in an elaborate scheme to predict ratings for new TV shows. Studio audience techniques gave us a rough indication of winners and dogs, but didn't help any when it came to gauging the influence of time-slot competition from other networks. Experimentally, we tried the television listing approach: Printing up schedules with show descriptions much like the *TV Guide*, we asked people to tell us which shows they'd probably select for viewing. Worked great the first time we did it. All the new shows got the ratings we predicted in the Nielsens that came out later on. But we were lulled into thinking we had a winning new technique, and did not realize that the year when we did the study was characterized by few changes in network programming. The following year, immense upheavals in programming occurred, and the technique didn't work at all. The moral is, if you can't predict something as simple as TV viewing, how can you possibly predict something as woolly as market shares on new brands . . . without some form of test marketing or STM?

DANGER NUMBER 78: Ability of Consumers to Remember Purchases

The consumer's memory is so fallible that it is totally impractical to compute volumetric product usage data from personal interviews, or even to divide them into light vs. heavy users.

Consumers either forget, or never did know, how much product they buy and use. This has been seen time and time again. Whenever you try to make volume projections based on respondents' usage claims, you end up with a market estimate several times the size of what you know actually to exist.

Several years ago the Attwood Research Company in the United Kingdom, which ran a purchase panel, decided to quantify such inaccuracies.[2]

They interviewed the members of their diary-keeping panel and found that their purchase frequency claims were off by anywhere from 16 percent to 192 percent, depending on the product category. Keeping a diary may have made these folks even more accurate than ordinary housewives, so Attwood went out and got a sample of non-diary keepers and computed their error range. It was from 36 percent to a whopping 296 percent. In general, the lower the actual purchase frequency, the higher the error rate.

Even more disturbing, you can't even delineate the light users from the heavy users by such questioning methods. This is something that most researchers do all the time, so listen carefully to the following: A significant number of people would be seriously misclassified if you tried to do this. The Attwood experiment showed that for tea users, for example, 77 percent would have been incorrectly classified; for furniture and floor polish users it wasn't as bad; not quite half (41 percent) were wrongly classified. But this can still kill your analysis of the heavy vs. light user. It turns it into absolute nonsense. Plainly, you can't enjoy the fruits of a light vs. heavy breakout analysis when less than half of your respondents have been correctly pigeonholed.

Need comic relief? One of the more amusing aspects of the Attwood study was their observation that "the irony of this situation is that many housewives, who correctly report their purchasing level at the interview, will be downgraded in the light vs. heavy buyer classification because they will be overtaken, so to speak, by housewives who have exaggerated buying claims." Funny, but it doesn't help you, does it?

This is a pretty old study, and there have been others since, but Attwood's is kind of a classic, and its British thoroughness of approach (or its thoroughly British approach) is still technically comforting. Would it be safe to say that today researchers are more sophisticated; that few would dare attempt to derive volumetric indications from personal interviews? I wish it were so. But it goes on all the time. And few of us are free from *guilt* on the heavy vs. light user thing . . . which may have even more profound implications because it touches on strategic issues and on media planning, both of which areas involve big bucks.

DANGER NUMBER 79: Small Test Markets

The smaller the geographic area, the greater the likelihood that something will go wrong in your test market.

When Doral cigarettes (one of the most successful new cigarette introductions in recent history) were under development, the brand group, anxious to try what was then called a *mini-test-market*, spoke eloquently on its behalf and finally got its way. And so it was on to little Medford, Oregon, which had only one company salesman, who—quite accurately—assumed the harsh glare of the corporate spotlight would be focused on him. I no longer recall his name, but I would presume he's gone far in his career. He put Doral on the map in Medford, Oregon: virtually 100 percent distribution in the first few days, never any out-of-stock, point-of-purchase displays you wouldn't believe, and—get this—on the front page of the local newspaper a shot of him presenting a complimentary carton of Dorals to the mayor of Medford! It was not exactly what the conservative researcher could term an *unblemished test market*. Nor was it what the brand group had in mind.

In another case, we went to the tiny town of Hamburg, Arkansas, to test a plastic container for Prince Albert Smoking (i.e., pipe) Tobacco. Sales at first weren't too good. No one seemed to want to give up the metal tin, which old-timers liked to store their fishhooks in, etc. But then . . . a rumor started to make the rounds. I can't say who started it; maybe a salesman. This was back when the Vietnam War was still on, and the rumor consisted of the story that the company was helping the war effort by converting to plastic, thus saving metal. Sales edged upwards, but subsequent tests of the plastic container in much bigger geographic areas gave the real answer: nix. This experience gave the research group additional problems: they had a rough time finding enough people to interview for their continuous tracking study. They must have interviewed everybody in town several times over. Interviewees became *family*. Respondents were saying things like: "Cousin Abner said to tell you he's not goin' to be home next week, so could you call him tonight instead?" and "Jonesy's General Store wants to know if they can get more of them free pipe tampers to give out," etc. It was fun, but t'warn't research.

Potentially, the same kind of problem affects—but probably goes undetected—the cable/scanner kind of test market. A salesman, it must be remembered, is motivated by the most exquisite management incentive tool ever devised: *fear*. When he knows (or suspects) his stores are under closer than normal scrutiny, he really swings into action. He's not stupid. When he sees a supermarket with scanners, when others in the same chain don't have scanners, he knows something is up. Do you think the store manager isn't going to blow your cover? Within three days the savvy salesman will have all the details he needs to save his own skin.

In most cases this will make a huge difference. Point-of-purchase (POP) does count, and if you're testing a new campaign and the rep is in there loading the shelves and building stupendous displays, you may be leaping to faulty conclusions when you conclude your test market is intact, because you've been raped without knowing it. *Virginitas vel castitas corruptas non.*[3] Naturally, if your use of the cable/scanner facility or of the minimarket is more cautious (e.g., to see which of two campaigns works better), you may not have to worry as much since the pollution will be common to both stimuli.

Of course, you could always try to reason with the nice salesman. Just ask him to lay off. And, after you succeed in that, maybe you could do something to prevent all these tornados we keep getting here in the Midwest.

DANGER NUMBER 80: Timing of Advertising in Test Markets

The sequence of events in a test market should copy the national plan's but it often doesn't.

It goes without saying that everything you intend to do when you go national you should also do in the test market. However, in too many cases, certain *seemingly* minor exceptions are made; and some of them, especially those regarding the timing of the start of your advertising, can invalidate the results of the test market.

I suppose all of us have voiced objections to schemes putting the media weight in the test market far above the level the brand could sustain if it went national. Skulduggery works where the researcher is not eternally vigilant and wary of such malfeasance.

Advertising is the one glitch that is most often overlooked—especially the precise timing of when the advertising is supposed to start. Though it goes against all the precepts of scientific management, test markets are often launched with less planning than national efforts. The popular excuse is that there's never enough time to make all the right media buys, etc.; and the consequence is having the brand introduced, getting fairly complete distribution, and perhaps even sampled, before its commercials get on TV.

This practice clashes with the conventional wisdom of advertising strategists. Judgment tells us that if the advertising is any good at all, it will have some influence over how the product is perceived. (For some product categories, perception is everything.) If your customers try your product before they have the benefit of exposure to your commercials, they may fail to experience the euphoria you had intended. In fact, for those cases where I actually had a chance to follow the brands that did it *both* ways (that is, beginning after full distribution was attained vs. beginning with start of sell-in), there were sharp differences in attitudes, repurchase levels, and market shares. In all cases the superior result was gained when the advertising started *before* anyone could have had a chance to try the product. In the interest of full disclosure, and not intending to be gratuitously cynical, I must stress that these cases all happened to involve successful advertising; conceivably, advertising with a negative value—assuming there can be such a thing—would produce the opposite results.

The grand message to the conscientious researcher is to leave no stone unturned in trying to make test markets ring true. Media timing is one of the biggest problems because effective distribution levels are reached *much faster* in a test market—due to your sales force getting spotlight fever—thus putting product in the hands of consumers before your commercials are aired.

DANGER NUMBER 81: Samples versus Coupons

This is not a job for store audits, unless there is a healthy dose of consumer research accompanying it.

Apart from fat rebates, the characteristic way of bringing out a new brand is with sampling or couponing programs, or both. It is also automatic to try to find out which combination is the most productive.

Accordingly, many companies incorporate tests of the introductory promotion into their test markets. One market will get the sampling, another will get the couponing. In my experience, for some reason that probably has to do with localized variances in shopping habits or trade structures, city differences are usually so great that such comparisons are not reliable. (The situation is even more extreme outside the United States.) Some cable/scanner operators have detected the same problem.[4]

If you aren't using a cable/scanner service, the best way to compare sampling to couponing is to checkerboard the same city with both promotional methods, and use a Usage and Attitude study. Based on some previously expressed concerns (see Danger Number 79: Small Test Markets) about the many distortions overzealous salesmen can inflict on scanner test stores, my sympathies go with the door-to-door, eyeball-to-eyeball interview where you can get verified on-hand measurements on the brand.

DANGER NUMBER 82: Asking about Sample Receipt

Consumers won't, or can't, answer questions about sample receipt honestly.

Once in a while researchers are asked to field studies to see how much effect sampling programs had. Sometimes they are even required to locate people who received the samples in order to get certain information from them (like checking on the integrity and competence of the field crew that was supposed to deliver the samples, etc.). In both cases the questionnaire usually asks if the householder got the sample.

Asking the householder if she received a sample of any consumer brand is the *reverse* of asking a used car salesman if the car you are thinking of buying is in good condition. Neither atmosphere encourages honesty.

The consumer's immediate compulsion is to say *no*, because then, she thinks, you will make it up to her and give her one. Others, who may not be so greedy, won't even remember receiving the sample. Though marketing people often find this hard to accept, it just wasn't a big thing in her life. All told, your efforts to reconstruct the base of people who were sampled will be severely compromised.

Plan ahead; use maps to show the sampled areas and interview in those areas. Not all homes will have gotten the sample, some having been stolen or tossed down manholes by delivery crews, but that represents the real-world sampling program.

DANGER NUMBER 83: Screening Premium Items

Mass screening of potential premiums is a job for the monadic approach. Rankings are misleading.

There are lots of means of evaluating the ultimate sales generating power of premiums, and even of comparing them to other promotional tools like sampling, couponing, and rebates. But in the very preliminary stages of any sound merchandising program, hundreds, even thousands, of premium articles will be under consideration, with even more waiting in the pipeline to be pushed by eager novelty manufacturers.

Most active premium-using companies need some kind of fast and inexpensive technique for screening these items. Judgment will naturally rule out most of them, but there will still be too many left to permit highly concentrated research on each. If the promotion will be foisted mainly by print advertising, mail panels can be used to judge their potential; but if otherwise, the actual physical item has to be subjected to an evaluation test.

Many companies use some kind of central location test to screen premiums (and then follow up with a more refined test later on). In the more standard of these tests they will display several premium items and have respondents rank them in order of preference.

This method runs the risk of incurring the dreaded *split preference*. Its results won't be the same as when each premium article gets rated *separately*. Intuitively, the individual rating must be considered the most reliable—it more closely approaches the situation occurring in the market. Plainly, consumers only get one premium item for acceptance or rejection, not several. It's comparable to the tomfoolery we inflict on ourselves in presidential primaries. If three candidates—two liberals and one conservative—run on a party ticket, the liberals run the biggest risk of losing—even though the combined liberal vote would exceed the conservative's. Plurality politics is not very satisfactory, nor is plurality selection of premiums.

One easily implementable technique for solving this problem, which at the same time lets you handle many items in one shot, is the *ballot box*. Display your premiums on a table, with a bank of ballot boxes—each one expressing an attitude rating (excellent, very good, fair, etc.)—behind them. Give the respondents a deck of IBM cards, each card identifying an item, and let them vote by putting the cards in the ballot box representing their feelings about the premium. Rating ten or more premiums in one whack is no problem for most respondents.

The first time I did it this way I made the stupid mistake of imprinting the name of the premium article on the card and noticed that women were just reading off the name of the item instead of looking at the actual premium before they voted. To avoid this subsequently I gave each item a code number, thus forcing their inspection of the items up for assessment.

Not to be picky, but if it's more convenient, your ballot box device can consist of a single, multicompartment construction with a slot for each rating interval. Now, you're going to ask: which goes at the top—the positive or the negative ratings? Well, I've tested this too, and it doesn't make any difference . . . both'll give you the same answer.

In addition to being cheap, this kind of test is also replicable. When you split the test—showing some items to half your sample, other items to the other half, and keeping a couple of items common to both groups—you'll get the same ratings on the controls. Not only, therefore, does this endorse the soundness of the technique, it also says that it truly provides an *individual* assessment of each item, and that the cohort items have no bearing on results.

Because of the logistics of central location tests you are never going to be confident that your sample is sound, and it is always prudent to provide a couple of control items in every premium array. If they get scores at odds with their norms, then you know you've got a sampling problem and can reschedule the study.

It's not a simple matter to learn if this method can predict market results. You always have far too many variables intervening to make a sound scientific determination feasible. One of the more subtle of these is that *premium success*, to many merchandising managers, is an amorphous term; a lot of them use poorly analyzed data to shape their judgments. Still, what evidence there is, is comforting. In tests where I have inserted controls with known track records, I've yet to see a premium with a successful past score low or one that flopped score high. As research techniques go, that's about all you really need to give them your blessing; many don't even give that much solace.

DANGER NUMBER 84: Evaluating Premiums

Premium evaluations often suffer from excessive methodology and little common sense.

Once you winnow out scores of premium candidates to a manageable few, the merchandising moguls may want you to take a closer look at what remains. The screening efforts you used heretofore to unearth the most alluring candidates are pretty limited, and any further information you can give them should help them to strengthen their programs for implementing the premium in some forthcoming promotion. For example, you may end up doing detailed attitude studies on each item they are seriously considering. Two commonsense observations on this are:

1. If merchandising management wants consumers to make comparative evaluations among different candidates (some occasions will call for this), make them assure you all the items are honestly being considered for the same class of promotion. If the premium supplier is offering to sponsor this test, check that all articles are of near equal value.

2. Make sure when you frame the questions that you don't tend to emphasize what consumers like—rather than what they would, in actual prac-

tice, use. Example: a test in France where the agency had narrowed down several candidates to one—a woman's handbag—and the task was to evaluate several different colors. They asked, innocently enough, which one was best liked, and a red handbag won easily. But someone, more observant of bourgeois fashion than the rest of us, pointed out that few women in France were ever seen carrying red handbags. Repeating the test, this time asking which one they'd likely buy if they were in the market for a handbag, the black one came out victorious. With hindsight it was obvious that red looked nicer but didn't *go* the way black did. I don't know how you can consistently avoid problems like this, especially when premium evaluation gets you into product areas you aren't familiar with, but it helps to start off being skeptical about any traditional questioning technique.

DANGER NUMBER 85: Brand Identification on Premium Tests

Divulging the whole story of the promotion (brand, price, etc.) doesn't help make the test more predictive.

Some feel each premium must be tested in context with the brand it's slated for. Isolated flukes may require this sort of elaborate presentation, but generally this is not so. Premiums are pretty much evaluated by the consumer on the basis of how much she wants the article, not in connection with brand or product type.

I've tested premiums alone, and then again banded to brand packages, and have never got any difference in results. But the approach does raise irritating peripheral issues that may throw the unsuspecting a lot of silly curves. Consumers are prone to muddy the waters with a profusion of comments like, "Well, I don't like that brand much." Stuff like that may not bother my readers who are able to flush out all extraneous comments that housewives are prone to give; but the uninitiated merchandising manager, who may just happen to make a field visit when he hears *all* the respondents (i.e., three or four) make comments like that, could very well return to his office and either (1) kill all further work on that premium, (2) make up his mind that the brand in question is not appropriate for any premiums, or (3) resolve never to submit any premium item to research in the future.

DANGER NUMBER 86: Name Tests

A good rule of thumb is that most name tests completely miss the boat.

Believe it or not, the standard test for new names still remains the one where consumers are shown a list of candidates and are asked which one they like best.

Erudite readers will be shocked by this; many will refuse to believe it. They should be grateful they have sufficient judgment to spot the dangers such approaches can lead to. Some attempt to overcome the weaknesses of such errant methodologies by interjecting mentions of product category; although, at the other end of the lunacy continuum, I've met old-line researchers who've told me they thought that introduced a bias into the test. Neither extreme is any good.

Needless to say, the point is this: whenever you let the respondent don the mantle of the expert, *you* put on the dunce cap because you have removed her entirely from the only role she knows well enough to help you—that of an ordinary consumer. And ordinary consumers don't agonize over brand names.

The only effective way you can test a name is *without* the respondent knowing it. The best way to do this is through the *sensation transfer* technique devised by the late Louis Cheskin. To my utter and continuing amazement, whenever they hear of it, marketing novices treat it like some incredible breakthrough. Each year, it seems, Cheskin's sensation transference philosophy is rediscovered. (I've borrowed heavily from it for my discussion on concept and advertising tests, in Danger Number 24: The Entertainment Syndrome.)

If you belong to the school that says that although the name is very important to the marketing process it works *sotto voce*, then what you have to do, according to Cheskin, is pack up some product in packages bearing the test names and give them to people to use as if you were doing a paired comparison product test. This method comes from the *dirty trick department*, the dirty trick being that the actual product is the same in both packages. (No, Virginia, you don't tell the respondents this!) When they give one of the products a whopping big preference, you know that one name works a hell of a lot better than the other. And you get your answer in a way that comes as close to replicating actual market conditions as you can get. What's more, it also gives you a believable crack at finding out what connotations the name delivers in terms of product performance benefits (as revealed in the reasons for preference).

In about six experimental studies, I've found this method will frequently give you a different winning name than the more direct *simple preference* method. A priori, the sensation transfer method would be considered preeminent.

Now, to be perfectly frank, you can't always do this sort of test. In a real name search, you probably start off with about six pretty hot candidates and no one is going to let you spend the brand's entire budget just thrashing out name tests, regardless of how critical it is. In a pinch you can get by with asking, paired comparison fashion, "Which of these two brands would you most likely try/buy?" as you show the two names (preferably printed on some kind of a simplified package mock-up). Going a bit beyond this, you could devise a method that would attempt to delineate the connotations each name creates. Sometimes the marketing issues may mandate finding a name that creates a *particular* performance impression, so that the task of locating one with high *overall* appeal would take a back seat. For example, one of the toughest things to do in the cigarette business is to convincingly demonstrate to smokers that your low-tar blend has good taste (once, that is, you've exhausted all the obvious spin-offs from your superannuated 1950s brands). In such a situation you may be very happy to get a name that conjures up "rich tobacco taste," and not much care if smokers receive an overall favorable impression from it, since you can take care of that with *media heaviosa*.

The task for the researcher here is clear: show the test names and ask which'd probably have the richest tobacco taste. (Once having screened several promising names you'd then choose the best and employ the sensation transference approach.) Name association tests are reliable as screening tools provided you have your respondent focus on the product and not on the name. However, there is one problem with this form of testing: people will gravitate toward a name best fitting their logical expectations. This doesn't say a name can't logically fit the product (as does "Quaker 100% Natural Cereal"), but simply that other names lacking the logic may have stronger emotional power but still lose out in such tests.

Seldom do test names have strange pronunciations; nor are they difficult to pronounce because of some unusual spelling. Normally, things are pretty easy. However, when you try to use an English name in a foreign land you can run into trouble, and a name test under those circumstances should have someone actually speak the name, as well as show it in its written form. But make sure you provide field personnel with a phonetic spelling so they get it right; otherwise, they are bound to find a limitless number of ways to say it.

DANGER NUMBER 87: Name Tests by Free-Form Methods

People are not imaginative enough to help select names by open-ended methods.

In one such method you show respondents a test name and ask them to imagine what the product it represents would be like; i.e., what advantages and disadvantages it would probably possess. But let's face it—they don't give you much information when you do this. They might say a few bland things like, "Oh, it would taste nice, I suppose," but you always have the feeling they are dreadfully embarrassed and say something just to please you. If you've ever witnessed any interviews like this, it's hard to believe the respondents really feel what they say. And you seldom get much discrimination among the names you're looking at. The major strategic flaw with this approach is that people do not react to names in this manner; they are oblivious to them, but the method forces them to focus on them.

One free-form technique, the association test, where you show name candidates cold—without linking them to any particular product—and ask what kind of product the respondents think each represents, is a good way of screening for negatives. If you were bringing out a new soft drink and your prized name candidate made people think of crankcase oil you'd want to know this. I don't know of any reasonable way of validating this technique, however. You either have to accept or reject it on judgment.

DANGER NUMBER 88: Package Design Tests

If they know you're testing packages, respondents go loony on you.

(See Danger Number 86: Name Tests. Package tests run into almost the same problems and require essentially the same measures to solve them.)

DANGER NUMBER 89: Simulated Usage Test for Package Evaluation

When it's impossible to have enough experimental packages made up for a sensation transfer in-home test, do not abandon entirely the spirit of this approach and revert to less sophisticated techniques.

The sensation transfer design, which I feel is ideal for evaluating package designs, just as it is for names, often runs into a practical snag—management tells you to get stuffed when you ask the art department to silk-screen a couple hundred experimental packages. Instead of having a snit, you can be resourceful and approximate the test design by showing consumers mock-ups of the design candidates and telling them you're giving out free samples . . . and that they can have any of the "products" they see. Their judgments will be based solely on the graphics.

(You get around management's cost strictures by pretending you're out of the very one the consumer wants and giving her, as a substitute, some old blind test product you've been trying to get rid of. It's another one from the dirty tricks department, but who gets hurt?)

DANGER NUMBER 90: Presentation Position in Package Tests

Researchers easily go overboard and festoon the interviewers with a burden of unnecessary procedural details.

One terribly recherché technical question is the following: When showing two package designs to consumers for their evaluation, does it make any difference which is on the right and which is on the left; i.e., should positions be rotated on a strict basis?

Answer: I have actually tested this, although not more than five or six times, since there are usually more urgent issues to worry about. The answer is, it doesn't make any difference. So, we all have one less thing to worry about now.

This weighty finding carries through intact into other kinds of show tests, such as those that are dramatically reenacted in detergent commercials where bubbling ingenues point to the pile of towels that is whiter, fluffier, or whatever.

If you do ask the field personnel to rotate positions you will not thereupon be sucked into some recondite methodological quicksand, so you have nothing to be concerned with if you do it as a matter of course. However, it is nice to know, if you are otherwise scrupulous about such things and you've just done a show test and rotation of presentation position never occurred to you, that this is one time an oversight won't kill you.

DANGER NUMBER 91: Package Research—Current versus New

It's almost impossible to test a new package against a current one. Many hidden problems abound.

All previous comments on package tests have to be taken with a grain of sodium chloride when you are charged with formulating the research program for an updated package on an already established brand.

It is here you'll run into a lot of different sources of bias. People who like the *new* will tend to vote in favor of new package designs, and traditionalists, especially those strongly commited to the brand, will resist them. The latter will have trouble believing you haven't made any change in the formula. If you are using a new package design to support a reformulation, then you are on safer ground.

If no formula changes are intended, but marketing just wants to modernize an old package design, you may be able to get some useful insights with a sensation transfer study if you take extreme pains to inform your respondents that the different packages represent only very slight changes in formula. This is still rather risky and must be handled carefully. Be certain (this goes without saying, I suppose) to include a large subsample of current users in the test. This is one of those occasions when you may be justified in reserving judgment on the technique until you can see the results. I must confess that a lot of marketing people would not feel comfortable fooling around with any research—including this method—that attempts to pit a new package design against a current one, especially when the current has been kicking around for a long time. While package research here is probably better than just winging it, anyone contemplating a visible change on a profitable brand without a test market is overly audacious.

Apart from the techniques, another snag in testing new packages dwells in the nature of changes that can be made on them. You beg the obvious once you put users in a position of looking at the package more closely than they would normally. In the process of revitalizing package graphics, oftentimes outmoded details are omitted that consumers would deem crucial under such artificial circumstances. Sometimes these are just plain silly and it clearly pays to allow for some open-ended responses so you know just what is happening. Here's an example of how stupid this can get. I once evaluated a new package for a floor cleaner that, in a perfectly understandable move toward modernity and to encourage broader use of the product, removed a picture of a female mop-wielder scrubbing her linoleum floor.

Respondents said things like, "Now I won't know what the product is for." Nonsense like that you can live without. However, had we not asked reasons for preference we'd not have appreciated the flimsy base on which the overall preference was couched. On the other hand, there are inadvertent design lapses that can be of immense significance to consumers. The Camel cigarette experience is a case in point. The story of how Camel removed the pyramid from its package and suffered a colossal sales decline has become legendary, but the details are wrong. What actually happened was that in the desire to clean up the package graphics someone removed more than just the pyramid—they also dropped the reference to Turkish tobacco. Obviously, a confirmed Camel smoker, carrying the pack with him day and night, would be disturbed at this suggestion of such a major blend change.

When revised copy signals a formula change, you get your regular customer's back up—making it impossible to get his blessing on those updating efforts that most packages need from time to time. Unless you obtain reasons for preference you won't learn how important such changes are. Even when you conduct a sensation transfer study, you might want to consider also asking for open-end reasons for preference on the package, as well as on the product. Usually you will just get a lot of useless comments, but occasionally it might spare you a packaging disaster.

DANGER NUMBER 92: "Spot" Tests (Including Taste Tests) versus In-Home Tests

They exaggerate the influence of the single variable being tested.

A *spot test* is where you test just one variable in a product that has many variables. For example, you may wish to know what color (or color intensity) to put in your soft drink, hamburger patty, mouthwash, etc. Or you may be concerned about the perfume in your toilet soap, shampoo, or car polish. It would be too costly to test every feasible variable in an in-home use test, no matter how reassuring such an approach. So the normal temptation is to select some cheap method, such as a show test or a sniff test out at a mall or in a central location facility, where you can collect hundreds of judgments in a hurry and at very low cost. It doesn't take long for a woman to smell a pair of soap bars and tell you which she likes better. Once her nostrils recover, she can even do another pair for you, so you get two tests for the price of one. And, following the typical central location test format, you might also get her to look at that new green shade for your mouthwash while she's there. It's so cheap and fast compared to most of the research we do, but the question is: how good are tests like this? Also, how far can you go with them? And are taste tests the same thing or something a little bit different?

In trying to answer this question, you can't duck the halo effect issue. Naturally, you expect the color of a mouthwash to have some influence over the user's reaction to the overall product. Change the color, and you automatically change the perception of its taste, its germ-killing properties, and so on.

Some argue that no variable operates in a vacuum; they all have halo effects, but, in addition, some variables have to be considered more important than others. Example: the flavor of a fast-food hamburger is more important than the color of the sauce that goes on top of it. So how do you isolate one variable (like sauce color) and get a valid reading on it?

If all this were so, then spot tests would be unsafe. If unsafe, then no self-respecting researcher should do them. But the alternative is just as bad: all these variables would have to be decided on judgment, since no company could afford to test them all in the only manner absolving the ills plaguing the spot test; namely, in-home use tests for everything that R&D comes up with, from a color change to a perfume change.

Over the years I've had the good fortune to be able to compare the spot test result to the in-home result, under very nicely controlled conditions meeting rigorous scientific standards, for a smattering of different types of variables among food and general household products. My conclusion is that any feature with low *conscious* impact, but fairly high halo effect properties (like the color of a mouthwash) will make much less noise (i.e., a weak preference, etc.) in the in-home test than in the spot test. Considering the sniff test, I found in one comparison (encompassing eight cases) that the spot test's average spread was 37:63 (in answer to the simple question, "Which odor do you like better?"). In the in-home version, which involved a blind test of the same pairs of products with the test perfumes, this odor preference settled down to a more conservative 46:54 (in answer to a direct question on odor preference, and, as in all cases where the two numbers add up to an even 100, with the no preferences eliminated). You also get fewer jerks in the spot test who are unable to state a preference (only 3 percent), whereas in-home it was rather high (27 percent).

The implication here—and we were clearly dealing with an important halo effect variable, mainly in household cleaning products, and not cosmetics or health and beauty aids (HBAs)—is that sniff tests give you an *exaggerated* result, but will not lie to you. If you decided to go with the perfume they said was better, you would find *gentle* confirmation of this decision in a test involving the entire product under normal usage conditions. From what we all know about consumer marketing, this is to be expected. Normal people don't buy a floor cleaner expressly because they consciously like the perfume. So, when you consult them about the product's odor directly, you would expect them to give it less attention when making an overall assessment of the product than when you only let them smell it and limit your investigation to a single question about odor. Also, once the entire product is put under evaluation, the halo effect goes underground like it's supposed to, and the true influences it exerts come out in other ways.

Suffice it to say, even with a halo effect stimulus like perfume in an otherwise mundane product category, you can still rely on the spot test's assessment of the variable.

I must hasten to point out that in all of these cases the spot tests took a simple view of the variable in question. We did not try to ascertain halo effects by asking something like, "Which of these products, just by smelling them, do you think would clean better?" Presumably, this line of questioning would produce a somewhat different response, but I regret that I don't have enough matched cases to report definitively on how it would compare with the in-home use test. The problem with pushing it in that manner is that you don't always know what the halo effect is or where its effect will be felt. In a laundry detergent it could connote cleaning or whitening power, or both. Then again, if you're dealing with an entirely different class of perfumes, you might have a fabric softening or an ease-on-fabric connotation. Consequently, you are much safer with the blunter and less elegant, "Which perfume do you like better?" as a simple expedience. Readers will want to review their files for spot test vs. in-home test comparisons in their own product categories and within the frames of reference of their own unique marketing strategies before leaping to conclusions.

Maybe my experiences with perfume tests were just plain luck. What about a show test . . . one where the color of the product is the variable put under the microscope? And I'm still talking about products where color is incidental, not pivotal, as in clothes or home-decorating items.

I recall six cases where spot tests paired up the same colors as in-home use tests. (It is amusing, by the way, how many cases had to be invalidated because R&D, based only on results of the show tests, altered the colors before commencing the in-home phase.) The net conclusion is that show tests don't do as good a job as the sniff tests examined above. Maybe we should have expected this. For one thing, though color is important, the average respondent in the in-home test environment appears quite unwilling to put a lot of conscious stress on appearance. Our comparisons suffered from a tremendous incidence of no preferences in the appearance direct question (going all the way to 86 percent in one case). So you are faced with a variable where the spot tests would give you a resounding preference but, in about half the cases, the in-home tests failed to endorse it.

Still, the practical finding is that in no case would you risk a marketing disaster by following the results of the spot test. The worst-thing scenario would be for it to make a certain color *look* important when, in fact, it probably wouldn't make any difference to consumer perceptions. Now, if changing the color cost you nothing you could safely follow the spot test result; but if, as in a pet food for example, a color change required extensive balancing with other product components plus a probable cost increase, you'd want to go easy on overusing the show test.

Of course, none of this tells you much about halo effect. Looking at a comparison of the show test vs. the overall blind test preference throws little light on this. It still says the same thing: half the time the show test succeeds; half the time it fails to predict overall blind test preferences. All that this means may be that the color halo was not the only operational halo effect in the test.

For some highly personal types of products, the ability of the inexpensive show test to forecast blind test results may be more solid. As this would vary by product category, I would hesitate to make a sweeping statement. In cigarette marketing, for example, where you have a paucity of real physical product differentiation, you can get a lot of mileage out of show tests when you couple them with taste tests. As an illustration, most tobacco folks will know what happens when you take a menthol cigarette, dye the filter tow green, and pit it against the regular white tow in a *puff test* (as it is antiquatedly called). Predictably, smokers will detect a marked increase in menthol delivery in the green-colored product. (Even if you actually saw the technician dipping the stuff in the green dye, it would be almost impossible not to experience the extra menthol kick yourself.)

Taste tests are a different kettle of fish, to use an unsavory metaphor. Flavor is the eminent central fact of any food product. And the taste test is a much more reliable predictor of in-home usage results. Still, the problems of coping with the product in the kitchen (the oven that always overheats, and so forth), subjecting it to family group approval, etc., can make any comparisons between taste tests and in-home tests unscientific. But this is just an academic issue anyway. You have to use taste tests—lots of them—if you want to run a successful food company. There's no way around it. Where most food companies err is in never getting around to doing the in-home test, so that they end up being totally dependent on taste tests of food cooked by technicians in professional-grade ovens . . . and served at *room* temperature.

Obviously, the last word on the spot test has yet to be penned. This exploration is not as definitive as the methodological investigations have allowed us to be on most other subjects. The astounding thing is how often spot tests are taken on absolute faith—with nary an internal validation study being undertaken.

DANGER NUMBER 93: Applicability of Sniff Tests

Perfume sniff tests have serious limitations.

More perfume is used to mask or enhance the features of HBA and household products than is sold in expensive little bottles. The sniff tests that are used to evaluate these in-product essences are very troublesome. For example, they don't work well in differentiating intensity levels of the same perfume. Perfume level is always a difficult thing to test reliably. Sometimes you simply cannot get a useful answer even from in-home tests.

Nor are in-product perfume tests always good indicators of marketing direction. The experienced marketer knows enough to allow his or her own judgment to overrule the perfume test when it would be at odds with his marketing strategy. He would realize, for example, that his ammonia-scented cleaner would get drubbed in a blunt sniff test against a lemon scent if the question were simply, "Which odor do you like better?" Yet would he want to give up the marvelous cleaning connotation ammonia gives him? I doubt that Ivory bar soap wins many sniff tests, but its unique odor goes with the territory.

While there are practical reasons for asking "Which odor/perfume/smell/scent (everyone thinks everyone else's word for it is wrong) do you like better?" since it does nicely isolate the factor, there are, I feel, much better ways of asking the question. For general purposes I prefer something like: "Considering just the smell, which of these two products would you probably buy?" If smoking out connotations, you could ask something like, "Which of these products, just from smelling them, do you think would taste better/clean better, etc.?" The goal should be to try to develop as much information as possible about the factor and how it actually functions, rather than to assume it works in a vacuum. Few odors lack halo effect clout. In most cases their halos are more important than their intrinsic qualities.

DANGER NUMBER 94: Sensory Fatigue in Sniff Tests

Everyone knows the human nose loses ability to discern perfumes when called on to do too much work, but there are a lot of wrong notions about this.

First let me say that I'm wary of sensory fatigue in sniff tests and advise that you always insist on respondents breathing and exhaling through a Kleenex before testing each perfume. And it goes without saying you'd want to strictly rotate which product is tested first. Lastly, while I wouldn't volunteer to test more than one pair in a single sitting, if I had to I'd alternate the sniff tests with some other kind of test (like a show test or concept study) as a relaxant.

Having said all that, I can report that olfactory fatigue isn't always as serious as some people think. It depends on the nature of the perfume. I've seen sniff tests of toilet bars where housewives were quite capable of testing two pairs consecutively—without biasing the second pair's test. But, to be honest, I've also seen cases where extreme bias occurred.

The point is that olfactory fatigue has become sort of a research profession orthodoxy, but like dogmatism everywhere, it is only half true. You may be able to save a lot of money and time if you can double up on perfume tests.

DANGER NUMBER 95: Sensory Fatigue in Show Tests

In taking unnecessary pains to avoid eyeball fatigue, some researchers overlook more troublesome design flaws in color testing, etc.

There is no evidence that subsequent pairs are influenced by prior pairs in show tests. While taste and smell, connected as they are, can suffer losses of sensitivity after repeated usage, unless extreme differences of light intensity are involved, the sense of sight does not. Most folks probably haven't been worrying about this anyway, but some of our research colleagues get awfully fastidious on things like sensory fatigue and can tend to go overboard.

While sensory fatigue is not an issue with visual testing, *mental fatigue* is. When you have lots of colors to test it's always better to limit the respondent's judgment to pairs of colors, and to resist strongly the temptation to show them all at one time in a ranking assignment. This way you avoid the dreaded *split preference*. People who go for the blue-green end of the rainbow will split off among all the blues and greens in your array of test colors . . . and make that one red color you stuck in there the undisputed winner, via a plurality victory. But by pairing them off in a round robin you'd probably see that one of the blues or greens would have emerged victorious.

I recall trying to pick a color for a floor cleaner. In the paired comparison, round-robin show test a dark green shade was the clear-cut winner. But when we showed four colors at one time in a ranking ordeal, amber was first, light green second, pink third, and (guess what?) dark green was last—the exact opposite of the intuitively more appealing round-robin test.

I think all of this is obvious to research pros who are constantly occupied with look-testing, but I've halted a lot of research in the planning stages—in companies that seldom have the need for this type of test—that was about to fall into these kinds of errors.

DANGER NUMBER 96: Participation in Meetings

Marketing researchers cannot participate effectively in meetings with marketing or general management.

Once in a blue moon marketing researchers get invited to chips-are-down meetings to watch Bushido executives review the current scene, bark commands, and formulate massive programs; sometimes, in the process, invoking research as a maulstick for their decisions.

As a rule, invitations to such confabs come only moments before they begin; or, if given in advance, no agenda is made available. No matter how he (or she) attempts to prepare for it, the researcher will not know the issues or be cognizant of the political intrigues concealed in the laconic verbal karate which will only bore him, forcing his thoughts to awandering and causing him to lose the train of the conversation. Suddenly, thoughts elsewhere, he's asked to endorse someone's statements. Fortunately for him, brief spans of the spoken word can be retrieved from the ether and no one—he can only hope—will notice his inattentiveness. But the real problem is in trying to answer this question—any question—in the environment of such meetings.

You see, lay folks think researchers remember every piece of unruly data they've ever published. This, of course, is hilarious. If nonresearchers could see the stacks of printouts, with all those "Let's do it just to see what we get" kinds of breakouts, or the phalanx of purged tables rejected for redundancy, they'd know it ain't possible. Moreover, usually only the top dogs of the research department, few of whom ever have time to read all the reports their troops issue, get hauled into these meetings. So when, out of the blue, the chief marketing pooh-bah asks, whiskey-voiced, "Aren't I right, Charlie? Aren't those test market attitudes good enough to take us national?" (a question that is rigged so as to totally defy any reasonable response), the researcher must choose from one of two scenarios.

The first being the instant cave-in: "Right, Bob," making the on-a-first-name-basis clear to all at the outset, "they're certainly about the best we've seen lately for that kind of product at this time of year." Ironically, he could still have agreed with Bob even if the question instead had been, "Aren't I right, Charlie? Aren't these attitudes the worst we've had and shouldn't we hold off national expansion?" I'm not saying Charlie is more a sycophant than anyone else in the meeting. The point is that nothing is black and white here. Poor Charlie may have a vague feel for what this study showed; but unless he gets a chance to analyze it and adequate time to present his findings, he cannot possibly unravel the complexities of such big marketing issues as whether to go national, or not. But knowing no one is going to let him have the floor for more than thirty seconds, he has to make it fast. And he can hardly avoid coming across like an apple-polishing weasel.

Now, the other scenario is where Charlie challenges the Big Boss. This does not cause the gasps from the audience that you might expect. In fact, most of them are winking at one another. But by the time he gets his exegesis started, everyone starts shuffling in their chairs, because poor Charlie is dwelling on the damn details again. What else can he do if he wants to make the issues clear and give a balanced report? But his reluctant audience, with snobbery encoded in every movement, resents the intromittency of his picayune delivery. And with such performances, he damages his reputation little by little.

There are corporate environments where the research department is treated with more respect, but in most they are not involved in the decision process at the right time, and so the above scenarios inevitably must unfold.

There is enough blame to go around for everyone though, and there are two managerial or administrative problems that make the researcher's contribution to meetings less than what it could be.

One starts with the ultimately self-destructive marketing V.P. who likes to have only nonoogamous wimps in his staff departments. People who don't know how to cause trouble, or to be more accurate, who have *forgotten* how, eventually wilt on the corporate vine because their potential intellectual inputs are never needed. They're just there to churn out the numbers. So little opportunity exists for hearty involvement that they never get immersed deeply enough in their data to develop a mature judgment about them.

The other problem originates with the researchers. Too many of them give visible signs of glee every time their company suffers a setback. They only seem to have a good time when market shares are dropping, competitors are coming out with breakthrough products, or the feds are issuing restrictive new sanctions. They have no positive identification with corporate success. They are hard to work with, much less confide in.

The solution to both problems lies in a totally new way of looking at marketing, one that places emphasis more on strategy than on tactics (see Chapter 9). This frees everyone from the need to use research for dismissing self-doubts and for supporting foregone decisions and puts the researcher in a role where his analytical talents can best be used.

DANGER NUMBER 97: Interpretive Logic

Take care that your frame of reference doesn't cloud your judgment when reviewing research results.

The following item appeared on the front page of the *Wall Street Journal* on March 23, 1982:

Jobless Ills: Unemployed workers' children are more likely to get ill and for longer periods than the offspring of those still working, a University of North Carolina study suggests. The youngsters seem most vulnerable at the time of a layoff. Afterwards, the risk drops.

Simple enough presentation of the alleged facts. But what does it all mean?

To the Potomac mentality the problem would look serious and in dire need of immediate federal government intervention. The social tinkerers would cry: "We need programs, work programs, to get these daddies off the streets and their kiddies back in school where they belong."

That would be one way of using the research. But to the conservative, who, it must be admitted, has a much more realistic grasp of human nature, the problem would not be all that bad: "The fathers have nothing to do so they go fishing a lot. They take their kids with them."

Not all marketing research has two sides to it, but many studies do, and things like this can slip by you very easily, especially when the faulty interpretation appeals to your personal biases. *Prenez garde.*

DANGER NUMBER 98: Offshore Research versus the United States

With rare exceptions, most of the world is not yet ready for marketing research.

At the risk of being unfashionably thought an American patriot, with qualified sympathies and apologies to cited nations, and shooting for brevity, I have this to say about the following countries' comparative abilities in marketing research:

Argentina. One of the world's economic mysteries—a country that's got everything, competent researchers included, but can't turn assets into success. Research community helped by combined American and British exposure in the past, but now grossly out of date. Engaging but antiquated research designs and concerns ensue.

Australia. Very good, almost like the United Kingdom with a smattering of the breeziness of the United States circa 1955. A joy working with the research community here. Same goes for New Zealand, which probably won't appreciate being lumped in with the Aussies.

Benelux. (This includes Belgium, the Netherlands, and Luxembourg, for those that will ask.) Good journeyman research, but surprisingly less open to developments from more important nations than one would expect from longtime trading nations like these.

Brazil. Not yet good enough, but getting there. Held back by old-fashioned ideas. Contrary to popular notion, when you get this far south there isn't much contact with the United States and your assumptions may not be theirs, even though they have many of the same marketing problems.

Canada. Very good. Easily better than most of the rest of the world. The trouble is its very proximity to the United States—and this pervades all of its marketing, not just its research. Canadians see so much of the United States that they think they know all about it. But they've only seen it superficially, making their thinking shallow in comparison to their U.S. cohorts. It's like *2001*, where the Venusians prepared comfortable quarters for the astronaut from what they telescopically discerned of earthly habitats. Among the accoutrements they gave him was a book, which turns out to be full of unintelligible squiggles. Canadians, thinking they are capable of emulating the Yanks, often see only squiggles.

Central America. Does not compute.

Colombia. Somewhere between Venezuela and Brazil—not geographically, but technically.

France. Mediocre. Incapable of listening to anyone from the globe's many superior nations, they inflict on themselves a dreadful technical inferiority in their research, which is usually crippled by careless design and badly laid out questionnaires.

Indonesia. Terrible.

Italy. Simply hopeless. Getting by only on charm.

Japan. Economic success based mainly on technology, not marketing. Tactical rather than strategic in research orientation. So far (touch wood) they have nothing to teach us in the marketing research realm.

Mexico. Fair. Hard workers, not at all like their popular stereotype; in fact, they'll wear you out. Watch out for that fieldwork though; check addresses on questionnaires for nonexistent houses, etc.

Philippines. Some research firms here are quite good. Strong past and present U.S. influence.

Scandinavia. Unreliable, opinionated, bogged down in quaint motivation research of the 1950s. Heavily influenced by academics and other intellectuals who may, in fact, never have done a single interview, judging by the way they talk. Research here is unbelievably expensive due to sordid womb-to-tomb wage and employment laws. Though Nordic languages are understood by only a tiny fraction of the world's population, the Scandinavian's arrogance (or bashfulness) precludes having reports translated into more serviceable languages—even for the U.S. head office, so a lot of dreck must slip by.

Southeast Asia. Not bad; varies by country.

United Kingdom. Superb technique control and execution, all the way from the fieldwork to analysis. Very reliable profession with high standards. Somewhat weak on linkage to marketing community. Americans would be bored with British lust for detail, but it's something they should crib.

United States of America. Excellent mainly because of enormous budgets. Big problem: excessive computerization leading to danger of turning the whole mess into one big, beautiful, but unfathomable and untrustworthy analog. Researchers going in opposite direction from rest of business community; losing respect due to extreme introspection and strategic clumsiness. Least interesting and most narrowly educated of the world's researchers. But the most effective. Which must mean something very profound.

Venezuela. Good research community. Unfortunate tendency to assume they are on same level as their U.S. counterparts. Similar in this regard to Canada; in fact, Venezuelans are amazingly like Canadians in many regards.

West Germany. Excellent capabilities; very thorough; a bit too trusting of psychological theory, making them occasionally appear dilettantish in eyes of upper management.

NOTES

1. *Old marketing research joke:*
   FIRST RESEARCHER: Hi. How's your wife?
   SECOND RESEARCHER: Compared with what?
2. *Journal of Advertising Research*, September 1967, p. 17.
3. A maxim meaning, "Virginity or chastity, once violated, cannot be restored."
4. ". . . multi-city test market programs using cable tv and supermarket scanners carry too many variables." *Advertising Age*, March 15, 1982, p. 74: "AdTel Shows New Service Results."

9 • *Marketing Research Comes of Age*

To the vigilant executive or to anyone else who views the apparent death throes of the corporate era and the unfolding enactment of America's own *Paradise Lost* as a continuing cliff-hanger of quarterly profit hyping, there are many villains. While shareholders would gladly ship the whole crew of short-term thinkers to Devil's Island for an extended vacation draining swamps, perhaps none more than the marketing person deserves punishment of the most exquisite and lasting variety.

THE DECLINE AND DEMISE OF MARKETING?

Declining in the eyes of management (only 30 percent rate marketing "very satisfactory," according to a 1981 American Marketing Association survey),[1] marketing managers are accused of possessing a merely superficial understanding of strategy. To marketing people, *strategy* is comparable to the kid-stuff work of puerile professional athletes they read about on the sports page and seek to emulate in real life. . . . Marketing's principal limitation is the short-term horizon of its technocrat minions, the marketing researchers. Long, long ago, marketing people shirked the executive accountability of making judgment decisions, substituting research where plain talk and logic once held sway. They thus became addicted to a style of marketing research incapable of furnishing anything more than a tactical *fix*. It is not then surprising that marketing decisions, which cannot be made without such security-blanket support data, do not ascend to the stratosphere of strategic management that professional planners know to be the only true way to corporate enlightenment and profits.

Unquestionably, the time has arrived for marketing researchers to lend a collective ear to some revolutionary new concepts that will free their field from its present dismal imprisonment in tactics and advance it into an area of immensely greater freedom for itself and infinitely enhanced value to the corporation it serves. The strategic orientation of research, though highly innovative and uncommon at present, is being followed already by a few brave pioneers.

The effectiveness of the strategic approach dwells not in its design so much as in its analysis. The aggressive, informed analyst can entwine the data of his surveys with the various market *attractiveness* or market *matrix* constructs used by the company planning staff and, more importantly, hook it all up to their planning philosophies as well. You can't do that with orthodox research methods without closing one eye and stretching the numbers like mad.

But, as with any other view of research, there are dangers. Being new, most of the dangers are interpretive and definitional, rather than ones of technical finesse. The latter will no doubt come later, as the discipline seasons.

DANGER NUMBER 99: A Strategic Look at Marketing

Marketing is digging its own grave by championing policies that are out of step with economic realities.

"Marketing—a word that single-handedly destroyed Detroit."—Francis Ford Coppola.[2]

The chief goal of the enlightened corporation is cash. It is cash (an economic value), not profit (an accounting concept) that enhances corporate wealth and the price of its stock. Interesting findings from the work of strategic planners show how marketing *and* research executives can devise strategies to boost cash flow. Strategists have various ways of depicting the cash flow consequences of operational effort. Shown below is a simplified (and perhaps somewhat antiquated though still generally serviceable) approach that reveals the cash flow outcome of different marketing situations:

35	good future cash flow	poor future cash flow
MARKET GROWTH RATE	good cash flow now	poor cash flow now
0	**+**	**-**

RELATIVE MARKET SHARE

Although some efficient businesses can have a positive cash flow even when they fall into the quadrants on the right—due to the *experience curve effect*—the general marketing goal should be to get your products into the left-hand quadrants via marketing superiority, product differentiation, and aggressive and skillful segmentation and flanker brands. Strategy oriented market research can obviously help. The product's market share strategy is probably one of its most crucial strategies and the following observations are in order:

• *Growth Strategy*. This is a cash user. Innovate, always be first, because followers seldom prosper. Advertising and marketing will fail unless supported by product quality. Share of media dollars is crucial—Nielsen showed that market leaders who keep their dominance spend at or above a rate equal to their market share. Even if a pay-out plan looks good, a discounted cash flow analysis may prove otherwise because of inflation and high capital costs. Always calculate the *net present value* of marketing proposals.

• *Holding Strategy*. This saves cash. For future wealth enhancement (the shareholder's goal) segment the market now with line extensions and spin-offs. Different pricing moves may be opportune now (they usually aren't with other share strategies). Umbrella advertising strategy (cut back on parent brand's weight, and heavy up on spin-off's) may help to conserve cash. But this should be test marketed first.

• *Harvesting Share*. This is a guaranteed cash producer, but at the end there is nothing left of the business. Instead of pulling product off market immediately, it is better to let it die a slow death by depriving it of marketing support and letting it throw off cash. Be cautious of trade reaction; frequent harvesting can damage relations.

Strategic planning is rightfully a part of marketing management, and the best place to start exploiting the findings of strategic planning (in order to improve cash flow and return on investment) is in the marketing research area. The research department can combine strategic planning and consumer research; it can bridge these two disciplines (both of which are applied sciences) and show you how to plan research programs that impact directly on return on investment and cash flow. Few research staffs are now equipped to do this, but they have the right native talents for it and need only to get the go-ahead from management.

DANGER NUMBER 100: Optimization of Research Resources

Analytical talents are frittered away on trivial research projects.

All the pursuits of the marketing research staff can be planned and implemented for both tactical and strategic purposes at the *same* time. But most companies expect the research unit to focus on only the tactical. This is a shocking waste, and an administrative crime.

Research is one of the *few purely analytical* operations in the business world. Clearly, it is what the mind does with the data that counts—and what counts today is palpably the strategic concern. Ask any chief executive officer. Ask any security analyst. Tactics are fun . . . but it's strategy that governs your financial results.

The intellectual foundation of the new strategic marketing research must be built upon the great cornerstones of the Laws of Business Strategy. From the PIMS program, and elsewhere, we can know with a comfortable level of certitude the strategic profit agents that marketing people are accountable for, some of which loom large in the old ROI equation: market share, market growth rate, product quality, R&D expenditures, price, and value.

The framework we erect on top of this foundation will necessarily vary by project type, but if we stick to a reasonable semblance of logic we will be able to produce analytical data of a truly long-term perspective (while at the same time satisfy the needs of the short-termer who probably commissioned the study in the first place—so everyone's going to be happy).

The big danger is in failing to recognize the primacy of strategy in the design of the research program, starting with the annual budget and working on down to the individual projects. Lead time is needed. It cannot be done all at the last minute.

DANGER NUMBER 101: The Strategic Focus Group Interview

The train of strategic thought is quickly shifted when commonplace qualitative research precedes the quantitative.

In the *romance of marketing* an adventure begins with the qualitative phase of the research commonly referred to as the *focus group*. It is possible to do very good focus groups, but most are *deadly*. Few moderators know much, if anything at all, about strategy. They are good on simple tactical things. They know, for example, how crucial it is for a shampoo to make a lot of suds, and they can sure ask penetrating questions about that. But, without prior exposure to Boston Consulting Group (BCG) bubble charts and other market matrices, or to the several concerns facing management, they are of no help exploring hypotheses related to those marketing options that govern ROI and cash flow.

The strategic researcher would regard the focus group method as a supreme source of early hypotheses on the strategic scenarios marketing can deploy to raise the ROI of a given product or profit center: segmentation scenarios, product differentiation scenarios, offensive and defensive strategies, and the harvesting/divesting scenario. Focus groups, when validated by structured research programs, can be a significant constituent in the overall effort to enhance profitability. Here then are a few thoughts on how to get the most out of them:

The session moderator must understand the product's strategic position. This requires more than just a knowledge of marketing. He or she must know the brand's options (physical, budgetary, thematic, political, etc.)

and what competition is doing or might do, and must use this intelligence to build a useful discussion outline and, more importantly, to keep his group talking on the subject by preventing the wasteful, time-consuming sorties into extraneous areas that seem, as a rule, to take up so much of the traditional session's energy. He has to induce his respondents to explore all the main strategic issues as they affect themselves. Everything else is garbage and the marketing people have heard it all before.

The strategic approach to the focus group provides more information than the old mode and positions this data a lot better. Strategic focus groups are also ideal for acquisition and merger programs and are extremely helpful for discovering attitudes about a company within the investment community. (See Chapter 10.)

The orthodox, garden-variety moderator is ill equipped to help develop new strategies or improve the implementation of current strategies because he hasn't made a formal study of strategic management and planning. Few would even know what this is when you come right down to it. It is, therefore, smart to choose your moderator with great care.

ORGANIZATION OF STRATEGIC FOCUS GROUP OUTLINE

The most effective method for organizing strategic issues into a manageable discussion outline is as follows:

1. Introduction and Warm-up. Cover this messy little tactical part (on product usage, awareness, etc.) fast, before the group gets the idea the whole session is going to be this boring and they conk out on you—killing any chance for an interesting and useful session.

2. Product Category Strategic Vulnerabilities. Explore areas like whether consumers mentally group the category's brands into coherent units. This lets you match your strategic business unit or segment determinations with theirs, and sometimes they are very divergent. How do they assess product quality; i.e., what criteria do they use, and is this a major determination of brand choice, etc.? Also investigate other relevant issues affecting strategies in the category as a whole.

3. Brand Strengths and Differentiation Aspects. This concentrates on your company's own brand and includes elements like an overall ranking vis-à-vis competition. Discuss how consumers make such judgments; i.e., what criteria do they really employ, etc.? Question how they would propose improving your brand . . . to make it superior to competition; e.g., what needs could you satisfy that competition is ignoring or not handling well enough. Get a detailed coverage of each major product attribute or performance benefit, and emphasize the extent to which it serves to differentiate your brand in the market; how important it is in brand selection decisions. (Most consumers may not know the answers to this, but their

comments will be helpful and revealing nonetheless.) Make a detailed exploration of what *quality* really means in this product category and how it applies to your brand.

4. Gap Analysis of Consumer Benefits. Examine all the things the ideal product could do to satisfy the consumer against what current brands are actually doing.

5. Image Points. This will serve to reveal the consumer's overall feelings about the product category compared to what they once were. Discuss why any shifts in attitudes have occurred. Inroads of substitute products, changing lifestyles, etc., may have a profound impact on how your category is now regarded by consumers.

Most key specific issues can be analyzed quite fully within this proposed framework. The report writing task is better left in the hands of someone who speaks the language of strategic management. In this way enough cerebral fodder can come out of a batch of strategic focus groups to keep marketing folks busy for several days. Later, of course, you will do some kind of quantitative research to add statistical clout to this. Just because you've now gone *strategic* doesn't mean you can become cavalier.

DANGER NUMBER 102: *The Differentiation Spectrum*

The me-too syndrome is prolonged or perpetuated by research failing to zero in on its true causes.

The strategic manager would have no trouble accepting the notion that me-too products are more likely to flop than those that are highly differentiated. In fact, it is now an article of faith in the strategic planning profession that *meaningful* product differentiation is mandatory for real financial *success* in any business, where success is measured in terms of return on investment and cash flow phenomena.

The traditional research effort generally fails to explore the question of product differentiation deeply and thoroughly enough to make a useful contribution to the market planning process. In the course of obtaining consumer attitudes, full attention must be devoted to making a thorough assessment of how the product differentiates itself (or fails to do so) from competition, whether in its own product category or in other categories serving as feasible substitutes.

One of the more critical components of product differentiation is what criteria consumers use when they evaluate the product. These may not necessarily be the same criteria used by your R&D personnel, or they may not be regarded in exactly the same way. I can remember testing a table syrup and learning that consumers chided our brand for being *thinner* and *runnier* compared to the market leader, which they regarded as the ideal for *thickness*. Pointing out to R&D, in the most diplomatic way possible, that we had a *viscosity* problem merely generated stonewalling until, finally, a showdown meeting was arranged at the lab, whereat white-coated R&D technicians went through various demonstrations, none of which I or our marketing people fully appreciated, showing that both products had exactly the same viscosity. Chagrined, I finally, in desperation—or maybe I was just fooling around at this point—put a drop of each syrup on a large dinner plate, held the plate vertical, and forced everyone to watch as our brand skid to the finish line an easy first, while competition just sat there.

"See," I said, "ours isn't viscous enough."

"No," they retorted, "you're obviously not technically competent in such matters. What you were witnessing was just a difference in surface tension."

"Same difference," I thought, but to the marketing people the point had been made. We wondered privately among ourselves later why the word *viscosity* didn't work here, and I still don't know, but the point is that there is always a very real danger that consumers and technocrats can look at the same phenomenon and see two totally different problems. And, to get back to the initial premise, this is certainly not a good first step on the road to solving a me-too problem.

Beyond determining how consumers assess the alacrity of a product to make itself meaningfully different is the requirement that the researcher find out how important these factors are to consumers. Some aren't going to be important at all. *Importance*, as I have noted in previous Dangers, is tough to ascertain. It can be explored partially in focus groups or other qualitative research, and partially by itemizing each differentiation factor (which will extend from performance traits, esthetic qualities, and so on) and trying to make a determination of how *interesting* each is to the consumer. If it's interesting, maybe you can make it also important. But if it's boring, probably not. One sign of a factor's interest level is its apparent complexity and the extent to which its complexity is easy to discuss. (Of course, in the end it will be a matter of marketing judgment whether this is sufficiently appealing to offer a good marketing opportunity—and this becomes a subject for concept testing.)

The more intense the differentiation, the more successfully a brand can compete. Therefore, no thought or idea should be ignored in the exploration of what constitutes differentiation. Usually it is a complex assembly of factors and interfaces.

DANGER NUMBER 103: The Consumer's Perception of Segments

Segmentation's here for keeps, but profits are bridled when consumers disagree with marketing on what constitutes a segment.

All modern marketing and business analysis employs the market segment (the strategist's strategic business unit is just about the same thing) as the prime focus of strategy development, goal setting, and performance evaluation. But it's not always certain that consumers see the product's segmentation the same way marketing people do. Who cares what they see? Well, it can make a big difference in a lot of ways. One example: In the breakfast cereal market, manufacturers regard the presweetened brands as the *children's* segment and thus pitch most of their advertising at kids. That's fine, as far as it goes, but it ignores the fact that many adults also prefer the presweetened *ready-to-eats*. Several other industries have products that they assume, because of their advertising strategies, appeal to limited demographic segments when, in fact, they have broader, additional appeals they fail to exploit. Some Detroit auto firms have stumbled into this kind of marketing planning trap. Perhaps Chrysler's me-too marketing problems could have been largely avoided years ago by rejecting the traditional automaker's tendency to segmentize on the basis of narrow parameters. So the problem can be more serious than it may at first sound, and the research must take great pains to determine what brands (and even other kinds of products) consumers view as comprising given segments. This is rather difficult to translate into questionnaire queries, since few respondents know what a segment is, but you can give them examples to make them familiar with the concept and then go on to find out what brands they consider to be in direct competition with one another so that they form a segment. The key point here is to find how they'd respond to the logic of your brand pitting itself against these in a herculean differentiation attempt. Since visible, unequivocal differentiation is *the* goal, you must ascertain precisely what it is you are going to differentiate yourself from.

This might all seem rather effete compared to the usual marketing research concerns, but advanced strategic thinking opens up a whole new game—with new things to worry about and new parameters to delineate and define. One thing though, the net result—a better financial outcome—is more certain, so it's worth addressing these issues even though it may not be as clear how it all fits together as it is with some of the more simplistic tactical things in which traditional researchers are absorbed. *Nihil sine labore.*

DANGER NUMBER 104: Consumer's Product Knowledge

Research must not stop with brand attitudes, since this curtails potential success, but must go on to define the complete mental baggage consumers bring to the product.

It's no surprise that there is a lot more to devising marketing strategies than just fussing about your own brand's product formulation, packaging, advertising, and so on. But strategy formulation can make it imperative that you look into areas that your research normally overlooks, or which it fails to position conveniently for your use. Even before you put your commercial on the air, consumers already have a vast store of knowledge—some correct, some wrong; some relevant, some not—about the product and perhaps even about your company.

Before it's too late and your plans are all nailed down, the research should be put to work exploring everything swirling about in the consumer's mind that may have some bearing on how she receives your brand. This will involve a lengthy list of topics: What kinds of associations (visual or conceptual images, mnemonic potentials, etc.) does she have regarding the product or brand? Are her product performance criteria well defined; does she have *expressed* goals for this kind of product or is it still a wide-open proposition up for grabs? Can she effectively defend her brand selections in this category—for example, by citing a lot of details—or is her expertise level impoverished? Does she actually compare different brands—explicitly or implicitly—and if so, what *kinds* of information does she seem to draw on? What kind of information would she be interested in having? Lastly, is she exposed to much outside information about this product category; e.g., is it a product that the media has selected for particular attention because of an alleged health problem, like salt, fat, or tobacco? If so, to what extent is this counterproductive to your efforts or intentions? Can you address these issues or is it better to ignore them? Well, there's more, but this should give you an idea of what the research should go on after here.

Unless you fully explore all the key issues surrounding your product category and determine how much real or supposed information the consumer has on each, your efforts to research the category will be superficial and your ability to devise a successful marketing strategy will be seriously attenuated.

DANGER NUMBER 105: Consumer Vocabulary

Conventional research drops the ball in discovering if the consumer can even discuss your product effectively. Result: you may be talking under their heads.

It's one thing to talk over the consumer's head in your advertising, and most good advertising research helps you avoid this. But it's entirely another thing to err in the opposite direction, and to talk down to them. Do we know when we do this?

The consumer has no ability to ponder your product that *words* do not give her. Words are more than language. They are the stuff of thought (which sounds like something Carl Sagan might have said). It is incumbent on the researcher to determine how articulate the consumer is on the subject of your product category and to pass judgment on how much word power she possesses and to what extent it can be exploited in your communications.

This is a critical point when devising your strategy, since a limited vocabulary presents obstacles you'd better know about. You may need to devote part of your budget to building a new vocabulary before the consumer will appreciate what you are trying to communicate. This is not unusual: many brands have attitudinal profiles showing where advertising copy worked its way into the consumer lexicon. (People talk of the *wet-strength* of paper towels, for example.) Once there were no good ways to express the mental concepts that are now commonplace in these categories.

Know what the problem is in this regard before sitting down to write the copy strategy.

DANGER NUMBER 106: Perceptions of Quality

Quality, a major profit control agent, is passed over too lightly in conventional research.

Any serious study of the factorial determinants of ROI will show that paramount among them is the quality of a product relative to its competition—quality being defined as it occurs in the eyes of the end user. It can be demonstrated, for example, that the relatively high-quality product will have several times the ROI and cash flow of the lower-quality competitor, will usually have a bigger market share, and can get by quite nicely with lower marketing budgets.

Research in the past has concerned itself with only the superficial and more obvious aspects of quality, but given the tremendous power it has over profits much more work must be done on it before coherent strategies can be evolved.

I have already said enough about the glories of the open-end approach. It should be doubly obvious here that, if the subject of quality is to be explored in thoroughgoing fashion, full vent must be given to the consumer's definition of quality, and the research must not, therefore, freeze itself into a predetermined list of product attributes. Quality is such a broad issue that you can virtually exhaust the patience of any reasonable respondent once you elect to explore it fully, and you don't want to limit your strategy development flexibility by the tunnel vision of a research technician's *shopping list*.

Include the consumer's criteria for judging quality (this, in itself, could disinter a wide spectrum of unexpected factors) and a determination if really diligent, hard choices are made among the brand options, or if the consumer's selection tends to be wishy-washy, sporadic, or promotion-induced.

Another useful issue to explore is where the consumer perceives the quality coming through. In some products this'll be strongest during actual use, but in others it is a manifestation of appearance, odor, or feel. Every possible physical and mental aspect of the product should be covered, and the research should be able to lead to some safe assumptions about how each enters into the consumer assessment of the brand's quality. The same must also be obtained on all logical, key competitors so as to provide both R&D and marketing with the broadest possible rundown on the brand's competitive strengths and weaknesses regarding its *relative quality*. This in turn should be applied to the task of improving or exploiting the quality factor in the brand's strategy, either separately or as a *value* strategy execution in conjunction with pricing policies.

DANGER NUMBER 107: Perceptions of Competitive Dominance

Leadership provides its own momentum and is a key profit factor, but most research doesn't know how to capitalize on it.

Leadership can be in the mind of the beholder. True leadership (that is, dominant market shares) spells fat profits, while nonleadership (small market shares) can mean diminutive profits, or (gulp!) no profit at all if things are really bad.

Market share is usually seen as an objective—what you strive for by having good marketing strategies. But it can also be a useful *sales aid* in itself to the extent that market leadership, or dominance, translates into something of positive significance to consumers. For example, if consumers perceive a brand to have *leadership*, they may assume it got there by merit. Moreover, marketing communications may be employed to strengthen this consumer impression.

First, the research has to determine how the consumer perceives the market—what brands she thinks dominate it, their relative importance, which has the greater market *presence* (a net impression of noise, excitement, and attention-getting in the geographic market), and what specific characteristics go into the idea of leadership (sales, history, distribution, technology, corporate backing, etc.).

Once the consumer's market perceptions have been traced, marketing strategists can examine them to see if they present their brands with any opportunities (or problems) that they can address. Leadership, more than being a goal (sales volume), has a profound cognitive impact on attitudes, and for this reason its study should be incorporated in all strategy research.

DANGER NUMBER 108: Strategic Vulnerabilities

Conventional research is too introspective to detect the constant perils most brands face in trying to implement their strategies.

All brands live in danger of forces from the outside—threats from competition, from products not considered in the same category, from things beyond the immediate market like technological changes and new governmental regulations—which usually slip by undetected until too late. The only perils orthodox research easily detects are the inherent, brand-based, parochial weaknesses.

A good market study must in some way examine all the micro/macro issues that may come to bear on the product. This will include obtaining good information on a broadly defined spectrum of consumer behavior and attitudes, fears and needs, to let the product group see not just the threats but—more importantly—the opportunities they can adjust their strategies to and translate into marketing action.

One important issue here is the question of how personalized the product has become. Obviously, products (even more so, brands) that have personal importance to the consumer (beer and wine, for example) are less strategically vulnerable to deterioration from outside forces than products that have little personal connection (like flashlight batteries). Hence it's critical to determine the extent to which consumers have a coherent personalized philosophy about the product. Is there a strong personal involvement; is discussion about it easy or forced, enthusiastic or lethargic? The research must also determine if there is an emotional payoff to the user, or if usage is merely a dull and very practical matter. The personal significance of a product may be a pivotal consideration in the brand's strategy (as part of its anti-me-too thrust, for example), and surely it has a direct bearing on the brand's advertising.

Another aspect of the brand's strategic vulnerability is its *goodwill*. Every brand has some portion of goodwill: some have more than others; and some may even have its negative, flip side, *badwill*. The question here always is, "Does the brand have enough goodwill to sustain its consumer franchise . . . for a while longer; or to serve as the base for future marketing ventures?" Most myopic product managers assume they have loads of goodwill, but you should really make a point of researching it to be sure. Why was Camel regular, for example, able to hang in there as the cigarette market evolved from regular to filter to low tar to ultra-low tar, sometimes flourishing, sometimes listing to port, but always making a comeback and, in effect, displaying buoyant and healthy measures of long-term consumer goodwill while other oldtime brands, like Lucky Strike and Chesterfield, were unable to match Camel's performance? Did they not all have the same amount of consumer goodwill at one time? Was Camel the only brand that knew how to exploit it? The ultimate question, regarding chiefly the older brand: "Is your brand aegis an asset to the corporation or a liability?" Goodwill is one of the most neglected elements of consumer research. It's hard to define, hard to nail down, but critical in the long run for warding off outside forces as part and parcel of strong marketing strategies. Research into the nature of it is of paramount importance if you want to make your peril-prone brand relatively invincible.

NOTES

1. *Advertising Age*, September 21, 1981, p. 36: "Marketing Scores Low in Executive Poll."

2. National Public Radio, February 9, 1982: "All Things Considered."

10 • *Financial Communications: Research to the Rescue*

To the heavy breathers in the offices just down the corridor from the chief executive officer everything I've talked about up to now—even including our brave-new-world attempt to bond research to profit-oriented applications and strategic thinking in brand and strategic business unit problems—is all just chicken feed. While we marketing staffers have all the fun and the plural martini lunches, it is clearly up in the executive suites where the big fish are being fried. For this is where all eyeballs are on the Big Board. Stock price is all that really matters here.

The researcher, with his enviable analytical talents, above all others can contribute by dispensing stiff doses of the strategic research medicine described in the preceding chapter; for he will thereby be ready when it becomes urgent for his company to discern exactly what the investment community knows and feels about it. When the chips are down, a strategic inflection on research is the *only* way that makes any sense. Common logic dictates that, while your earnings prospects have much to do with how investors set the price level on your stock, it is your business strategies that exert the most powerful influence over your stock market fortunes. Since they *alone* determine the size of your earnings, it is, intuitively, to your strategies that sophisticated investors (security analysts, brokers, fund managers, serious individuals, etc.) look when making appraisals, but they are often untutored on how to define and assess a strategy.

This knowledge gap is a key actionable opportunity—not a problem—for the corporation. When a company can make an accurate determination of what misconceptions investors have about its *true* business strategies and then predetermine (via concept testing) the most compelling way to communicate them, it will make an impressive improvement in how it relates to the investment community. The ultimate goal, of course, is to engineer an increase in its stock price. With good strategic research, this task should be much more assured than with the orthodox research approaches.

DANGER NUMBER 109: Financial Communications Research

Conventional financial communications research is too shallow to be of any use to anyone.

Whether used for general purposes or because of a recent flurry of mergers, acquisitions, or divestitures, conventional research used to gauge

corporate attitudinal profiles is restricted to a narrow list of bland, pedestrian, and utterly useless benchmarks. For example, research will get ratings
on your company's management ability ("Is their management better than
average, just average, or below average?"), on your "growth prospects,"
on your "technology leadership," on whether you make "quality
products," etc. All are fairly predictable and do not require much thinking.
They'll even impose social worker nonsense in questions on "how much
your company cares about people. . . . " Such hackneyed lists of attributes
and topics appear to have popped off the pages of dusty old college texts or
from the student movement manifestos of the sixties. It really must take
nerve to be able to bluff the chief executive officer into accepting this sort of
junk as the last word on what the investment community thinks about his
company.

Traditional corporate research totally neglects any acknowledgment of
the quantum leaps made in the art of business analysis in the past decade or
so. This dangerous orthodoxy fails to recognize that, in the main, business
strategies are divisional (and even product or market segment oriented)
more than corporate, and that they are multifactored (e.g., growth alone is
neither good nor bad and cannot be understood without a broader assessment of other factors like market share, capital intensity, industry environment, rate of technology change, etc.). While the modern-day way of looking at your assembly of business strategies undeniably makes your company
totally different from any other you've ever seen, heard about, or studied,
the traditional research is incapable of discovering this uniqueness. *Yet, it is
uniqueness—the point of differentiation—that could be giving your
company the attention-getting, memorable story required to make the
Street take notice and respond intelligently.*

Marketing executives will know that we're talking here about the good
old unique selling proposition and all that it says about marketing. It
shouldn't come as news to anyone that financial relations *is* marketing. The
mystery is why it's done so badly. Financial communications are handled
with less finesse than we in marketing commonly dedicate to the average
ballpoint pen commercial. But where are real marketing skills needed more
than in selling the corporation to the investment community?

DANGER NUMBER 110: Corporate Research Components

*Impressive advances in corporate research are ignored in most financial
relations studies with the investment community.*

You only cope effectively with the various investment publics when you
can pinpoint how bereft they are of a basic appreciation of your strategies.
Thus, your research must thoroughly probe how well you have heretofore
communicated this, whether intentionally or accidently, but your research
methods must not assume your audience has a sophisticated understanding
of strategic management. Although some are moving toward this point,

most are not yet that sophisticated. (Importantly though, surveys report that security analysts are more interested in a company's business strategies than anything else.)

You should precede any quantitative polling of the members of the investment community by qualitative research such as focus groups, but for both qualitative and quantitative studies, the following elements must be considered:

Overall Awareness. Have the respondent outline, in his own words, the company's overall corporate and business strategies. Use probes such as, "What are some of the specific factors or elements in these strategies that the company feels will help to ensure/promote a successful future?" but don't expect this to yield much the first few times you do it. At present, as a rule, corporate strategies aren't well known (that becomes the job of the financial relations staff). You'll get lots of pedestrian responses ("They want to grow faster." And, "They want to diversify," etc.), and this question—obviously—only serves to show the extent of the current information base.

Attitudes. Although they probably won't have much awareness of your business strategies, you still need to know their attitudes about them *as they are perceived*, since even attitudes founded on the most bizarre kinds of misinformation govern investors' behavior . . . in the same way they cause wars and topple governments. Questions like the following are submitted for your approval in this twilight zone of probing the hidden recesses of the Wall Street mind: "I'd like to get your impressions/reactions to the company's strategies: what is it you, as an investment professional, like about the company's strategies? What else . . . ?" Then (naturally) ask what they don't like. Once you get them talking along these lines you'll find you can elevate their thinking beyond the usual sophomore levels at which such matters are discussed in the conventional research with investment mavens. Most have been interviewed many times before and will give you the Sunday Business Page treatment if they think you are one of those run-of-the-mill researchers who stumbles over all the big words like *supplysider* and *breakupvalue*. Let them know you mean business and they'll increase the amperage.

Variations on the preceding can be used if your business situation has some unique problems and if this approach is inappropriate. In other words, you really have to conduct a thorough assessment of your own strategic condition and devise your own *ad hoc* questions to fully explore the investment community's relevant attitudes. Just don't become specific, at this stage, about the detailed components of your strategies; this comes next.

Scalar Geographic Multivariate Perceptual Mapping. Now that you've got a measurement of the current investment community's mental inventory of attitudes safely tucked away, you can launch into more interesting matters. In this section you can take about a dozen of the key strategic factors forming the guts of your basic ROI equations. Example: your ability to enhance your returns not only by having a high market share but also by having—at the same time—the right amount of vertical integration (one of the more common pairs of strategic factors cited in the strategic management literature). To researchers and financial relations people, who are now saying to themselves, "Hell, I can't get my hands on that sort of analysis; so forget it," I have this message: Go see the head corporate planner. This stuff is his stock-in-trade. Make him figure it out for you. That's his job.

Have respondents (you'll have to encourage or urge them to think a bit about this) rate your company's proficiency on these factors or pairs of factors. Do the same thing for some competitive companies (but choose only those that investors would compare to yours naturally). If you've got access to the right software you can have those strange-looking multidimensional charts drawn up showing where all the companies group—only this time you're going to have some decent data to do your analysis on (at least now it's going to have some bearing on stock prices). Now you can see which strategic factors made you what you are in the eyes of the investment community, and what problems you must address to move yourself to a better position on the map.

(I promised not to expound on multivariate analysis in this book, but this is one time I'm tempted to break that promise, since here such analysis can be very useful—although I still wouldn't take it in and dump it on the chief executive's lap. For him you need the one-page summary, all words, no formulas. Well, most readers probably don't need a lecture on this sort of thing and the potential it offers here. For those that would like to know more, there are many good texts available in any library.)

Evaluation of Specific Strategic Factors. Once having rated them you may want to discover more about how investors think of your company's posture on some of these factors; e.g., "How has the quest for greater vertical integration been a part of the company's overall strategic thrust?" and "How do you feel about this?" or even "What does this mean to you?" and so forth. Again, don't anticipate that the feedback will be in the strategic planner's language; it will, in fact, be kind of crude, but you are trying to determine the awareness and attitudinal deposit in *their minds* so you can recommend more effective communication programs. After all, you cannot devise more effective programs until you define the problem. You may need to simplify your language somewhat. . . . My wording is given only to show the basic idea and not to tell you how to write the actual questionnaire, which really has to be a custom job.

Perhaps the greatest value in this kind of research is in its use as a tracking study. By establishing a base in your first study and then repeating the same study a year or so later you can tell, with immense scientific precision, how well your financial relations program is succeeding. Hence, the first time you do it, it won't mean a whole lot.

Concepts. You may want to try out different ideas on how you can position your company to the Street. Brief statements of different positionings can be read to the respondents for their reactions, just like any advertising concept screening.

This, of course, is only a brief accounting of a very idealized approach using strategic inputs on corporate level market studies. Your corporation is unique and requires its own *ad hoc* applications of these principles. The important thing is to go beyond the trite, worn-out pedestrian research methodologies that most financial communication programs fall victim to and to recognize this underlying truth: *a business owes its success to its strategies, and strategies are what ultimately govern its stock price.* Unarguably, it is imperative to know exactly how much—or how little—investors know about, and appreciate, your strategies so that unfavorable or inaccurate perceptions can be rectified.

Before I get too carried away here, however, I will admit that, from a practical point of view, the remedy for a poor corporate attitude profile on the Street would not involve divulging your complete strategic plan. Rather, it would, with suitable literary flourish, use it as a basis for differentiating your company and supporting your claim that it is a worthy investment.

Obviously, the financial communications that would emanate from this would never have the analytical intensity of the professional planner's commentaries, the world at large having little patience with such serious tomes, but they would be founded on substantive data, which, in itself, would constitute a major turning point in the annals of corporate advertising and image building.

If you want to heal the sick and faltering corporate image, this is the process, because everything must begin with unassailable problem definition—and this is the way to get there.

DANGER NUMBER 111: *True Role of Researcher*

Most companies sell their researchers short. Their true potential is seldom tapped.

In the last two chapters I outlined new and substantially more elegant approaches to market research, both at the product and the corporate levels. Concepts in strategic management are used to deliver decision-basing information that can actually help the company enhance its long-term profitability.

For too long, marketing research has been asked to bestow on the corporate world only a short-term, tactical range of its competence. These new approaches would improve the marketing research profession's stature in the business world.

The researcher is the *complete analytical being*. He can absorb the lore of the strategic management profession with little trouble. Once he incorporates its thinking into his work, he can, at the product level, still supply tactical directions while simultaneously providing strategic direction. And at the corporate level, he can give top management a much better grasp of why its corporate stock fails to command a higher price, and what financial communications to implement to improve this.

Analysis is the key component. The researcher who can creatively and energetically combine the mundane tabulations of questionnaire responses with the more intellectually challenging precepts of strategic management will make a stronger contribution to the corporate fortunes.

These new approaches represent steps toward altering our national journey toward economic oblivion. By finally, at long last, providing a universally applicable marketing intelligence system that addresses the long term, we can turn our backs on the deplorable month-to-month obsession that has rendered us at first prodigal and now impotent, thus halting a formidable threat to the free enterprise system. In a small way, of course.

• *Postscript*

A PLEA

I hope it is not too apparent that this book has many shortcomings. Of the dangers just covered herein, not all are of major concern. Some are those small nagging things that hold you up when you're trying to plan a job—the types of things you never get a chance to test but which frequently slow you down, or on which your clients may later challenge you. Others, of course, are central to our very profession.

Many of my opinions, in spite of the careful research on which they are all based, will continue to be controversial. To be thoroughly scientific all would need further testing, but—and here's the rub—none of us ever has the budget this demands. Also, I'm sure there are hundreds of similar dangers that remain uncovered by this book.

I am hoping that some readers will have something to add. If you would like to tell me about some of your experiments, I would gratefully consider them for the revised edition of this book a few years from now. You can contact me through the publisher. We'll use your name and give you full credit, but only if you say it's okay.

Ideally, the revised book should have not only many new dangers to explore, but it should also contain rebuttals on the dangers in the present edition, giving contrary evidence. Down the road a bit the ultimate would be the final tome: where total resolution is found. That may be only a dream. But, for now, we have a long way to go.

If you have a contribution, even if it totally disagrees with what I've said, I'd sure like to hear from you. If you have something that confirms any of my positions, so much the better. Whatever you've got, please let me see it.

• *Suggested Readings*

Adler, Lee, and Mayer, Charles S. *Managing the Marketing Research Function.* Chicago: American Marketing Association, 1977.

Alt, Mick, and Brighton, Malcolm. "Analysing Data: Or Telling Stories?" *Journal of the Market Research Society* (October 1981): 209–19.

Bellenger, Danny, Bernhardt, Kenneth L., and Goldstucker, Jac L. *Qualitative Research in Marketing.* Chicago: American Marketing Association, 1976.

Cheskin, Louis. *Why People Buy.* New York: Liveright, 1959.

Chisnall, Peter M. *Marketing Research: Analysis & Measurement.* (Maidenhead, U.K.: McGraw-Hill Book Co., 1973.

Criteria for Marketing and Advertising Research. New York: Advertising Research Foundation, 1953. (No author.)

Davis, E. J. *Experimental Marketing.* Sunburg-on-Thames, U.K.: Thomas Nelson & Sons, 1970.

Dichter, Ernest. *Getting Motivated by Ernest Dichter.* New York: Pergamon Press, 1979.

Dommermuth, William P. *The Use of Sampling in Marketing Research.* Chicago: American Marketing Association, 1975.

Haller, Terry. "ARF Convention Reports Sound Like Reports from 1954 Conference: Where's Progress?" *Advertising Age* (November 19, 1979): 72.

_____. "Corporate Ads Doomed." *Advertising Age* (January 25, 1982): 47.

_____. "Corporate Ads Need to Get Specific." *Marketing Executive's Digest* (October 1981): 8.

_____. "Day-After Recall to Persist Despite JWT Study; Other Criteria Looming." *Marketing News* (May 18, 1979): 9.

_____. "The Day Hegel Took on Wall Street." *Financial Analysts Journal* (January/February 1982): 10.

_____. "Escape Route from Wimpdom." *Advertising Age* (October 26, 1981): S-12.

_____. "Fixing the Corporate Image." *Journal of Business Strategy* (Summer 1981. Vol. 2, no. 1): 65.

_____. "How to Get More Mileage out of Your Corporate Advertising." *Journal of Business Strategy* (Spring 1981. Vol. 1, no. 4): 72.

_____. "Let's Not Bury Paired Comparison." *Journal of Advertising Research* (September 1966): 29.

_____. "Marketers: Strategically Plan Recovery of Corporate Power." *Advertising Age* (July 1979): 41.

_____. "An Organizational Structure to Help You in the 80s." *Advertising Age* (August 25, 1980): 45.

———. "Predicting Recall of TV Commercials." *Journal of Advertising Research* (October 1972): 43.

———. "Selecting Corporate Advertising Themes." *Journal of Business Strategy* (Fall 1981. Vol. 2, no. 2): 85.

———. "Strategic Planning: Key to Corporate Power for Marketers." *Marketing Times* (May/June 1980): 26.

———. "Using Public Opinion Surveys." *Litigation* (Winter 1982. Vol. 8, no. 2): 17.

Henault, Georges-Maurice. *Le Comportement du Consommateur.* Quebec City: Les Presses de l'Universite du Quebec, 1973.

Henry, Harry. *Perspectives in Management, Marketing and Research.* London: Crosby Lockwood & Son, 1971.

Hofer, Charles. *Strategy Formulation: Analytical Concepts.* St. Paul, Minn.: West Publishing Co., 1978.

Hofer, Charles, and Haller, Terry. "GlobeScan: A Way to Better International Risk Assessment." *Journal of Business Strategy* (Fall 1980. Vol. 1, no. 2): 41–55.

———. "International Risk/Reward Assessment." *Advanced Management Report* (1981. Vol. 3, no. 2): 7.

Holbrook, Morris B. *A Study of Communication in Advertising.* Ann Arbor, Mich.: Xerox University Microfilm, 1975.

Levine, Philip. *Attitude Research Bridges the Atlantic.* Chicago: American Marketing Association, 1975.

Lief, Alfred. *It Floats: the Story of Procter & Gamble.* New York: Rinehart, 1958.

Morgan, Fred W., Jr. "An Analysis of Experimental Buying Behavior." *Journal of the Academy of Marketing Science* (Winter 1978. Vol. 6, no. 1): 12–24.

Scitovsky, Tibor. *The Joyless Economy.* New York: Oxford University Press, 1976.

Seligman, Daniel. "Keeping Up: Poll Watching." *Fortune* (April 19, 1982): 55.

Weller, Don G. *Who Buys—A Study of the Consumer.* London: Ebenezer Baylis & Son, 1974.

Zaltman, Gerald, and Burger, Philip C. *Marketing Research: Fundamentals and Dynamics.* Hinsdale, Ill.: Dryden Press, 1975.

Zaltman, Gerald, and Wallendorf, Melanie. *Consumer Behavior: Basic Findings and Management Implications.* New York: John Wiley & Sons, 1979.

Index

About the Author
TERRY HALLER has worked in an executive capacity in marketing, marketing research, and corporate planning for Procter & Gamble, R.J. Reynolds, and Quaker Oats. Currently, he is the president of the Chicago Research Company, chairman of the Financial Communications Center, an editor of the *Journal of Business Strategy*, and a member of the Chicago United Way Communication Advisory Council.